Georg Stauth, Samuli Schielke (eds.)
Dimensions of Locality

GEORG STAUTH, SAMULI SCHIELKE (EDS.)
Dimensions of Locality
Muslim Saints, their Place and Space
(Yearbook of the Sociology of Islam No. 8)

[transcript]

This volume was printed by support of the Deutsche Forschungsgemeinschaft DFG and the Sonderforschungsbereich 295 »Kulturelle und sprachliche Kontakte« at the Johannes Gutenberg-Universität Mainz.

Bibliographic information published by the Deutsche Nationalbibliothek
The Deutsche Nationalbibliothek lists this publication in the Deutsche Nationalbibliografie; detailed bibliographic data are available in the Internet at http://dnb.d-nb.de

© 2008 transcript Verlag, Bielefeld

All rights reserved. No part of this book may be reprinted or reproduced or utilized in any form or by any electronic, mechanical, or other means, now known or hereafter invented, including photocopying and recording, or in any information storage or retrieval system, without permission in writing from the publisher.

Cover layout: Kordula Röckenhaus, Bielefeld
Typeset by: Jörg Burkhard, Bielefeld
Printed by: Majuskel Medienproduktion GmbH, Wetzlar
ISBN 978-3-89942-968-8

Table of Contents

Introduction   7
SAMULI SCHIELKE AND GEORG STAUTH

Part 1: Conceptual Spaces

Chapter 1
Sufi Regional Cults in South Asia and Indonesia:
Towards a Comparative Analysis   25
PNINA WERBNER

Chapter 2
(Re)Imagining Space: Dreams and Saint Shrines in Egypt   47
AMIRA MITTERMAIER

Chapter 3
Remixing Songs, Remaking MULIDS:
The Merging Spaces of Dance Music and Saint Festivals in Egypt   67
JENNIFER PETERSON

Chapter 4
Notes on Locality, Connectedness, and Saintliness   89
ARMANDO SALVATORE

Part 2: Contested Places

Chapter 5
Saints (*awliya'*), Public Places and Modernity in Egypt   103
AHMED A. ZAYED

Chapter 6
Islam on both Sides: Religion and Locality in Western Burkina Faso   125
KATJA WERTHMANN

Chapter 7
The Making of a 'Harari' City in Ethiopia:
Constructing and Contesting Saintly Places in Harar   149
PATRICK DESPLAT

Chapter 8
Merchants and *Mujahidin*:
Beliefs about Muslim Saints and the History of Towns in Egypt   169
SOUZAN EL SAIED YOUSEF MOSA

Abstracts   183

On the Authors and Editors of the Yearbook   189

Introduction

Samuli Schielke and Georg Stauth

The shrines of Muslim saints can be found in a number of similar forms around the world: a tombstone, often surrounded by a quadratic structure and covered by a dome, sometimes standing alone, sometimes attached to a mosque. And around the world, these shrines are special places. Not only do they mark natural boundaries, roads, and villages, they also constitute places: i.e. standing on central squares and crossroads, giving names to towns, attracting pious seekers of relief, pilgrims, students, trade, and festivals. The desire to gain the blessings of the sheikh, to stand—if only for a brief moment—under his *baraka* and, in many cases, to gain a sense of the aura of the sheikh's place is as prevalent among modern Muslims as it was in earlier periods. The sheikh's charisma and the aura of his place seem to incorporate and radiate divine power. The singularity of the places makes them stand out from and dominate their surroundings, they appear as intersections of the human and divine, the religious, and the secular, and of conflicting and contradicting claims.

The reference to locality forms a very important dimension within all world religions where the ideas of return to origins and of an imminent physical presence of the transcendent in specific places play a foundational and ideological role. Like Judaism and Christianity—and perhaps even more so—Islam as a world religion is based on a highly abstract and absolute notion of the transcendent which its followers establish and celebrate at very specific sites: Mecca, Medina, Jerusalem, and the vast and complex landscapes of mosques and saintly places around the world.

This importance of saintly places has, however, become increasingly complicated and troubled by different currents building on modern modes of cultural authentication. Modern reformist movements within Islam, particularly those of Wahhabi and Salafi orientation, have denied the possibility and need for any mediation within the dichotomy of God and His servants and, as a result, have furiously attacked—in both word and deed—localized cults of Muslim saints. At the same time, this religious opposition to saintly places has gone hand in hand with their nationalist valorization as 'culture', strongly aided by modern archaeology and anthropology, which have contributed—sometimes unwittingly, sometimes willingly—to the belief that local cults are a separate cultural reality away from and opposed to what they have deemed orthodox universal Islam. In response, anthropologists have recently tried to develop more nuanced views on Islamic dogma and practice. It is within this complex context of the local and local saint cults that we wish to locate the contributions to this volume.

Looking at localized cults of Muslim saints around the world it is striking to note that, wherever one goes, they are often described by local intellectuals, reformist Muslims, and many Western observers as local syncretisms, continuities of local, pre-Islamic traditions under the cloak of Islam. In Egypt, the shrines of Muslim saints are sometimes claimed to be superficially Islamized sites of Pharaonic gods or Christian saints. In the Indian sub-continent, they are sometimes told as belonging to Hindu deities turned into Muslims. However, on closer examination, it is striking how similar the concepts of sainthood, the beliefs in *baraka* and miracles, and even the physical structure of saints' shrines are around the Muslim world. In addition, the festive traditions around these sites show striking similarities in form and atmosphere in Morocco, Egypt, and Pakistan, although in each country one will hear from folklorists and reformist Muslims alike that these are very special and unique local traditions, in reality not religious at all, but communal customs that predate Islam.

Thus if we are to enquire about the relationship between locality and sainthood and their importance for Islam as a world religion, we must question and reflect on the various claims that 'local specificity' is the key to understanding the very significance of the local. In fact, claims to continuity, competing theories of the origin of a saint and varying and often contradicting *modes of authentication*—that is, of ways to imagine and to argue for historical, territorial and normative foundations of a religion, a nation, a culture, or any other such imagined community—significantly contribute to the kind of importance and dimensions that are assigned to a location. The same physical structure becomes a very different thing, depending on whether it is interpreted as the manifestation of the universal truth and divine aura of Islam, as a key site of local identity, or as a trace of a pre-Islamic past. And, in each case, the kind of authenticity it is attached to, the kind of territorial and collective imagination, and the kind of relationship of the transcendent with the world of humans and things appear in a different configuration.

Like followers of all religions, Muslims in our time relate to locality, sanctity, and the transcendent on different levels. It is from this angle that we might address the components of locality viewing them in relation to the categories of the saintly and the sacred in Islam, and to their sociological significance.

The focus of this volume, therefore, is on locality. Building on immanence—in the very sense of the presence of the deceased saint at his place—we wish to develop here a complementary view to that pursued in Volume 5 of this *Yearbook*. It struck us there that the manifest continuity of 'extraworldly' orientations and soteriological needs of the modern subject are finding a parallel expression in Sufism and the veneration of saints in Islam. We wanted to show that the coincidence of extra-worldly salvational attitudes and individualism form a new, 'modern' category today, and that this certainly features in cultural attitudes in Islam. However, in contrast to the issue of the cultural needs of the modern subject raised in Volume 5, the present volume stresses a different type of interplay of the realities of the sacred: i.e. the immanence of the place and the powerful totality of any locality seen to be inspirited.

By following the perspective of the place, this volume attempts to overcome the misgivings of Weberian dichotomies and to look to modern forms of appropriating religious ideas in terms of their manifest immanence in modern life. This perhaps provides a better key for understanding the claims and practices of local authentication in religion and art and seeing their expressions in Islam (and other world religions). Rather than focusing on questions of identity construction and modern self-constitution and on Weber's conceptual antagonisms, we attempt to depart from the strategic use of 'Islam' as an explanatory paradigm and the accompanying dichotomy of Islam and non-Islam. Instead, the book takes the construction of saints and places as a primary level of reflection and analysis, looking at the dynamic and competing imaginaries of aura and modes of authentication at work.

Some—although not all—of the papers included in this volume were presented at a small conference titled 'Saintly Places in Islam' which was organized by the Research Group 'Saintly Places and the Veneration of Saints in Egypt and Ethiopia' of the DFG Collaborative Research Centre 295, 'Cultural and Linguistic Contacts' at the University of Mainz in Haus Noth Gottes near Mainz in June 2006. The large number of contributions on Egypt derives in part from the editors' own research orientation and, in part, from a strong Egyptian presence at this conference. We would like to avail of this opportunity to thank our Egyptian counterparts, Professors Mahmoud Auda and Ahmad Zayed in Cairo, who directed an Egyptian research group in the field, and our colleagues in Mainz and specifically the speakers of the Collaborative Research Centre 295, Professors Walter Bisang, Ursula Verhoeven and Thomas Bierschenk, for their unconditional support.

Continuity and Authenticity

The many localized expressions of Islam have also become a subject of study ever since the emergence of European scholarly interest in the Muslim world. The, perhaps, oldest approach to their study had its focus on continuity, the aim of finding a true core, or at least a positive trace, of earlier worship in the practices of contemporary Muslims. In this view, a saint's shrine and mosque is 'really' a temple in disguise, an unchanging essence behind a changing appearance. Largely abandoned in contemporary Western historiography and anthropology, this approach enjoys continued popularity in the folklore and social sciences of many Muslim countries, in particular Egypt.

There is no doubt that where people are educated and socialized, and in turn educate and socialize the next generation, there is continuity in human history. But how continuity takes place, and how it is imagined by people remembering and reconstructing the past, requires closer examination. Take, for example, the topic of an essential continuity of the Pharaonic tradition in current Egyptian cloaks of Christianity and Islam granting an essential Egyptian Islamic specificity. This notion of a 'genius of the place', of an inner lasting essence of a location, has great poetic (and, potentially, ideological) power, but remains problematic in view of both historical evidence and its heuristic value as such.

There is no archaeological or documentary evidence for a direct continuity of gods as saints. Furthermore, from the mediaeval period of the Islamization of rural Egypt, there is only one documented case of a Christian saint becoming a Muslim one. Far more often, however, we find evidence for the establishment of new Islamic sanctuaries that compete with the existing Christian ones (Mayeur-Jaouen 2005). However, there is, of course, the fact that some mosques and *maqams* (shrines) have been built on top of churches which, in turn, were built on top of temples. This has been cited by both Egyptian and European scholars as a case for essential continuity. The problem, however, is that the appearance of a saint at former site of Pharaonic, Greek, Roman, or Christian worship, stands for a specific way of building authenticity and cultural recognition that explicitly denies continuity in the sense of *genius loci*. The construction of a mosque over a pre-Islamic site of worship is an act of symbolical and physical triumph, of the defeat and replacement of the preceding cult. As such it is the instigation of the symbolic rule of the new religion, an expression of cultural break rather than continuity in essence.

At the same time, there is no doubt that the physical presence of pre-Islamic objects has always been acknowledged by Muslims, often with some ambiguity. Symbolic triumph implies recognition which, in turn, is a tool of the authentication and reconstruction of essence. It remains therefore important to analyze the changing and varying forms in which Islamic thought and practice relates to elements and expressions of Pharaonic history (El Daly 2005). If we want to understand how saintly places are constituted in relation to their surrounding settlements, other sanctuaries, and the wider religious and political ideologies of a society, the search for an unchanging essence behind changing facades does not help us in analytical terms. It is, however, an important clue for understanding the different modes of authentication at work. The search for unchanging 'traces' is in itself one of these imagined histories, or modes of authentication, embedded as it is in romantic and nationalist imagination, but also in religious reformist polemics against the cult of saints. It is a distinctively modern point of view that stands in clear contrast to the way people in earlier periods dealt with the history of a site and with the material traces of earlier cults found at the sites or near the shrines of Muslim saints. In the mediaeval period of Islamization, liberal use was made of Pharaonic, Roman and Christian elements—stones, columns, etc.—in the construction of mosques. This was hardly a friendly gesture at the time, but a powerful demonstration of victory: i.e. the demolition of temples and churches and use of their stones to build mosques. In the contemporary period, however, these stones and columns have become a part of the nationalist romantic imagination of the cult of saints as unchanging Egyptian culture—an image which the Muslims who venerate saints do not share. Thus, once ambiguous signs of the victory of Islam, the physical traces of earlier cults now become at once secular symbols of national identity and potential targets of reformist attacks. For those, in turn, who continue to venerate the saints and their places as Islamic holy places, removing pre-Islamic objects becomes a way of reclaiming the Islamic nature of a contested site (see Stauth 2008).

Beyond the Local and the Universal

Another very important and more sophisticated but nevertheless highly problematic approach to the local in Islam has come from the field of the anthropology in association with the concept of little and great traditions. This notion, originally developed by Robert Redfield (1960: 40-59), was most notably adopted by Ernest Gellner who, in his famous and eloquent analysis of Islam in Morocco, claims that there is an essential dichotomy within Islam between a universal, abstract, rationalist, and puritan Great Tradition and a local, mystical, ecstatic, and popular Small Tradition. He goes on to claim that the 'central' variant of Islam is in fact the one more compatible with modernity (Gellner 1981: 4-5). This, of course, is what many modernists of both secular and Islamic coloring claimed throughout the 20th century. Gellner, however, disregards that this opposition is a construct of the 19th and 20th centuries' own historical imagination. He reproduces a reformist imagination of true versus marginal forms of religion in an ingenious way but fails to problematize the claim that scholarly, purist approaches are central and others marginal.

On closer examination, however, the dichotomies between puritan and ecstatic, egalitarian and hierarchical, and metropolitan and folk Islam turn out to be very inaccurate: scholars have been mystics and mystics have been scholars throughout the history of Islam. The very notion of some beliefs being 'folk', or 'popular' is a modern one (Schielke 2007). The veneration of Muslim saints, today deemed marginal by some, was firmly and clearly a part of orthodox Islam from the middle ages to the 20th century, and while the question as to how saints should be venerated was subject to major controversy, their status as mediators between the human and the transcendent and as sources of religious authority was subject to far less questioning (see, for example, the history of as-Sayyid Ahmad al-Badawi, Egypt's major Muslim saint in Mayeur-Jaouen 2004). Thus what Gellner deems the small 'folk' traditions of Islam may not be so 'small' at all. Mysticism, the cult of Muslim saints, festive traditions, magic, etc. are all intimately part of and make reference to the 'great' universal framework of Islam and just as peasants recite the Qur'an and hold on to 'central' traditions such as prayer and fasting, scholars and members of urban bourgeoisie have engaged in mysticism and magic.

A less dichotomous approach that attempts to avoid the ideological trap into which Gellner falls, has been offered by Clifford Geertz (1968) who argues that the universal discourse of religion is always localized in a specific cultural context which will make 'Indonesian Islam' substantially different from 'Moroccan Islam', even when they share the same doctrinal discourse. However, the problem in both Geertz's and Gellner's approaches is that they represent the relationship of the local to the universal as something fairly static and the difference between the two as more or less clear. In consequence, they thus fail to look at the ways people in any given local setting aim for the transcendent and locate themselves in it—a much more complex process that cannot be described by the simple opposition of the local and the universal.

A number of scholars of the history and contemporary practice of Islam and Islamic devotional cults (Abu-Zahra 1997; Werbner/Basu 1998; Sedgwick 2005; Soares 2005) have pointed out that while Islam as a religion always has been localized, it has never been disconnected from universalist discourses and trans-local networks. In *Embodying Charisma*, Werbner and Basu argue that rather than the localization of Islam, an Islamization of the local is the more accurate version of the story. Perhaps the most powerful model of a localized Islam, namely that of an 'African Islam' or 'black Islam' that was once promoted by the French colonial administration and that has long inspired the anthropology of Muslim societies in Africa, has been effectively demolished by contemporary Africanists (see, for example, Soares 2005) who show that not only have Muslims in Africa, whatever their doctrinal orientations may be, never subscribed to an 'African Islam' but to just Islam, they also have been well connected with the global movements of Sufism, legal scholarship, and most recently Salafi reformism. The local in relation to the various expressions of a world religion, it seems, is not really a category opposed to the universal and global, but something more complex.

One way to cope with this complexity would be to follow Talal Asad (1986) who has argued that rather than trying to distinguish different layers or forms of Islam, one should recognize that Muslims around the world search guidance, make arguments, and relate to the founding texts of the Qur'an and the Sunna. While they disagree and debate, their debates are characterized by the shared reference to the scripture and the attempt to maintain coherence. This view of Islam as a 'discursive tradition' has been greeted enthusiastically by many scholars of contemporary Islam (Abu-Zahra 1997; Mahmood 2005; Soares 2005; Hirschkind 2006). Because its approach to plurality within Islam is not dichotomizing, it may at an intial glance appear very promising in accounting for such contested practices as local pilgrimages, shrines, and the veneration of saints.

However, the problem remains that this type of universalist perspective involves a sort of 'orthodoxization' reducing discourse to the interpretation of scripture with the aim of regulating normative practice and creating coherence. In doing this, it favors approaches to religion that do exactly that, and overlooks approaches that do not. There can be no doubt that Muslims continuously relate their religious practice and ideas to the universalizing discourses of Islam, and this renders obsolete many of the juxtapositions between the universal and the local, or between orthodoxy and popular religion. However that is not the whole story. While Asad points to the right direction, his notion of tradition does not really offer a way of understanding the problem of locality and localized cults in their complexity. By focusing so exclusively on discourse and by conflating the historical genealogy of a discourse with the ideological imagination of its own history, the notion of discursive tradition has three blind spots that are important to mention here.

The first are traditions which are not transmitted in the form of discourse but materially. While they take their orientation from the universalizing blueprints of Mecca and Medina, the shrines of Muslim saints are based on a more complex kind of imagination and transmission than is evoked by the concept of 'discursive tradition.' A more holistic common sense of the shape, form, and practices related to a saintly place can be far more determining than explicit references to the scripture.

The second blind spot are the historical transformations of 'tradition' in the course of shifting social and political hegemonies. The orthodox Islam of 18th-century scholarly and saintly establishments was radically different to the orthodox Islam of 21st century social movements and do-it-yourself religious manuals. And yet believers of the 21st century see themselves as being in the unbroken and authentic tradition of objectively true Islam.

Finally, Islam is only one of the many parameters that are important when people relate to cities, villages, landscapes, and the place of the sacred and saintly within them. As many of the authors in this volume show, modern nationalism, urban planning, and ethnic conflicts contribute to the formation, contestation, and transformation of not only saintly places but also their religious imagination in a way that cannot be explained by the 'discursive tradition' of Islam.

The contributions in this volume present a more complex approach, looking at the ways sacred and saintly locality is established, imagined, and authenticated under complex and specific circumstances but always involving claims for wider, even universal (but not necessarily religious), validity. This, indeed, forms a specific component of what might be called discursive connectedness. Rather than taking Islam as the primary level of analysis and trying to explain what Islam 'is', we attempt to show how the local specificity and the historical and inter-local connectedness of a site and the beliefs and rituals relating to it are imagined and constructed (in the physical sense too) in a given historical and social setting.

Locations and Localities

The authors of this volume take up the issue of locality and sanctity from different perspectives, and yet their approaches all share the problematization of 'place' or 'location' in the banal sense: the limits and history of a place, the landscapes and territories it belongs to, its position in a political or religious imaginary, and its physical and conceptual structure, can all be and are being questioned, rethought, and remade by people who live in, visit, use, and plan them.

The perspectives of the contributions to this volume can be roughly divided into three groups. Werbner and Salvatore develop more general analysis perspectives, working on what may be called a communicative theory of locality and sanctity. Basing their analysis on empirical work and anthropological fieldwork, Desplat, Mittermaier, Peterson, and Werthmann make their field of research the starting point for wider questions and theorizing that move beyond the customary dichotomies of tradition and modernity, sacred and profane, Sufi and reformist Islam, or Islam and non-Islam. Zayed and Mosa, finally, take a special position in the volume since their research, conducted at Egyptian research institutions about Egyptian sites, is not only engaged in fieldwork but also forms part of the contestation of saintly places. As a folklorist, Souzanne Mosa problematizes Islamist claims to the history of a city but also presents an established point of view about the 'folkloricity' of the cult of saints. As a sociologist, Ahmed Zayed engages in a wider public debate on the shape of modernity in Egypt—and doing so questions the consensus of equating the cult of saints with folklore.

Locality appears in different dimensions in the contributions in this volume. First, it can be understood in the immediate sense of *place*, the historical continuum of practices in a location essentially defined through a reference to its past and continuity. As such, the aura of saintly locality is a product of historical imagination. The saint, ultimately localized by his or her shrine, is the carrier of local histories and identity. As a result, his or her character and deeds can change along with the interpretations and emphases of local history. As the contributions of Desplat, Mosa, and Werthmann show, claims to a place, its description as belonging to a religion, an ethnic group, or a clan, always imply a different way of imagining the place itself. When Islamists claim a Muslim saint to be a Jew and Sufis counter that, on the contrary, he was a *jihad* hero, when the middle classes of Harar claim the saints of the city as 'theirs' in opposition not only to Salafi reformism but also to other ethnic groups in the city, not only the saint but his or her identity with a town, village, family, or ethnic group stands in question. Contesting a saint's shrine becomes, as a result, a contestation of the identities and values of the people who relate to it.

Secondly, locality and the aura of the saintly place emerge in the sense of *landscape* or *territory*, the interrelationship of various locations to each other, and the hierarchies between them. These landscapes can take forms of highly organized movements, as Werbner shows in her contribution in which she brings in the level of regional cults as an important and often neglected category between the reference to a universal religious ideology and the localized practice at a specific site. As Desplat shows, such landscapes can also be very detailed and material, as is the case with the hierarchies of saints in Harar and the network of shrines and other sacred places in the countryside around the city. Such landscapes need not, however, be coherent or harmonious. On the contrary, as Werthmann shows in her comparison of the two saintly/sacred sites near Bobo-Dioulasso, they can stand in explicit contrast to each other and thus present very different forms of sanctity that contribute less to a coherent hierarchy than to a pluralistic landscape of different levels of connectiveness and discourse, and different material, organizational, and communal interests.

Third, sacred locality emerges in the more abstract sense of *space*, the structure and organization of a world apart. Here the notion of aura, or *baraka*, or charisma, becomes central as the principle of spatial organization. Zayed and Mittermaier, in particular, juxtapose the geometrical, functional order of the modern city to the imagination and organization of saints' shrines, their surroundings, and the (urban) landscape they constitute. While adopting very different perspectives, both argue that the saintly/sacred space of shrines is a world apart, structured according to spiritual hierarchies and open to different kinds of use and meaning. It is this at once open and esoteric character that has made saintly space so problematic for proponents of modern systematic rationality—of Salafi reformist and secular varieties alike. The modernist and reformist imagination of religion, society, and space highlight systematic rationality giving everything and everyone a place and a purpose, and spectacular hierarchies that prescribe knowledge and communication as a top-down process where the role of the public is to receive knowledge. In contrast, the imaginary and physical spaces of saints shrines, surrounding squares, and the landscapes they constitute are characterized by the moment of intersection: between the human and the transcendent, between pious and profane practices, between different social classes, and between open and protected (or 'public' and 'private') spaces. Ambiguous by default, saintly space cannot be put to the service of any grand project of reform or development and contains a degree of autonomy that continues to trouble those who believe that society and religion should be structured according to clear boundaries and ruled by universal laws.

Fourth, space, in turn, emerges as a metaphor for a *state of being* in the contributions of Mittermaier and Peterson. Focusing on dreams, Mittermaier highlights the importance of imaginary spaces. In doing so, she demonstrates the extent to which locality on all levels is a category of imagination: the history and meaning of a place, the details of a landscape stretching beyond the horizon, the hierarchies and structures of a space, all exist primarily on the level of imagination that provides 'a mode of perception and an order of reality' (Mittermaier in this volume), in which the history, the extension, and the structure of a site become meaningful. In a further step, Peterson shows that space as constituted through imagination can develop into an independent mode of action and experience that need not be in a direct relation with physical space. Peterson argues that the spatial arrangement of a saints-day festival as they exist around the Muslim world is essentially characterized by its temporality. The space of a festival is thus always a time-space: a structure of things related to a very specific moment in which more is allowed and things work differently than otherwise. Referring to the genre of *moulid* pop music, Peterson shows how this time-space of festive joy can become independent from its original site to a certain degree: when *moulid* develops into a category of experience characterized by *haysa*, fun, joy, and dancing, it becomes a metonymical space, not so much denoting any particular location and its structures than a modality of action that is described by reference to the spatial and temporal event of the festival.

Finally, Salvatore introduces charisma and relationality as a possible perspective for the study of the sacred, sainthood, and saintly locality. Critically engaging Western theoretical approaches to the concept of charisma, a category that has been used with considerable—and questionable—ease in opposition to rational authority and organization, Salvatore argues that we must see charisma as a relational principle based on the need for a connecting link between the human and the transcendent, or in more general terms, the specific and the universal. While Salvatore's approach does not center on the question of locality, the way he highlights relationality as the key moment of charisma could contribute to a more nuanced understanding of how exactly places can 'be' saintly, 'have' *baraka*, 'radiate' aura, and 'embody' charisma.

Sanctity and the Sacred

The three holy cities of Mecca, Medina, and Jerusalem each are bestowed with a special relationship to the transcendent: Mecca as the core site of the pilgrimage and the physical and imaginary center of Islam, Medina as the site of the victory of the Prophet Muhammad, Islam's charismatic mediator par excellence, and Jerusalem as the site of Muhammad's ascension to Heaven. These sites have also developed into paradigmatic examples of localized sanctity around the Islamic world. This is most evident with the tomb and mosque of the Prophet in Medina. The tomb, built at the site of Muhammad's house, and the mosque which, after successive extensions, has come to surround the tomb from all sides, serve as the blueprint of practically every Muslim saint's shrine around the world.

Far from being the absolute and mystical opposite of the profane world, the sacred embodied by these sites is a dynamic category that can be and has been imagined differently. More than that, different concepts of the sacred are often at work at the same time. The authors of this volume repeatedly discuss different, at times coexisting, at times mutually hostile, notions of sacredness, sanctity, and charisma. Different notions of sanctity and sacredness go hand in hand with ways of imagining and structuring locality and its meaning, in other words, different modes of authentication.

The customary terminology of Islam has several terms that can be more or less accurately translated in terms of sacredness and sanctity. The Arabic root QDS serves as source for terms that describe the transcendent and absolute holiness of God, such as in *muqaddas* (holy), al-Qaddûs ('Holy', one of the names of God) and al-Quds (Jerusalem, literally 'sanctuary'). From the root HRM are derived terms which describe sacredness in terms of protectedness, taboo, and opposition to the profane, such as *haram* (protected sanctuary, especially denoting the sacred districts of the three holy sites of Islam) and *harâm* (forbidden, taboo; sacred). Finally, the root BRK is a source for terms that describe spiritual power, most notably *baraka*—a complex notion that involves the divine aura, charisma or power of a person, object or a site, material beneficial power, and protection.

If the notions of holy/*muqaddas* and sanctuary/*haram* highlight the opposition between the human and the transcendent, and consequently the explicitly otherworldly nature of sacred space, the notion of *baraka* stresses the possibility of contact and mediation. It is no coincidence that *baraka* is the essential and most important quality of Muslim saintly places. By the virtue of the divine grace, the saint, a pilgrimage site, can be a source of protection, power, healing, wealth, and peace. In the Muslim faith, the Qur'an, holy places, pious people, and pious deeds radiate this beneficiary power that emanates from God and can be physically transmitted and received, be it by reading the Qur'an, by undertaking the pilgrimage to Mecca, by receiving the blessings of a religious person, or—although this is strongly contested in our time—by visiting the tomb of a pious person who enjoys a special grace of God that makes him a friend of God (*wali Allah*), in other words a saint.

Even where it has been established in clear contrast to pre-Islamic cults, the sanctity of a Muslim saint's shrine is of a kind that always carries an inclusive momentum that does not respect the clear limits of sacred and profane, Islam and non-Islam. In this volume Werthmann shows that elements of Islam can be incorporated into animism just as elements of animism can be incorporated in Islam. Furthermore, as Werthmann's juxtaposition of the sacrificial site of Dafra and the saints' tombs of Darsalamy shows, not only the places themselves, also the kinds of sacredness/sanctity ascribed to them are different.

The notion of *baraka* goes hand in hand with modes of authentication with their primary reference to divine grace and mediation embodied by the deceased saint, and a form of discursive connectedness that present localized mediation and universal transcendental truth as compatible. By the virtue of its *baraka*, its aura of the extraordinary, a major sanctuary is open to a much wider array of people and practices than a holy site defined by purity and opposition to the profane would be.

It is precisely this openness that has become a major issue in the intense criticism and often physical attacks on Islamic saintly places over the past century. If the sacred has a taste of license at the saintly place constituted by *baraka*, in another, distinctively modern notion of sanctity and the sacred, this is unthinkable. The often furious indignation of Muslim reformists about the participation of women, the openness of a saint's festival to the profane atmosphere of a fair, the ecstatic and spontaneous nature of religious performance, and the occasional presence of pre-Islamic objects are telling of a deep split in the ways the relationship of a sacred place with its history, landscape, and structure is being imagined.

The Place, Connectedness and Paradigms of Authentication

It is thus not merely the 'locality' (in sense of being specific to a particular place) as opposed to 'universality' of saintly places that has made them a favorite target of Salafism and developmental modernism, and an ambiguous icon of nationalism during the past century. Nor are the attempts to defend and to redefine saintly places merely a move from the 'local' to the 'universal'.

It is necessary here to return to the notions of aura and discursive connectedness. The special 'aura' of places, the imaginary yet immanent quality that makes them extraordinary, meaningful, powerful, and part of something greater can be thought of in different ways—and each way involves a different kind of connectedness, a different way of feeling about a place, of seeing it carry meanings and fitting into a bigger picture. The success of establishing and stabilizing the presence of the saint in a given place over a long period of time depends largely on successful modes of authentication, that is, re-imagining the place in terms of its origin (history) and establishing this imaginary as manifest (also changing) physical structures and ritual practices. But what happens when these imaginary histories and connections become contested? How do people attempt to defend, redefine, or replace the aura of a saintly place? The 'aura' of a place and its discursive and imaginary connectedness are intimately interwoven, and if one changes, the other will be affected.

By way of conclusion, we take up three juxtapositions that make clearer the ways in which the aura and the connections of a saintly place can be and are being imagined by present-day Muslims: *baraka* versus systemic rationality, cultural versus religious authentication, and city versus countryside.

The first juxtaposition presents *baraka* and systemic rationality as two opposing principles of organizing not only religion but social practice in general: inclusive as opposed to exclusive, the sacred as a source of power and protection—thence with an air of license—as opposed to the sacred as established by rational study and moral practice—therefore with an emphasis on discipline and purity. The inclusive nature of saintly places becomes a threat not only to the purity of the rational sanctity of revivalist Islam, but also to developmentalist modernist notions of public order and rationality. For the modernist notion of society as an organic system structured by over-arching norms and purposes, spaces that are characterized by openness rather than order are very problematic. As a result, the *baraka* of a saintly place becomes fundamentally problematic for the projects of modernity and Islamic reform because of its inherent ambiguity, openness to Islam and non-Islam, religious and secular practices, hierarchy and anarchy, local and trans-local dimensions.

The second juxtaposition presents a religious mode of authenticity deriving from the presence of a saint's body and the connectedness of the site to a grand history of Islam as opposed to a secular national mode of authenticity deriving from the cultural and regional specificity and very long but locally grounded history of the site. From a nationalist point of view, a site with a very long history radiates the continuous presence of something that is essentially 'ours', but precisely this presence can make it inauthentic in a religious imagination that takes the break between paganism and Islam as a key mark of authenticity. As a result, this puts people who venerate and defend Muslim saintly places in an ambiguous position whereby they have access to different levels of authenticity which, however, each may jeopardize the legitimacy of the site in a different way. Nationalist modernist middle classes and elites, on the other hand, face a different kind of ambiguity where saintly places present a threat to their religious and civilizational imagination, on the one hand, and an asset for their nationalist cultural narratives, on the other.

The third juxtaposition is the most complex of the three and presents modernist imaginaries of the village and the city as two modes of locality and social and civic order, the first imagined as culturally authentic but territorially limited and civilizationally backward, the other presented as culturally alienated, globally connected, and modern. The saint's shrine, in this imagination, is part of the village (regardless of the fact that most major shrines stand in cities) or of old city districts and resilient to the dynamics of urbanity and global modernity. This imagination is, in a way, an attempt to resolve the ambiguity of the first two juxtapositions, but when we look at the actual influence of the nation-state and urbanization on rural saints, a very different picture emerges. Mosa and Zayed, themselves arguing within the paradigm of modernity as a normative discourse on society, paradoxically show how 'city' and 'state' not only 'limit' the space of the saintly place by marginalizing it to the backward village, but also contribute to a de-territorialization of the saint. While their perspective is a modernizationist one, they present an intense interplay between different groups around a saint's place and the dynamics of saintly locality that makes obsolete the modernist dichotomy of city and village. While the Muslim saint in a modern city dominated by nationalist order and Salafi religious movements survives by undergoing many and often surprising transformations, saint cults in village milieus experience similar if not the same transformations in their physical and imaginary connectedness.

Finally, it is essential to stress that these contestations take place in complex ways which, while intimately related to the temporal imaginary of modernity, do not follow commonplace narratives of modernization. The flourishing regional Sufi cults (Werbner), the ambiguous balancing of the Harari middle-classes between religious and cultural authentication (Desplat), the dream spaces that compete with the modernist structures of Cairo (Mittermaier), the re-invention of the saint's festival as dance music (Peterson), the shifting boundaries between Islam and animism in Bobo-Dioulasso (Werthmann), and the omnipresence of peripheral modernity in Egyptian countryside (Zayed) all indicate that locality and the aura of saintly places cannot be thought of in terms of local-universal oppositions. Instead, it is established, contested, and remade as part of different outlooks on both the specific place as well as the world as a whole.

References

Abu-Zahra, Nadia (1997) *The Pure and Powerful: Studies in Contemporary Muslim Society*, Berkshire: Ithaca Press.

Asad, Talal (1986) *The Idea of an Anthropology of Islam* (Occasional Papers Series), Washington, DC: Center for Contemporary Arab Studies, Georgetown University.

El Daly, Okasha (2005) *Egyptology: The Missing Millennium. Ancient Egypt in Medieval Arabic Writings*, London: UCL.

Geertz, Clifford (1968) *Islam Observed: Religious Development in Morocco and Indonesia*, New Haven and London: Yale University Press.

Gellner, Ernest (1981) *Muslim Society*, Cambridge: Cambridge University Press.

Hirschkind, Charles (2006) "Cassette Ethics: Public Piety and Popular Media in Egypt". In: Birgit Meyer/Annelies Moors (eds.) *Religion, Media, and the Public Sphere*, Bloomington: Indiana University Press, pp. 29-52.

Mahmood, Saba (2005) *Politics of Piety: The Islamic Revival and the Feminist Subject*, Princeton: Princeton University Press.

Mayer-Jaouen, Catherine (2004) *Histoire d'un pèlerinage légendaire en Islam: Le mouled de Tantâ du XIIIe siècle a nos jours*, Paris: Aubier.

Mayeur-Jaouen, Catherine (2005) *Pèlerinages d'Égypte: Histoire de la piété copte et musulmane (XVe-XXe siècles)*, Paris: Éditions de l'EHESS.

Redfield, Robert (1960) *Peasant Society and Culture*, Chicago: The University of Chicago Press.

Schielke, Samuli (2007) "Hegemonic Encounters: Criticism of Saints-day Festivals and the Formation of Modern Islam in late 19th and early 20th-century Egypt". *Die Welt des Islams* 47/3-4, pp. 319-355.

Sedgwick, Mark (2005) *Saints and Sons: The Making and Remaking of the Rashidi Ahmadi Sufi Order, 1799-2000*, Leiden: Brill.

Soares, Benjamin (2005) *Islam and the Prayer Economy: History and Authority in a Malian Town*, Edinburgh: Edinburgh University Press.

Stauth, Georg (2008) *Ägyptische heilige Orte II: Zwischen den Steinen des Pharao und islamischer Moderne. Konstruktionen, Inszenierungen und Landschaften der Heiligen im Nildelta: Fuwa—Sa al-Hagar (Sais)*, Bielefeld: transcript.

Werbner, Pnina/Basu, Helene (eds.) (1998) *Embodying Charisma: Modernity, Locality and the Performance of Emotion in Sufi Cults*, London: Routledge.

Part 1: Conceptual Spaces

Chapter 1

Sufi Regional Cults in South Asia and Indonesia: Towards a Comparative Analysis

Pnina Werbner

Introduction

To compare Sufi orders across different places separated by thousands of miles of sea and land, and by radically different cultural milieus, is in many senses to seek the global in the local rather than the local in the global. Either way, charting difference and similarity in Sufism as an embodied tradition requires attention, beyond mystical philosophical and ethical ideas, to the ritual performances and religious organizational patterns that shape Sufi orders and cults in widely separated locations. We need, in other words, to seek to understand comparatively four interrelated symbolic complexes: first, the sacred division of labor—the ritual roles that perpetuate and reproduce a Sufi order focused on a particular sacred center; second, sacred exchanges between places and persons, often across great distances; third, the sacred 'region', its catchment area, and the sanctified central places that shape it; and fourth, the sacred indexical events—the rituals—that co-ordinate and revitalize organizational and symbolic unities and enable managerial and logistical planning and decision making. Comparison requires that we examine the way in which these four dimensions of ritual sanctification and performance are linked, and are embedded in a particular symbolic logic and local environment.

In this chapter I use the notion of 'cult' in its anthropological sense, i.e. to refer to organized ritual and symbolic practices performed in space and over time, often cyclically, by a defined group of devotees, kinsmen, initiates, supplicants, pilgrims, or disciples. The notion of a 'regional cult' drew on the geographical analysis of regional markets to refer to cults which extend beyond a locally demarcated and bounded administrative order (see R. Werbner 1977). Regional cults are, importantly, 'cults of the middle range', neither a world religion nor a local, parochially focused set of ritual practices. Regional cult *analysis* refers to the theorization of the complex, ambivalent relations between the politics, economics, ritual, and belief at the cult center, considered in its wider geographical and political context, as these relations are played out historically, over time, and as they affect shifting power relations between sacred and temporal authority. Spirituality and territorial politics are often conflictual, at least publicly, but at the same time politicians seek the support of priests or saints at the center of regional cults, able to mobilize the masses, while the latter often draw legitimacy from recognition (and material support) granted by temporal rulers.

The Sufi cult or sub-order I studied in Pakistan (see P. Werbner 2003), was in many senses remarkably similar organizationally to other, *non-Muslim* regional cults and pilgrimage systems in Africa, Latin America, and Europe (for examples see the chapters in R. Werbner 1977). It also fitted the model of Sufi orders analysed by Trimingham (1971), which was mainly based on his extensive knowledge of Sufi orders in the Middle East and Africa.

The difficulty, of course, in trying to understand Sufism and comprehend its systematic ritual and symbolic logic and organization, is that in any particular locality, there is a wide range of Sufi saints, from major shrines of great antiquity, managed by descendants of the original saintly founder and guardians of his tomb, to minor saints with a highly localized clientele (see Troll 1989; Werbner/Basu 1998). In any generation, only some outstanding living saints succeed in founding major regional cults, Sufi sub-orders which extend widely beyond their immediate locality. My own study was about one such Sufi regional cult, whose founder, Zindapir, the 'living saint', had established his central lodge, a place of enchanting loveliness and tranquility, in a small valley in the North West Frontier Province of Pakistan.

During the saint's lifetime, his cult, from being regional, extended globally: to Britain and Europe, the Middle East, and even South Africa. Established during the 1940s, in the dying days of Empire, Zindapir began his career as an army tailor contractor for the seventh Baluch regiment, and his cult membership expanded through the recruitment of army personnel. These, in turn, recruited members of their families and, when they retired to civilian life, their co-villagers or townsmen. The cult expanded further as these soldiers went to work as labor migrants in the Gulf or Britain. Disciples were also recruited from among the stream of supplicants coming to the lodge to seek the saint's blessings or remedies for their afflictions, and from among casual visitors curious to see the saint and lodge itself, a place renowned for its beauty. Some disciples joined the cult after meeting Zindapir or his vicegerents (messengers) on the annual Hajj to Mecca.

These disciples and messengers of Zindapir met regularly to perform *zikr* at the lodge branches of the order, located throughout Pakistan. They gathered at Zindapir's central lodge weekly, monthly, and in most cases, annually, at the *'urs*, the three-day ritual festival commemorating the mystical 'marriage' of a deceased saint with God. Some pilgrims arrived for the festival as individuals, but most came in convoys of trucks and buses from particular branches of the order, traveling in some cases for over 24 hours, bearing with them sacrificial offerings of grain, butter, and animals. They returned bearing gifts from the saint—gowns or caps, and in some instances, the sacred soil of the lodge itself. During their three-day stay at the *'urs,* all the participants were fed and nurtured by the saint himself. The hundreds of beasts sacrificed, the hundreds of thousands of baked chappatis and nans, the enormous cauldrons of sweet and pilau rice distributed during the *'urs,* feed some 30,000 people over three days, a major logistical challenge. But the saint also feeds pilgrims to the lodge throughout the year, in what may be conceived of as a form of perpetual sacrifice. The lodge itself has been built with voluntary labor, usually in the weeks preceding the annual *'urs.* The crowds depart following the final *du'a,* the supplicatory prayer and benediction enunciated by the saint himself on behalf of the whole community.

These are the bare outlines of Sufi regional cult organization. The Sufi cultural concept which best captures the idea of a Sufi region is *wilayat.* *Wilayat,* a master concept in Sufi terminology, denotes a series of interrelated meanings: (secular) sovereignty over a region, the spiritual dominion of a saint, guardianship, a foreign land, friendship, intimacy with God, and union with the Deity. As a master concept, *wilayat* encapsulates the range of complex ideas defining the charismatic power of a saint—not only over transcendental spaces of mystical knowledge but as sovereign of the terrestrial spaces into which his sacred region extends. These, it must be stressed, remain unbounded and theoretically could reach the far corners of the earth. The term regional cult, a comparative, analytic term used to describe centrally focused, expansive and unbounded religious organizations, which extend across administrative borders and boundaries, seems particularly apt to capture this symbolic complexity. Saints do no command exclusive territories. On the contrary, the *wilayats* of different saints interpenetrate, and any one locality will be the abode of a range of saints, big and small, more or less respected, each with his or her own following.

Sufi Orders and Saintly Charisma in the Middle East and Pakistan

Trimingham (1971) speaks of Sufi *'ta'ifas',* sub-orders focused around a single living saint or his shrine. His description makes evident that *ta'ifas* are comparable to other regional cults in their basic central place organization. The sheikh, a living saint or his descendant, heads the *ta'ifa* by virtue of his powers of blessing. Under the sheikh are a number of *khalifas* appointed by him directly to take charge of districts or town centers. He reports that in a large order each regional *khalifa* may have sectional leaders under him (Trimingham 1971: 173-174, 179). The sacred centers and subcenters of the cult, known as *zawiya* in North Africa, and *darbars* or *dargahs* (royal courts) in Pakistan and India, are places of pilgrimage and ritual celebration, with the tomb of the founder being the "focal point of the organization, a center of veneration to which visitations (*ziyarat*) are made" (ibid.: 179). The center is regarded as sacred (*haram*), a place of sanctuary for refugees from vengeance.

The word *ta'ifa* was not used by members of Zindapir's regional cult (and appears to be unknown even in some parts of the Middle East). They spoke of the cult as a *tariqa*, but to distinguish it from the wider Naqshbandi order to which it was affiliated, it was known as *tariqa Naqshbandiyya Ghamkolia*. By appending the name of the cult center, Ghamkol, to their regional cult, they marked its distinctiveness as an autonomous organization. The saint at the head of the order, *Zindapir*, ('the living saint'), was by the time of my study the head of a vast, transnational regional cult, stretching throughout Pakistan to the Gulf, Britain, Afghanistan, and Southern Africa. He had founded the cult center in 1948, when he first secluded himself, according to the legend, in a cave on the hill of Ghamkol. At the time the place was a wilderness.

A key feature of Zindapir's cult organization was the way in which the exemplary center has replicated itself throughout the saint's region through scores of deliberate and conscious acts of mimesis. In different parts of the Punjab important khalifas of the saint reproduce in their manners, dress, and minute customs the image of Zindapir, along with the ethics and aesthetics of the cult he founded. In their own places they are addressed, much as Zindapir himself is, as *pir sahib*. Such mimesis, I want to suggest, creates a sense of unity across distance: the same sounds and images, the same ambience, are experienced by the traveler wherever he goes in the cult region. Along with this extraordinary mimetic resemblance, however, each khalifa also fosters his own distinctiveness, his own special way of being a Sufi.

In other ways, too, Trimingham's account accords with regional cult theory. He makes the point that *ta'ifas* "undergo cycles of expansion, stagnation, decay, and even death" (1971: 179), but that since there are "thousands of them, new ones [are] continually being formed" (ibid.: 172).[1]

One way to understand processes of Sufi regional cult formation to look at the way cults are founded and expand 'during the lifetime of an originary, living saint'. There are also cases, of course, in which saints are sanctified posthumously, their charisma 'discovered' by devout followers often decades and even centuries later.[2] The present chapter, however, aims to disclose what endows some men with extraordinary charismatic authority during their life

---

1　Sedgwick (2005) makes a similar point, in virtually the same words, about Sufi orders in the Middle East, without acknowledging Trimingham's original contribution.
2　I am grateful to the editors for this point. Such post-facto sanctifications nevertheless require the organizational talents and dedication of living devotees.

time, and hence the power to found new Sufi regional cults and expand their organizational ambit.

To comprehend how the charisma of a saint is constructed and underpins saintly authority requires a comparative analysis of the poetics of traveling theories; that is, the way that such myths tell, simultaneously, both a local and a global tale about Sufi mystical power everywhere, and the settlement of Sufis in virgin, barren or idolatrous lands, such as the lodge valley in Pakistan or industrial towns in Britain. Each Sufi cult is distinctive and embedded in a local cultural context. But, against a view of the radical plurality of Islam proposed, for example, by Clifford Geertz (1968), I want to suggest in this chapter that Sufism everywhere shares the same deep structural logic of ideas. These shape the ecological and cultural habitat and local habitus wherever Sufi saints settle. Such beliefs persist, I show, despite internal inconsistencies and evidence to the contrary, and remain powerfully compelling.

Sufi Myths and Legends:
Teasing out Comparisons between Morocco and Indonesia

In a groundbreaking essay, Clifford Geertz (1968), comparing Moroccan and Indonesian Islam, proposed that global religions are necessarily embedded in the taken-for-granteds of local cultural milieus. In criticizing Geertz, I am not suggesting that he is entirely wrong. It is quite likely that Moroccan Islam and Indonesian Islam are in many ways very different in their feel, their style, their religious emphases, the emotions evoked by particular symbols and rituals, the centrality of ritual and religion in the society, its symbolic importance, and so forth.

Against Geertz, however, I want to argue that Sufi Islam as a traveling religion may change radically but in a way which seems almost the opposite to that suggested by him. In theory, and often in practice, when a world religion encroaches into an already charged social field, both religious practice and scriptural exegesis are likely to be politicized and to *lose* the taken-for-granted, doxic transparency that they once possessed. Instead, such religions become highly self-conscious, reflexive ideologies. Intertextuality, in other words, relativizes all knowledge. Recognizing the intertextual dimensions of locally appropriated global religious texts is a critical theoretical advance for an understanding of the global and local politics of religion and its thrust towards greater reflexivity.

Two related questions are implied by the argument that traveling theories gain in reflexivity: first, whether global religious knowledge, locally contextualised, is produced within a charged political field, in what sense can it still be said to be commonsensical, taken-for-granted and embedded unreflectively in a local cultural ethos and world view, as Geertz proposed? Second, in what respect do traveling theories which change, *also stay the same*? In what respect is Sufi Islam one rather than many?

To address these questions, I want to follow Geertz in the first instance by shifting the focus to locally told narratives about saints and away from published sacred texts. Unlike Geertz, however, my aim is to explore the underlying structures—the moral fables—animating such narratives. The structural logic of these fables, I wish to argue, in being implicit is rarely questioned or challenged, even in politicized contexts. It provides believers with their sense of naturalized, taken-for-granted certainty. So much so that such fables or underlying plots, rather than being modified in travel, once adopted are a symbolic force reshaping the cultural environments they invade. This is so because, as Becker has argued, in most cultures,

knowledge of plot constraints is unstated background knowledge, like the knowledge of grammar and syntax. It is learned indirectly, first through fairy tales and nursery rhymes (and their equivalent in other cultures), and then from the various media that have access to children (Becker 1979: 217).

Hence, going against the anthropological tendency to stress the local, I propose that Sufi Islam, despite its apparent variety and concrete localism, embodies a global religious ideology within a social movement which everywhere fabulates the *possibility* (if not the actualization) of human perfection. Its shared implicit logic is revealed in the structural similarities between Sufi legends and modes of organization in widely dispersed localities, separated in time as well as in space. This is exemplified by the parallels in the plots of the myths reported by Geertz for Morocco and Indonesia (Figure 1).

Figure 1: Sufi Myths in Morocco and Indonesia (after Geertz 1968)

---

(1) Inner Jihad: Overcoming Inner Desires/Total Submission
Morocco: Saint Washes with Smallpox-Infested Water
Indonesia: Saint Stands in a River for 15 Years
RESULT: DIVINE KNOWLEDGE

(2) Outer Jihad: Overcoming External Evil/Lack of Faith
Morocco: Triumph over the Evil Sultan
Indonesia: Conversion of Rulers at the Exemplary Center
RESULT: SPIRITUAL POWER OVERCOMES TEMPORAL POWER

The very same myths told about an Indonesian and a Moroccan saint could *both* be told about Pakistani saints, or even about the very same saint. This is because the myths represent two important and linked dimensions of Sufi Islam—the inner *jihad* and the outer *jihad* (Figure 1). *Jihad* means struggle or battle. For Muslims there is an inner battle with their desires and appetites and an outer battle with infidels and non-believers.

The two myths in both localities, Indonesia and Morocco, tell a story of an ordeal overcome through faith in the Sufi teacher. In Morocco the hero washes the clothes of the teacher, covered in smallpox, and then washes in the dirty water. This ordeal, which is an act of faith, endows him with divine blessing from the teacher who, as a charismatic holy man, is an intermediary with God, and inevitably also with divine knowledge. In the Indonesian myth the hero undergoes a typical Sufi ordeal—he stands in a river for 15 years waiting for his teacher to return, and is endowed with divine knowledge for his patience. In both cases, according to Sufi doctrine, the heroes kill their *nafs*, their personal selfish and bodily desires or carnal self. The Indonesian hero's myth ends here, except that we know that the hero went on to Islamicize the center of the state. In the Moroccan myth, the hero has a confrontation with a powerful but evil monarch. This is the external *jihad*—the fight against evil or religious backsliders.

My own interpretation of the message of this latter myth is different from that suggested by Geertz, who interprets the myth as implying that the Moroccan ruler proves his credentials as descendant of the Prophet. I propose that the moral of this myth is that spiritual power is always above temporal power—the house of God and his dweller, the saint, is more powerful than the palace of the monarch and its dweller, the worldly ruler. Both may be descendents from the Prophet, but one is superior to the other by virtue of his spirituality and the monarch must therefore bow to him. The moral of the tale is that the rule of God is above the rule of man. Man does not make the law, he simply administers it.[3]

This same principle is exemplified by Zindapir in a series of morality tales about his encounter with secular authority.

Once an uncle of the Minister of Finance Mian Muhammad Yasin Khan Watto came to Pir Sahib. He was seriously ill, and had returned from England, diagnosed as suffering from an incurable illness. Pir Sahib cast *dam* (blew a Qur'anic verse for healing purposes) on him and said: 'Let him eat from the *langar*'s food and he will be cured'. Once healed, the Minister asked the Pir if he could make him, the Minister, his disciple, allow him to cast *dam* and provide the food for the *langar* for three days. Zindapir said: 'You will provide for the *langar* for three days but what will happen after that? I cannot make you partner, *sharik*, with God. Nor will I make you

---

[3] A similar message in contemporary Morocco is enunciated by Abd al Yasin, founder of the Justice and Charity Society, who rejects the authority of the King, according to Paul Heck (2006).

my disciple or allow you to cast *dam*.' (Story first told me by the Sheikh in October 1989)

The tapestry of legends, myths, and morality tales told by and about Zindapir objectify the saint's divine grace and power through concrete images and remembered encounters. At the same time, the powerful validity of the legends and morality tales springs dialectically from the observed ascetic practices of the Saint, which embody for his followers fundamental notions about human existence and sources of spiritual authority.

This dual basis for legitimized truth—saintly practice and concrete image—makes the legendary corpus about the saint impervious to factual inconsistencies. The 'myths' and 'legends' are conceived of as historically accurate, true, exemplary narratives about an extraordinary individual. If the myths contain self-evident truths which transcend the mundane and are not amenable to quotidian, common sense evaluation, this is because the subject of these tales, the living saint, is perceived to be an extramundane individual, a man outside and above the world, rather than in it.

This returns us to the question raised at the outset: to what extent is Sufism as a transnational religious movement differentially embedded in the common sense notions of specific cultural environments? I want to argue, against Geertz's relativist position, that the religious rationality and common sense values implicit in Sufism *transcend* cultural and geographical boundaries. The underlying logic of the fables constituting this religious imagination is the same logic, whether in Morocco, Iraq, Pakistan or Indonesia. It is based on a single and constant set of equations, starting from the ultimate value of self-denial or asceticism:

World renunciation (asceticism) = divine love and intimacy with God = divine 'hidden' knowledge = the ability to transform the world = the hegemony of spiritual authority over temporal power and authority.

The legends about powerful Sufis, from Indonesia and Morocco, which Geertz argues exemplify the contrastive localism of Islam, retell, in essence, the same fable or plot: (1) initiation through a physical and mental ordeal overcome; (2) the achievement of innate and instantaneous divine knowledge; (3) the triumphant encounter with temporal authority. The same legends can be found in Attar's 'Memorial of Saints' which records the lives of the early saints of Baghdad (Attar 1990). What differs are merely the ecological and historical details: a flowing river and exemplary center in Indonesia, desert sands and a fortress town in Morocco, the Baluch Regiment, an anti-colonial brigand's valley, and corrupt politicians in Pakistan. A single paradigmatic common sense plot upholds this legendary corpus, while the legends' local concrete details—regiments, rivers, and desert sands embody this common sense and suffuse it with axiomatic authority. But the symbolic structure underlying this common sense is as unitary as it is inexorable.

Indonesian Sufism: Teasing out Comparisons

This brings me finally to a comparison of South Asian and Indonesian Sufism. One of the difficulties of drawing such a comparison relates to the different terminology used to describe Sufi regional cults in Indonesia. The key elements—places, actors, and rituals—that sustain Indonesian regional cults are described by their indigenous names even in anthropological texts, and this makes comparison difficult to tease out. Nevertheless, the basic building blocks of the cults: saints, shrines, annual rituals, sacred exchange, central lodges, and their hierarchically ordered branches, all seem to be present in Indonesia.

Let me consider each of the different building blocks comprising Indonesian Sufi cults first, before exploring how they are interrelated. I draw on published texts, along with three doctoral theses and one masters thesis submitted to the Australian National University which are also crucial ethnographic documents in this comparative endeavor.[4]

As in South Asia, so too in Indonesia there are famous ancient Sufi shrines of celebrated *wali* which are places of pilgrimage for persons coming from the whole of Indonesia. As in South Asia, these major shrines often have associated with them whole villages of descendants who service the grave and its festivals, each with its own clientele. Such a village is described by Jeffery (1979) and by Pinto (1995) in their studies of the shrine of Nizam-uddin Auliya located in Delhi, and for Indonesia by Muhaimin (1995) in his description of the Buntet shrine complex in Cirebon, Java. My own focus here, however, is on the smaller Sufi regional cults whose extension is far more limited and local, focused on either a living saint or his shrine, which rise and fall periodically, waxing and waning over time.

The other point which needs to be made in advance of the comparative analysis is one established clearly by Mark Woodward (1989) and a range of other Indonesian scholars: namely, that Sufi mystical theosophy in Indonesia, along with the practice of *zikr,* the repetitive recollection of God's name, resemble practices and beliefs elsewhere in the Muslim world. The basic ideas of taking the oath of allegiance to a saint (*bai'at*), initiation, and 'travel' through different mystical stages on the Sufi path, self-denial, asceticism,

---

4   These are: Dhofier (1980); Zulkifli (1994); Muhaimin (1995); Jamhari (2000). For a survey of studies of Islam in Indonesia, with particular emphasis on anthropological studies of Islam, see Jamhari (2002) and for further references see the brief survey by Fox (2002).

control of the vital, selfish soul (*nafs*), and mystical epiphany are found in Indonesia as they are in the Middle East or South Asia. Second, as in South Asia, Sufism in Indonesia, known locally as 'traditional' Islam, has been under attack by Islamic and modernist reformists, who accuse it of unlawful syncretism and polytheism (*shirk*). While such highly politicized attacks are found throughout the Muslim world, and are often defined as an opposition between 'doctor' (*'alim*) and 'saint' (see Gellner 1981), in Indonesia, as in South Asia, the resistance to this attack has involved, it seems, an alliance of both saints and learned religious scholars or clerics (*'ulama*), a point to which I return below.[5] Following from this, like in South Asia and other parts of the Muslim world, a tendency to distinguish in Indonesia between practicing Sufis and the so-called superstitions surrounding the cult of saints' shrines has obscured the intrinsic *interdependency* of these two.

In Indonesia, saints are known honorifically as *kyai,* but also by a range of other titles: *wali* (usually reserved for big saints, including the nine founding saints in Java), *muqaddam, mursyid, serepah* (meaning elder), and *syeikh*. Important *kyai,* founders of their own lodges (*pesantren*) are regarded as charismatic figures, imbued with blessing, and this charisma is transmitted from father to son, much as it is in other parts of the Muslim world. Woodward acknowledges that "for many traditional students, relationships with *kyai* are elements in the *zuhud* (ascetic) complex. They see *kyai* as much as living saints as teachers, as much as sources of blessing as of knowledge" (Woodward 1989: 144). As in South Asia, in Indonesia too, high value is placed on asceticism even in the case of wealthy saints (ibid.: 145). Saints prepare amulets for supplicants and engage in healing, blessing, and exorcism as they do in South Asia (ibid.: 146).

Indonesian saintly lodges or *pesantren* (ibid.: 135) are most often rural, and they often own large tracts of land donated as religious endowments (*waqf*), by royal patrons (ibid.: 146) or through purchase. If the lodge is an old one, it usually includes the graves of the founders and their sons and grandsons. These are known as (*keramat*) and are the focus of an annual festival commemorating the death of the saint, usually called *khaul* or *kaul* in Indonesia. The lodge doubles up as a religious seminary for youth, mostly young men, which teaches a standard course in religious studies, with a traditional Sufi inflection. The centrality of teaching in the Indonesian lodges seems often to overshadow the centrality of saintly charisma and pilgrimage (*ziarah*) to a Sufi shrine characteristic of Pakistani and Middle Eastern central lodges. In Pakistan, Barelvi, Sufi-oriented, schools and seminaries are kept separate

---

5   Sufi-minded *'ulama* are also found in Egypt where Sufi orders continue to flourish.

from saints' lodges (on the growth in the number of these schools in Pakistan see Malik 1998).

Several ambiguities arise in the literature from the educational role of the *pesantren* Sufi lodges in Indonesia. The saint or his deputies (*khalifa, khulfat*, known in Indonesia also as *badal murshid*) who head the lodges are often described in English as 'teachers'. More usually in Sufi parlance, the saint as religious guide on the Sufi path is called a *murshid*. Saints in South Asia never officiate as religious officials in the mosque or in weddings and funerals. Unless they are minor saints, they never teach young children. These are tasks allocated to learned religious clerics who respect saintly traditions. The saint's role is confined to guiding his initiates (*murids*), healing supplicants, advising his flock and pronouncing *du'a*, a supplicatory prayer, benediction or blessing. In addition, the saint organizes the feeding of the multitudes in rituals, festivals, and weekly *zikr* meetings at the central lodge.

So who is the *kyai* in Indonesian Sufi Islam? Is he a teacher of young men and small children or a *murshid*, initiating and guiding his disciples?

The second ambiguity in the literature arises in relation to the organization of pesantren Sufi lodges in Indonesia. Woodward, following Dhofier (1980), describes the rise of a major Indonesia *kyai* saint, Hasyim Asy'ari, born in 1881, scion to a saintly family (Woodward 1989: 136). He began 'teaching' in his father's lodge at the age of 13 and later studied in Mecca. Returning to Java in 1899, he 'taught' briefly at his older brother's lodge before founding his own lodge, Pesantren Tebuireng at Cukir in East Java. Woodward says that "within ten years it was a major supplier of teachers to other *pesantren*". He reports that according to Dhofier (1982: 95-96), Asy'ari's students were sent to found their own lodges, many of which became institutions with over a thousand students.

The question is, were these so-called student-turned-teacher disciples promoted by the saint as his deputies and messengers (*khalifa*), being in some cases even aspiring *kyai* saints in their own right, or were they merely learned *'ulama*? One possibility is that in Indonesia two centrally focused, regional systems overlap, but only partially: one system is that of learned scholars, the *'ulama*, who remain connected to a major center of learning such as Tebureng in Easter Java, described by Dhofier (1999). Dhofier says that in its heyday there were 500 madrassas linked this lodge with 200,000 students, and it was the center of the NU (the Nahdatul 'Ulama,), an association of *'ulama*, with its circuit of meetings and conferences (see Hefner 2002: 144). Alternatively, one might look at the regional cults of the *kyai* or saints as comprising the sacred center along with its *khulafa*, sent by the saint to found new lodges, who continue to recognize their allegiance to their saint-guide, and to regard his lodge as the cult center. This view is lent support by Jamhari (2002)'s discussion of the central lodge in Buntet of a Tijanniya saint studied by Muhaimin

(1995: 346). Kyai Abbas acting as murshid, he says, 'organised and centralised' this Sufi order widely through the establishment of new lodges centerd on Buntet (Jamhari 2002: 19-20). Van Bruinessen (2003: 9) reports on an *'alim* who "succeeded his father Romly as the major Qadiriyya wa-Naqshbandi teacher of East Java and inherited a vast network of hundreds of local, mostly rural, groups of followers led by local deputies that went on expanding, and he established close contacts with members of the military and political establishment in Jakarta". He further reports that "in West Java, there was a rapidly expanding Qadiriya wa-Naqshbandiya network too, centered upon the pesantren of Suryalaya and its chief teacher, Abah Anom". Sila (2003: 3) reports on a popular order in Bandung which had 318 places of *manaqiban* (Sufi circles practicing collective reading of saintly hagiographies), with the number of students extending to tens of thousands throughout the city. Another order, Kadisiyya, was said to have founded four branches, spreading in several large cities in Indonesia, including Jakarta, with Cilegon as the headquarters (Sila 2003: 9). This particular founding saint claims direct inspiration from a hidden companion (*Uways*) of the Prophet. In one case, reported by Azra (2003: 5) a newly founded Sufi center which treated drug users through zikr, had developed transnational network throughout South East Asia. In other words, it had developed a new regional cult around the center.

How is such a far flung regional cult co-ordinated in Indonesia by the sacred center? We know nothing about these particular cults, but the literature contains some clues about the co-ordination of other Sufi regional cults in Indonesia. First, it seems that many saints are related to one another by kinship or marriage, and trace their origin as Sayyids to the Prophet's line of descent, as well as through a sacred genealogy (*silsila*) of teacher-disciples (Woodward 1989: 145).

In his own study of Jatinom, another lodge, Jamhari reports on a traditional celebration, named *Angkawiya,* commemorating the life of a deceased saint, to which people walked on foot some 30 kilometers to obtain *apem,* a pancake-like cake made of rice flour, coconut milk, sugar, salt, and oil (Jamhari 2000: 228). The festival, also known as *apenam* (ibid.: 205-215; 2002: 29), culminates in a ritual struggle by the attendant crowd for the pancakes, regarded as endowed with powerful blessing (*baraka),* thrown from a tall tower. As many as three tons of flour are donated by surrounding villagers, and the *apem* itself can only be baked by direct descendants of the saint (Jamhari 2000: 217, 226). The *apem* is arranged in a mountainous shape, in two types, one male, one female, representing the saint, Kyai Ageng Gribig, and his wife (ibid.: 226). Before its distribution a supplication (*du'a*) is made over it and during its distribution the crowds chant *dhikr* and address God, the Almighty and most powerful (ibid.: 227). Exegesis Jamhari obtained highlighted the spiritual aspect of the scramble, the 'striving' for *apem*. "This means that if in the *slametan* you obtained *apem*", one informant told Jamhari, "this indicates that you have obtained a spiritual blessing from Kyai Ageng Gribig" (the departed saint) (ibid.: 39). The *apem,* containing *baraka,* is not eaten but can be used in various ways: as a 'fertilizer' scattered over fields, to get rid of pest attacks, to protect a house (ibid.: 229).

We see here parallels with the *'urs* in Pakistan as an annual ritual festival at the sacred center, the abode of the saint, to which all the branches of a regional cult make pilgrimage. This is a moment of sacred exchange: the saint feeds the multitudes, slaughtering hundreds of animals in sacrifice, while disciples return from the lodge with gifts of white caps and cotton scarves. The moment of *du'a,* supplication, is a breathless moment of sacred *communitas.* Indeed, I have argued that the *'urs* is the organizational hub of Zindapir's and other Sufi regional cults. Woodward reports on the royal Sufi rituals at Yogyakarta, in which the sultan is said to attain mystical union with God and tens of thousands of people gathered are offered 'mountains' of sticky rice, highly charged with blessing (Woodward 1989: 179). Like the King of Morocco, Indonesian royals also claim direct descent from the Prophet. Dhofier (1999) reports that in the minor lodge at Tegalsari, at its heyday, during the annual *kaul* five cows, forty goats and hundreds of chickens were slaughtered for the festival. Jamhari reports that in the annual *kaul akbar* ceremony at the shrine of Sunan Tembayad, which lasts for a whole week, the cloth on the grave, the *pasang singep,* is changed and the old cloth is cut into handkerchief shapes and distributed to visitors, sometimes for a fee (Jamhari 2000: 127, 218). In Pakistan *dupatta,* green, red or black shawls, are carried through the lodge and laid on the saint's grave, much as they would be held over the bride's head at a *mehndi,* pre-wedding ritual, symbolizing his union, 'marriage' with God (Werbner 2003: 252-254, 269).

Van Bruinessen tells us that from 1950 to 1970, traditional *tariqas* such as the Naqshbandi, Qadri and Tijani, "expanded considerably and built up enormous rural followings, that had turned umbrella organizations into significant political actors" (2003: 13) with many top level army officers and politicians. This is very like the following built up by Zindapir. But what are these so-called umbrella organizations? Is he referring here to the regional cults formed around particular living saints, or are they the associations that joined these cults together? Once again organizational analysis and the use of vernacular terminology inhibit theoretical and conceptual comparisons with Sufi orders elsewhere. For example, according to van Bruinessen (ibid.) among the living saints that emerged were antinomian characters, but we are not told whether they were able to build regional cults, or whether they simply had a high-level clientele who believed in their magical powers of blessing.

A further weakness in this literature is that no distinction is made between (1) disciples, (2) supplicants to a saint seeking blessing or healing, and (3) 'groups' of disciples attending the sacred center, whether merely forming a *zikr* circle, or based at an alternative lodge. Second, we know little about how students are recruited to study at the lodge. How can a Javanese lodge attract young students in their teens from as far afield as Bali or Malaysia? Such recruitment from a vast catchment area implies connections—whether via key individuals or lodges located in peripheral areas.

Muhaimin (1995) contains the best ethnographic detail on the connections between different lodges. He reports on the many instances in which a saint sends delegates to found new lodges, much as Zindapir did in Pakistan and beyond it. The career of a saint usually begins as a young man with travel for learning, in which he may spend time at many different lodges, and often in the Hijaz, before returning to his original lodge and ultimately founding his own lodge. Over time a network of lodges emerges, linked through discipleship to the central lodge (see in particular Muhaimin 1995: 311, 351). There is a tendency for saints to recruit talented sons-in-law by marrying them to their daughters, and many lodges are connected by intricate kinship relations, since saints tend to marry endogamously with families tracing descent to the Prophet (ibid.: 317, 320). Lodges often celebrate the eleventh of the month (known in Pakistan as *gyarvi sharif*) much as they do in Pakistan, and Muhaimin reports regular visits from other branches to such celebrations. This, in addition to the annual ritual commemorating the saint's death, the *kaul*, celebrated in most central lodges in Java, although we are told little about the delegations from other lodges attending such festivals. It is also evident from the ethnography that most big saints go on regular circuits to visit outlying branches of the lodge.

As in other regional cults, large Sufi regional cults in Indonesia encompass a wide catchment area, including followers on other islands (Bali, Kalimantan, Sumatra) and beyond, in Singapore and Malaysia. They are thus inter-ethnic and trans-national. This is a distinctive feature of central place organizations and pilgrimage centers, which do not respect administrative and territorial boundaries. According to Richard Werbner, regional cults are, distinctively,

cults of the middle range—more far-reaching than any parochial cult of the little community, yet less inclusive in belief and membership than a world religion in its most universal form. Their central places are shrines in towns and villages, by crossroads or even in the wild, apart from human habitation, where great populations from various communities or their representatives, come to supplicate, sacrifice, or simply make pilgrimage. They are cults which have a topography of their own, conceptually defined by the people themselves and marked apart from other features of cultural landscapes by ritual activities. (R. Werbner 1977: ix)

Like other regional cults, Sufi cults are transregional, transnational, and transethnic. They interpenetrate with one another rather than generating contiguous, bounded territories. They leapfrog across major political and ethnic boundaries, creating their own sacred topographies and flows of goods and people. These override, rather than being congruent with, the political boundaries and subdivisions of nations, ethnic groups, or provinces (ibid.). For example, in the regional cult headed by Zindapir in the North West Frontier Province of Pakistan, followers within Pakistan were Pashtun, Punjabi, and Sindhi speakers. The cult extended into Afghanistan, and also had South African (Indian Muslim) followers, who are mainly Gujarati speakers. Zindapir's Murshid, Baba Qasim, had Hindu and Sikh followers. Zindapir was seeking to reach Christians in Sindh and was very welcoming to Christians, Japanese, and even a Jew like myself, since this proved his universal inclusiveness. There are still shrines both in India and Pakistan that have Muslim and Hindu followers (see, for example, Saheb 1998).

Regional cult analysis aims to disclose hidden structural interdependencies and ruptures between different domains of action: economic, ritual, political. Like other regional cults, Sufi regional cults are both linked to centers of political power and in tension with them. Various historical studies have highlighted the pragmatic tendencies of Sufism in South Asia which have enabled Sufi saints to accommodate to a variety of different political regimes and circumstances, over many centuries of imperial and postcolonial rule.[6] The relationship between the political center and the sacred center is a changing, historically contingent one, and in this sense, as in others, regional cults are historically evolving social formations.[7]

---

6   See, for example, Gilmartin (1984), (1988); Eaton (1978), (1984), (1993); Mann (1989); Liebeskind (1998); on North Africa see Eickelman (1976), (1977); Evans-Pritchard (1949).
7   An example of the complex, historically unstable relations between Sufi regional cults and indigenous political rulers in South Asia is highlighted in Susan Bayly's study of South India during the volatile pre-colonial period from the seventeenth to the early nineteenth centuries (Bayly 1989). Initially following the trade routes into the hinterland, Sufi regional cults drew extensive patronage from a wide variety of Muslim and Hindu petty kings and rulers who struggled to legitimize their rule by claiming spiritual dominion via important Sufi shrines or Hindu temples. The sacred networks of individual shrines extended well beyond a ruler's administrative territory and were thus perceived to be a source of power, so that displays of generosity towards a famous *dargah* became "important touchstone[s] in the competitive acts of state-building pursued by professing Hindu and Muslim rules" (ibid.: 221).

In a landmark study of sacred peripherality, Victor Turner defined pilgrimage centers as 'centers out there,' beyond the territorial political community, and in doing so opened up a whole new set of questions regarding ritual journeys as transformative movements (Turner 1974: ch. 5). Turner conceptualized pilgrimage centers as alternative loci of value within feudal-type societies. Like the rites of passage of tribal societies, he argued, the ritual movement in pilgrimage culminated in a liminal (or liminoid) moment of 'communitas' which was anti-structural and anti-hierarchical, releasing an egalitarian sociality and amity. Pilgrimage centers thus embodied an alternative ethical order, one uncircumscribed by territorially defined relations of power and authority.

In critiquing the series of dichotomous contrasts generated by Turner's theory—inclusive versus exclusive relations, peripherality versus centrality, generic versus particularistic sociality, egalitarian or homogeneous relations versus hierarchical or differentiated ones—regional cult analysis, as outlined above, aims to highlight the dialectic resulting from the complex *conjuncture* of these apparently opposed types of relationships, coexisting in a single cult (R. Werbner 1977: XII *passim*).

As the history of Sufism in South Asia shows, Sufi regional cults are inextricably intermeshed in regional politics. This is because Sufi cults are not simply inclusive. They foster an exclusive membership, and yet the sacred center and the major festivals around it are open to all. Relations between initiates are said to be (generic) relations of love and amity, stripped of any prior status, idealized as beyond conflict or division, yet the organization of regional cults is based around the ingathering of elective groups from particular, defined political and administrative communities—villages, towns, city neighborhoods—while cult relationships are often, as I show in my book (Werbner 2003), marred by interpersonal rivalries and jealousies. The egalitarianism between initiates comes alongside internal relations of hierarchy, and all disciples, whatever their rank, are subject to the absolute authority and discipline of the saint or his successors at the cult center. Indeed, worldly status, class and caste are implicitly recognized at the central lodge, while saintly descendants often vie bitterly for the succession after the decease of the founder.[8] If there is a moment of experienced communitas during the annual ritual at a Sufi regional cult center, it is the product of complex logistical planning, a highly disciplined division-of-labor, and constant vigilance on the part of the organizers.

In the face of criticisms leveled against Turner's theoretical model (R. Werbner 1977; Sallnow 1987; Eade/Sallnow 1991; and for India see Fuller

---

8   Caste is even more in evidence in the complex regional cult organization of the Swaminarayans of Gujarat who divide ascetics from lay followers and recognize divisions by caste among the ascetics (Williams 1984).

1993: 212-213), it seems more accurate to say that sacred pilgrimage creates not 'anti'-structure but 'counter'-structure. Nevertheless, Turner's key point, that pilgrimage centers and the cults they generate produce sacred geographies where alternative, non-temporal and non-administrative ethical orders are ritually embodied and enacted, still seems valid. In this spirit, regional cult theory, as proposed here, aims to conceptualize the dynamics of spatially alternative focal organizations to those centered on bounded, territorially based states or administrative units.

The literature also make clear the extent to which Sufi cults and orders are intermeshed with the politics of Indonesia, first with the politics of the court—royals claimed descent from the Prophet and officiated at major Sufi rituals—and later with the colonial and postcolonial governments. At the same time, most Indonesian saints guard their autonomy and refuse to be fully co-opted by any regime. This too is a widely found feature of Sufi saints and their cults.

Conclusion

Sufism always has its concrete, local manifestations. Without an adequate analytic terminology, however, and a conceptual framework linked to central place theory allowing for comparisons, the study of Indonesian Sufism seems doomed to remain locked in fragmentary descriptions and often fruitless debates about syncretism. Metaphors such as 'networks' are inadequate to describe the complex organizational logistics of Indonesian Sufi regional cults, especially because these networks are not documented ethnographically in detail and are sometimes said to consist of individuals, sometimes of groups or (in rare cases) of lodges (*pesantren*). Without serious consideration of hierarchy and authority relations within each regional cult or order, one has no sense of how such networks are constructed and maintained. Without serious attention to ritual performances as indexical events, the management of cult organization remains obscure, and no serious comparative analysis with South Asia or the Middle East is possible. Above all, we know very little about the kinds of sacred exchanges occurring at a central lodge—how are relations between saint and disciple or saint and *khalifa* embodied? What are the rituals that connect distant places? We do, however, get a hint of the prevalence of such sacred exchanges in accounts of the distribution of *apem,* sticky rice and sacrificial meat.

It is evident that, like in Pakistan and North Africa, in Indonesia as well Sufi centers rise and fall, wax and wane (see Dhofier 1980: 172, 235) as they do elsewhere. But the literature on Sufism in Indonesia lacks serious attention to the indexical dimensions of the annual saints' ritual, the *kaul* or its equivalent, which elsewhere, I have demonstrated, revitalizes the charisma of a saint and his dominion over an extensive catchment area, or *wilayat*. Too much attention, it seems to me, is paid to the educational, scholarly and intellectual dimensions of Indonesia Sufi cults, or the mapping in space of genealogical connections or chains of authority in the case of Sufi orders. These may not reflect actual organizational connections on the ground, but are often merely a way of conceptualizing space through the use of genealogies descent, familiar in the anthropological literature. In the case of Sufi genealogies, these trace the links from Pakistan or Indonesia to Mecca, the sacred center of Islam. To understand the charisma of a Sufi saint, and the cult he creates, sometimes expanded by his descendants, the need is to study contemporary Sufi regional cults or sub-orders, apart from the major global Sufi orders to which they recognize allegiance. The need, in other words, is to plot the actual relationships between branches and their disciples, and how these are sustained and revitalized through periodic ritual performance. This is a central theme in the regional cult theorization of Sufi orders.

In Trimingham's view, the larger orders were never viable organizations; their expansion took place, and continues to do so, via the *ta'ifas*. This was true of the Suharwardiyya order which was never, he says, a unified order but merely a "line of ascription from which derived hundreds of *ta'ifas*" (Trimingham 1971: 179). He continues:

Similarly with the Qadiriyya; the descendant of Abd al-Qadir in Baghdad is not recognized as their superior by an Arab Qadiri *ta'ifa*. Even the nineteenth-century Tijaniyya, as it expanded, has tended to lose its centralized authority. The shaikh of the central Darqawi *zawiya* has no control over the many offshoots (ibid.).

Only very small, parochial orders are coherent, he says, maintained by tours undertaken by the shaikh and his emissaries (ibid.).

Although lodges often imitate royal courts, the Weberian tension between bureaucratic or temporal authority and charismatic authority still holds true for autonomous Sufi lodges in South Asia.[9] Moreover, the capitalist, commodity economy is converted at a saint's lodge into a good-faith, moral economy through altruistic giving to the communal *langar*, a form of perpetual sacrifice[10]. Even more generally, the site of the saint's lodge is set apart as a space of voluntarism, expressive amity, and emotional good will, of *sukun*, tranquility and harmony. The bureaucratic state and its politicians, by contrast, are seen as menacing, corrupt, greedy and unfeeling. They are not truly 'rational' in the Weberian sense since they bend the rules to their selfish in-

---

9 For a discussion of Weber's notion of charisma, see Eisenstadt (1968), and for the debate as to whether charisma is located at the center or periphery, see Turner (1974); Shils (1965) and Geertz (1983).
10 On this see Werbner (2003).

terests; but they use the instruments of patriarchal domination to achieve their goals. Theirs is a charisma of unbridled power. By contrast the saint's charisma—and his achievement of subjective autonomy and freedom—is the product of his perceived (and projected) self-denial and self-mastery, of love and generosity.

But at the same time, as regional cult theory proposes, social structure is not effaced in Sufi regional cults, just as the mundane realities of politics, economics and social ranking cannot be made to disappear; instead, these structural and ordering elements are incorporated in new combinations, and negotiated in practice. Experientially, nevertheless, the lodges of Sufi saints are for supplicants and pilgrims a fleeting sanctuary from the 'real' world, a place of self-discovery and self-fashioning. A comparative analysis between Sufi cults in widely separated localities, using the range of analytic tools outlined in this chapter, enables us to begin to explore these complex interrelationships between power, authority, economics and religious experience in the contemporary world.

Acknowledgements

This paper was first presented at the conference on "Cultures, Nations, Identities and Migrations", 15-16 April 2004. I would like to thank participants at the conference and particularly Kathy Robinson for their insightful comments. In writing the paper, I benefited from a three-week fellowship at the Humanities Research Center, ANU, which enabled me to read some of the theses lodged in the ANU library. I have also benefited from the incisive and extremely helpful comments of the two editors of this volume, Samuli Schielke and Georg Stauth, I am grateful to them for compelling me to clarify my argument.

References

Attar, Farid al-Din (1990)[1966] *Muslim Saints and Mystics: Episodes from Tadhkirat al Auliyq'* (translated by A.J. Arberry), London: Arkana.
Azra, Asyumardi (2003) "Transnational Network and the Transformation of Indonesian Islam". Paper presented at the "International Conference on Sufism and the 'Modern' in Islam", Bogor, 4-6 September, 2003.
Bayly, Susan (1989) *Saints, Goddesses and Kings: Muslims and Christians in South Indian Society 1700-1900*, Cambridge: Cambridge University Press.
Becker, A.L. (1979) "Text-building, Epistemology, and Aesthetics in Javanese Shadow Theatre". In: A.L. Becker/Aram Yengoyen (eds.) *The Imagination of Reality*, Norwood: Ablex Publishing, pp. 211-243

van Bruinessen, Martin (2003) "Sufi Orders, Indigenous Mystical Traditions, and Islamic Reform in Indonesia: Some Counter-Intuitive Developments". Paper presented at the "International Conference on Sufism and the 'Modern' in Islam", Bogor, 4-6 September, 2003.

Dhofier, Zamankhsyari (1980) *The Pesantren Tradition: A Study of the Role of the Kyai in the Maintenance of the Traditional Ideology of Islam in Java* (Ph.D. thesis), The Australian National University.

Dhofier, Zamankhsyari (1982) *Tradisi Pesantren: Studi tentang Pandangan Hidup Kyai*, Jakarta: LP3ES.

Dhofier, Zamakhsyari (1999) *The Pesantren Tradition: The Role of Kyai in the Maintenance of Tradtional Religion in Java*, Arizona: Arizona State University.

Eade, John/Sallnow, Michael (1991) "Introduction". In: John Eade/Michael Sallnow (eds.) *Contesting the Sacred: The Anthropology of Christian Pilgrimage*, London: Routlege.

Eaton, Richard W. (1978) *Sufis of Bijapur, 1204-1760*, Berkeley: University of California Press.

Eaton, Richard W. (1984) "The Political and Religious Authority of the Shrine of Baba Farid". In: Barbara Daly Metcalf (ed.) *Moral Conduct and Authority: The Place of Adab in South Asian Islam*, Berkeley: University of California Press, pp. 333-356.

Eaton, Richard W. (1993) *The Rise of Islam on the Bengal Frontier, 1204-1760*, Berkeley: University of California Press.

Eickelman, Dale F. (1976) *Moroccan Islam*, Austin: University of Texas Press.

Eickelman, Dale F. (1977) "Ideological Change and Regional Cults: Maraboutism and Ties of 'Closeness' in Western Morocco". In: Ricahrd P. Werbner (ed.) *Regional Cults* (ASA Monographs No. 16), London/New York: Academic Press, pp. 3-28.

Eisenstadt, Shmuel N. (1968) *Max Weber and Institution Building: Selected Papers*, Chicago: University of Chicago Press.

Evans-Pritchard, E. E. (1949) *The Sanusi of Cyrenaica*, Oxford: Clarendon Press.

Fox, James J. (2002) "Towards a Social Anthropology of Islam in Indonesia". In Fu'ad Jabali/Jamhari (eds) *Islam in Indonesia: Islamic Studies and Social Transformation,* Montreal/Jakarta: Indonesia-Canada Higher Education Project, pp. 73-81.

Fuller, C. J. (1993) *The Camphor Flame: Popular Hinduism and Society in India*, Princeton, NJ: Princton University Press.

Geertz, Clifford (1968) *Islam Observed*, New Haven: Yale University Press.

Geertz, Clifford (1983) *Local Knowledge*, New York: Basic Books.

Gellner, Ernest (1981) *Muslim Society*, Cambridge: Cambridge University Press.

Gilmartin, David (1984) "Shrines, Succession, and Sources of Moral Authority". In: Barbara Daly Metcalf (ed.) *Moral Conduct and Authority: The Place of Adab in South Asian Islam*, Berkeley: University of California Press, pp. 221-240.

Gilmartin, David (1988) *Empire and Islam*, Berkeley: University of California.

Heck, Paul (2006) "The Politics of Sufism. Is There One?". Conference on "Exile and Tradition: Transnational Contemporary Sufism", Copenhagen 20-23 September 2006.

Hefner, Robert W. (2002) "Varieties of Muslim Politics: Civil vs. Statist Islam". In: Fu'ad Jabali/Jamhari (eds.) *Islam in Indonesia: Islamic Studies and Social Transformation,* Montreal/Jakarta: Indonesia-Canada Higher Education Project, pp. 136-151.

Jamhari (2000) *Popular Voices of Islam: Discourse on Muslim Orientations in South Central Java* (Ph.D. thesis), The Australian National University.

Jamhari (2002) "Javanese Islam: The Flow of Creed". *Studia Islamika* 9/2, pp. 3-45.

Jeffery, Patricia (1979) *Frogs in a Well*, London: Zed Books.

Liebeskind, Claudia (1998) *Piety on its Knees: Three Sufi Traditions in South Asia in Modern Times*, Delhi: Oxford University Press.

Malik, Jamal (1998) *Colonisation of Islam: Dissolution of Traditional Institutions in Pakistan*, Delhi: Manohar.

Mann, Elizabeth A. (1989) "Religion, Money and Status: Competititon for Resources at the Shrine of Shah Jamal, Aligarh". In: Christian W. Troll (ed.) *Muslim Shrines in India: Their Character, History and Significance*, Delhi: Oxford University Press, pp. 145-171.

Muhaimin, A. G. (1995) *The Islamic Traditions of Cirebon: Ibadat and Adat among Javanese Muslims,* (Ph.D. thesis), The Australian National University.

Pinto, Desiderio (1995) *Piri-Muridi Relationship: A Study of the Nizamuddin Dargah*, New Delhi: Manohar.

Saheb, S.A.A. (1998) "A Festival of Flags: Hindu-Muslim Devotion and the Sacralising of Localism at the Shrine of Nagor-e-Sharif". In: Pnina Werbner/Helene Basu (eds.) *Embodying Charisma: Modernity, Locality and the Performance of Emotion in Sufi Cults,* London: Routledge, pp. 55-76.

Sallnow, Michael J. (1987) *Pilgrims of the Andes: Regional Cults in Cusco*, Washington DC: Smithsonian Institution Press.

Sedgwick, Mark (2005) *Saints and Sons*, Leiden: Brill

Shils, Edward A. (1965) "Charisma, Order and Status". *American Sociological Review* 30/1, pp. 199-230.

Sila, Muhammad Adlin (2003) "*Tarekat Kadisiyyah:* an example of neo-tariqat searching for sympathy of urban people in Bandung". Paper presented at the "International Conference on Sufism and the 'Modern' in Islam", Bogor, 4-6 September, 2003.

Trimingham, J. S. (1971) *The Sufi Orders in Islam*, Oxford: Oxford University Press at the Clarendon Press.

Troll, Christian W. (ed.)(1989) *Muslim Shrines in India: Their Character, History and Significance*, Delhi: Oxford University Press.

Turner, Victor (1974) "Pilgrimages as Social Processes". In: Victor Turner *Dramas, Fields, and Metaphors*, Cornell: Cornell University Press, pp. 166-230.

Weber, Max (1948) *From Max Weber: Essays in Sociology*, London: Routledge/
Kegan Paul.

Werbner, Pnina (2003) *Pilgrims of Love: The Anthropology of a Global Sufi Cult*, London: Hurst Publishers/Bloomington: Indiana University Press.

Werbner, Pnina/Basu, Helene (1998) "Introduction: The Embodiment of Charisma". In: Pnina Werbner/Helene Basu (eds.) *Embodying Charisma: Modernity, Locality and the Performance of Emotion in Sufi Cults*, London: Routledge, pp. 3-27.

Werbner, Richard (1977) "Introduction". In: Richard Werbner (ed.) *Regional Cults*, London/New York: Academic Press.

Williams, Raymond B. (1984) *A New Face of Hinduism: The Swaminarayan Religion*, Cambridge: Cambridge University Press.

Woodward, Mark R. (1989) *Islam in Java: Normative Piety and Mysticism in the Sultanate of Yogyakarta*, Tuscon: The University of Arizona Press.

Zulkifli (1994) *Sufism in Java: The Role of the Pesantren in the Maintenance of Sufism in Java* (M.A.), The Australian National University.

Chapter 2

(Re)Imagining Space: Dreams and Saint Shrines in Egypt*

Amira Mittermaier

In 1867, when Khedive Ismail Pasha of Egypt traveled to France to visit the Exposition Universelle, Baron Haussmann personally received him and showed him the 'new Paris'. Inspired by his visit to the 'capital of modernity' (Harvey 2006), the Khedive appointed the French-educated minister Ali Mubarak to rebuild Cairo with open spaces and straight streets that would reflect and further the city's orderliness and social propriety.[1] The ensuing process of reordering which resulted in the construction of legible and easily-surveillable spaces has been read by Timothy Mitchell (1988) as an effect of modernity's colonizing and disciplinary power.[2] It aimed to impose onto Egypt not only a new 'modern' cityscape but also "a new conception of space, new forms of personhood, and a new means of manufacturing the experience of the real" (ibid.: ix). This paper is about two spaces that seem to run counter to this new conception of space and reality: the dream and the saint shrine.[3]

---

* I thank Alejandra Gonzalez-Jimenez, Jess Bier, Nadia Fadil, and the editors of the Yearbook, Georg Stauth and Samuli Schielke, for their helpful remarks on earlier drafts of this paper. I also gratefully acknowledge financial support from the Social Science Research Council, the Wenner Gren Foundation for Anthropological Research, and the Society of Fellows in the Humanities at Columbia University.

1 During their occupation the French had already built long, ruler-straight streets for military purposes, but for the most part the disciplinary order of modernity was imposed onto Cairo's city space by Muhammad Ali's grandson, Ismail Pasha, who was the Khedive of Egypt from 1863 to 1879. For details on Cairo's restructuring see Ali Mubarak's (1980) *al-Khitat al-Tawfiqiyya al-Jadida* and Janet Abu-Lughod's (1971) *Cairo: 1001 Years of the City Victorious*.

2 This is not to say that re-orderings of space have colonizing effects only in modernity. Gwendolyn Wright (1991) suggests parallels between colonial urban designs for Greek settlers in Turkey in the seventh century BC, Spanish conquistadors in Latin America in the sixteenth century, and more recent French, British, and Dutch colonial settlements. Michel Foucault (1984: 239), on the other hand, claims that a concern with the architectural requirements for the maintenance of order was heightened in eighteenth century Europe.

3 My fieldwork in Cairo in 2003 and 2004 was primarily concerned with discourses and practices surrounding dreams and visions, but for reasons that should be apparent from this paper, I also spent much time at saint shrines. A

Through considering the interplay between these two spaces, my discussion invites a re-imagining of space itself. Both the saint shrine and the dream diverge from the modern order that had so impressed the Khedive during his visit to Paris. Shrines break the order of straight lines and empty Cartesian space, and dreams open up possibilities of travel and interlocution that are foreclosed by the spatial and temporal restrictions of waking life. While both of these spaces seemingly subvert the order of modernity, I want to challenge materialist readings which view dreams as a form of false consciousness or which prioritize saint shrines as sites of resistance. Instead I suggest that understandings of saint shrines are incomplete unless they are conceptualized within a space which includes both the material and the imaginary. Importantly, 'imaginary' here does not equal 'unreal.' In the context of this paper the imagination is not the same as fantasy; it is both a *mode of perception* and an *order of reality*.[4] Attention to this kind of imagination, I suggest, can lead to a more nuanced view of religious everyday life in modern Egypt as it opens up spaces for understanding that move beyond dichotomies. Dreams and saints often inhabit an in-between-ness and direct our attention to interplays and ambiguities, thereby disrupting the antagonisms that pervade both liberal secularist and Salafi-oriented Muslim reformist discourses.

As in other places, the modernizing project had grand ambitions in Egypt, yet in practice its outcome was ambiguous and fragmentary. Alternative orders were not erased or replaced, but they were remade, reframed, and labeled as 'traditional.' The traditional/modern dichotomy is one particular outcome (and justification) of the modernizing project, and this dichotomy is today also mirrored in Cairo's cityscape. Whereas Haussmann had razed entire districts of Paris, Khedive Ismail Pasha decided to build a new city just west of the old Cairo. As in other colonial settings, two cities thus emerged side by side as architecturally and socially distinct entities: a New City that was planned on a drawing board, and an organically grown Old City.[5] Ali Mubarak's plans to also equip the Old City with open spaces and wide streets failed for the most part and, in addition to its winding alleys, Old Cairo kept most of its mosques and saint shrines. Supposedly, today there are more than 900 saint shrines in

---

note on translation: Rendering *awliya'* (literally the 'friends of God' or 'those close to God') as saints is problematic because of the Christian connotations attached to the latter term. Nevertheless, for the sake of readability, I use the term 'saints' throughout this paper to refer to the *awliya'*.

4 This model of the imagination is central to some Sufi cosmologies. See, e.g., Akkach (1997) and Corbin (1997) on Ibn al-'Arabi and the imagination, and Aaron (2002) and Moosa (2005) on al-Ghazali. Remnants and reformulations of this model play into contemporary dream-discourses in Egypt.
5 See Janet Abu-Lughod's article "Tale of Two Cities" (1965). See also Brinkley Messick (1993), especially chapter 12 "Spiral Texts", and Bourdieu (1977).

Cairo alone.[6] Besides the locally-known saints, famous members of the Prophet's family (*ahl al-bayt*) such as Imam al-Husayn, Sayyida Zaynab, Sayyida Nafisa, and Sayyida 'A'isha, are buried and revered in Egypt's capital. While the shrines generally are located outside of Cairo's modernized and more upper-class neighborhoods, they at times come face to face with urban planners' aspirations to ease the flow of traffic. Stories circulate in Egypt which describe how shrines (and their saints) literally deflected the order of modernity by refusing to give in to the demands of maximally functional city-plans. When shrines are to be moved or destroyed, shovels, pick axes, and other demolition tools break; workers suddenly get sick. Other stories describe how tombs were opened and a pleasant smell emanated from the saint's body which convinced the workers to leave the saint in his or her place. Shrines run counter to the checkerboard order of modernity not only because they refuse to be moved from their place, but also because they represent a non-linear spatial order. The closer one is to the shrine, the more one becomes immersed in its spiritual force, its *baraka*. Inside the shrines this spiritual power is most concentrated in the saint's tomb itself, so that visitors walk around or touch its enclosure (*maqsura*) to absorb some of its *baraka*. While also modern urban orders frequently have centers, as they are constructed around central squares, boulevards, government buildings, and shopping areas, the *baraka* of shrines is more inclusive and does not have the same degree of functional differentiation. Its high concentration inside the shrines extends into their surroundings in concentric and sometimes overlapping circles yet loses its force the further one gets away from the shrine.

Because of their *baraka* saint shrines also upset the order of modernity by attracting numerous visitors who come from nearby neighborhoods or from far away, and whose crowding convergence in the saintly spaces spoils the city's self-image as a modern metropolis. Whereas early hadith literatures as well as the fourteenth century Hanbalite scholar Ibn Taymiyya long ago condemned the practice of visiting saint shrines (*ziyara*), modernists and nationalists brought a new urgency to this critique since the turn of the twentieth century.[7] In spite of this critique, the shrines are continuously and devoutly visited. They are believed to be places where one's prayers get answered and where one can receive help or guidance. At shrines one meets not only peasant

---

6   This number was given to me by an employee at the Higher Council of Sufi Affairs in 2003.
7   See Samuli Schielke (2004) on *mulid*. On the Egyptian state's concern with 'superstitions' and 'excessive' Sufism more generally, see de Jong (1999) and Johansen (1995). What is 'superstition' and what orthodox Islam is of course always up for debate. Some reformist Muslims in Egypt acknowledge the prophetic potential of dream-visions but consider the visitation of shrines forbidden; others visit shrines but deem all dreams dangerously unreliable.

and working class Egyptians but also bankers, university professors, politicians, high school students, military officials and intellectuals. Believers treat the dead saints as real interlocutors and at times even address letters to them.[8] The fact that saints have postal addresses nicely illustrates the ways in which spiritual space spills over into material space. The focus of this paper is precisely this interplay between material and non-material spaces.

I propose that the space of the shrine can best be understood by also considering the imaginary geographies in which it partakes, and more specifically through its relation to dream-space. When conceptualizing dreams as space, one should remember that, as Lefebvre (1991: 3) has pointed out, "we are forever hearing about the space of this and/or the space of that: about literary space, ideological space, the space of the dream, psychoanalytic topologies, and so on and so forth", while it is rarely explained what 'space' is supposed to mean in these contexts. *Space*, as I use the term here, is not only produced through visible social and material relations but it is a broader realm that is socially or metaphysically imbued with meaning and power. Dreams can be thought of as space because dreamers move *in* and *through* dreams. Through dreams, furthermore, the dreamer's spirit can travel into the *barzakh*, a realm located between the human and the Divine, in which the spirits of the living and the dead meet. The dream thus offers a space for encounters. Dream-space is a socially meaningful space that interacts with, but cannot be reduced to, the material. To understand the dream spatially we might also turn to Foucault, who in one of his earliest writings, criticizes Freud for psychologizing the dream and argues that "the privilege [the dream] thus acquired in the realm of psychology deprived it of any privilege as a specific form of experience" (1993: 43). The dream, Foucault suggests, should be understood not as a mere 'rhapsody of images' but as a mode of being in the world. He argues that particular attention should be paid to the spatial dimensions of the dream experience since "much has been said about the temporal pulsations of the dream, its particular rhythms, the contradictions or paradoxes of its duration. Much less about dream space" (ibid. 60).

Dream-spaces, however, are not universal. They are shaped by historical contexts and beliefs concerning the nature of dreams. Yet, a study of dream-spaces poses an obvious methodological problem, as someone else's dreams can never be empirically verified. My interlocutors in Egypt sometimes pointed out to me that the Islamic tradition itself addresses this problematic relationship between dream-experience and dream-telling. A hadith warns that whoever lies about dreams will be gravely punished in the Hereafter as "the worst lie is that a person claims to have had a dream which he has not

---

8 The Egyptian sociologist Sayyid 'Uways (1965) studied a set of letters addressed to Imam al-Shafi'i in the 1960s. For a discussion of a more recent set of letters addressed to the same saint see Aymé Lebon (1997).

had".[9] Within the Islamic tradition of dream interpretation, furthermore, not all dreams are considered to be reliable and trustworthy. The tradition rather distinguishes between three kinds of dreams: dreams that are sent by the Devil or evil spirits; dreams mirroring the dreamers' wishes and worries; and dream-visions which the Prophet Muhammad defined as one of the forty-six parts of prophecy.[10] Telling dream-visions is an established mode of argumentation in Egypt, and dream-stories can consciously be told to establish authority. Far from wanting to embark onto the impossible endeavor of verifying or disproving particular dream-stories, I want to draw attention to the kinds of questions about space and conceptions of the real that such stories open up. All of the dreams that I recount were presented to me as truthful dream-visions (*ru'a*, sing. *ru'ya*). Not only are they taken to be prophetic but they also partake in a larger metaphysical geography. Dream-visions radically diverge from a psychological premise, reminding us that, as Vincent Crapanzano (1992: 142) has noted,

Much of what we in the West call psychological and locate in some sort of internal space ('in the head', 'in the mind', 'in the brain', 'in consciousness', 'in the psyche') is understood in many cultures in manifestly nonpsychological terms and located in other 'spaces'.

These *other spaces*, according to Islamic models of the imagination (*al-khayal*), are not loci inside the human consciousness, but they belong to an actual realm located between spirit and matter, between being and not-being, between the Divine and the human. Besides originating in this realm of in-between-ness, dream-visions are spaces of social relations that enable imaginary journeys which, in turn, often lead to saint shrines. Dream-visions are more than just reflections of the subconscious; they are a reality with potential material consequences.

This paper, in short, explores three geographies that intersect in contemporary Egypt: the order of modernity with its rectangular angles and straight lines; the order of the saint shrines from which concentric circles of *baraka* emanate; and the order of the dream-vision which seems to disregard spatial constraints altogether. Adopting Lefebvre's notion that neither imaginary nor material spaces can be understood in isolation, I examine how dream spaces spill over into, and are shaped by, material spaces and concrete spatial prac-

---

9   Sahih al-Bukhari, Vol. 9, Book 87, nos. 165, 167.
10 In Arabic the three kinds of dreams are referred to as *hulm*, *hadith nafsi*, and *ru'ya* respectively. The prophetic nature of dream-visions is affirmed by sound hadiths. See, e.g., Sahih Bukhari, Vol. 9, Book 87, nos. 116, 119. On the history of Islamic dream interpretation see, e.g., Lamoreaux (2002), Fahd (1966), Kinberg (1994), and Schimmel (1998).

tices. As will be shown, dreams find their materialization in visits to shrines and sometimes even in the building of shrines, whereas shrines (and saints) are materialized through dreams. My argument expands Lefebvre's notion of the production of space by incorporating a recognition of the fact that both the social and the material aspects of that production may take place in the imaginary realm, and thus that the imaginary realm is itself not entirely divorced from either the social or the material.

If we take seriously the interpenetration of the imaginary and the material, then we are also prevented from projecting counter-hegemonic ideologies onto the shrine. Precisely because saint shrines are spaces that counter the state-promoted order of modernity, reformist sensibilities, and patriarchic power relations, they have frequently been prioritized as sites of resistance. Fatima Mernissi refers to them as 'antiorthodox, antiestablishment' (1977: 105) spaces, and Michael Gilsenan (2000), in an article on the dreams of Egyptian peasant women, speaks of the 'disordering power' of dreams that invite women to visit the saint shrines whose powers are already 'resistant to worldly authorities'. Dreams in this view subversively invite believers to already-subversive spaces. Also, Marcia Hermansen suggests in an article on 'Dreams and Dreaming in Islam' that contemporary Muslim women can be empowered through dreaming because,

while women's dreams of saints commanding them to attend shrines are disparaged by scripturalist male religious authorities, such dreams allow the women to penetrate more public social spaces (2001: 84).

Attention to the imagination problematizes this public/private divide. Dreams do not only inspire believers to enter into the public sphere of mosques and shrines, but at times also enable believers to participate in religious realms that they might on a visible level not partake in.[11] Still, the act of visiting the shrines can easily be read as a subversive act. Dream-stories and dream-inspired visitations establish competing forms of order that relativise the seeming evidence that is needed to make the scholars' authority and the modern order seem objective and natural. Nevertheless, I suggest that *from the dreamer's point of view* such dream-stories are not subversive. When visiting a shrine in response to a visitational dream, the dreamer does not answer (or refuse to answer) to the state, to worldly authorities, to the law, or to scripturalist male religious authorities, but she responds to the saint (and the dream). Dream-stories, if taken seriously, thus invite us to think beyond a frame of resistance.[12] While dream-

---

11 Additionally, one might question whether shrines are best conceptualized as solely public spaces.
12 My argument here is in part inspired by Lila Abu-Lughod (1990) who has turned a critical eye to the romantization of resistance, and by Saba Mahmood

visions constitute links between dreamers and saints that evade state control, the laws of rationality, and modernity's spatial order, the interactions surrounding saint shrines for the believers themselves are not primarily subversive acts against state control or the orthodoxy. Dream-visions partake in larger metaphysical spatialities and logics of exchange. Dream-stories therefore do not so much *resist* the hegemonic order of modernity but rather *create* an alternative, but not purposively contrary, space within it.

Let me then turn to some concrete examples to illustrate the multiple spaces inhabited by believers. Drawing on conversations with, and stories told by, Egyptian interlocutors, the remainder of this paper describes four ways in which shrines and dream-visions are interrelated in contemporary Egypt: a) dreams move shrines in terms of their location; b) dreams move dreamers to visit shrines; c) dreams transport dreamers to shrines; and d) shrines shape dreams. Through tracing these multiple interplays, I aim to expand our understanding of both imaginary and material spaces.

Dreams Moving Shrines: Mashhad Ru'ya

We might first consider why shrines are built where they are. The most apparent answer is that the saint either died or was buried in that specific location. But there is another, less obvious possibility: some shrines are built *as a result of dreams*. The belief that deceased saints can announce by way of dream-visions where they want to be (re)buried, is evident, for instance, in the following story recounted by a middle-aged Egyptian woman who frequently visits Cairo's saint shrines:

Sidi Gharib—may God be content with him—was from Morocco. His name was 'Abdullah, and he was called Gharib ['stranger'] because he was fighting in the city of Suez and defending it. They say that, after he lost his leg in battle, he took the leg in his hand and used it as a sword. He was [buried] somewhere—we don't know where exactly—until he came in a dream [lit. in the sleep (*ga fi-l-manam*)] to Sheikh Hafiz, who was a good man, and asked him to take him out from where he was buried and to put him into a shrine. They tried to find his [initial] grave, but they couldn't find it, and then he came again to [Sheikh Hafiz]. He went back and dug deeper and found the body wrapped in white cloth with the leg next to it. The body was still intact, and a pure beautiful smell was emanating from it. The saints don't get eaten by worms. He took the body out and washed it and put it into a shrine as he

---

(2005) who points out that the very emphasis on resistance presupposes and reinscribes liberalist teleologies and concepts of agency.

had been told. Sidi Gharib now is buried in the mosque of the city of Suez, and they call the mosque 'Gharib'.[13]

Appearing twice by way of a dream-vision, Sidi Gharib insisted on being buried in a particular place, and he finally was. The dreamer, in this case a 'good man' and quite generally in such stories a famous person, saint or government official, is bound to execute the saint's request. Abu Hasan al-Shadhili's shrine is said to have been erected after he appeared to President Gamal 'Abd al-Nasser in a vision and requested for his tomb to be built at that specific location. One religious student who had always prayed in al-Sayyid Badawi's mosque in Tanta, supposedly appeared after his death to President Anwar al-Sadat and asked to be buried inside his favorite mosque. Sheikh Mutwalli Sha'rawi, a highly popular religious figure who died in 1998, appeared to President Mubarak who then initiated the building of the sheikh's shrine in Daqadus in the Nile Delta. I heard such stories from a number of Egyptians who frequent saints' tombs. Although the three Egyptian presidents, 'Abd al-Nasser, Sadat and Mubarak, are generally not thought of as very religious figures, these rumors illustrate the extent to which certain dreams are taken to be morally binding. Whether pious or not, the dreamer has to follow the dream-vision because instructions delivered in dreams are 'extremely clear', as a young woman explained to me—so clear that even the Egyptian presidents would not dare ignore them.[14]

In the stories above, the result of a fulfilled dream request is the building of a shrine in which the saint is then buried. Other times saints do not specify their burial place, but instead request a shrine which is merely a vision-site, referred to as *mashhad ru'ya* in Arabic. The term *mashhad* is the place-noun of the verb *shahida* (to witness, to be present). While according to Edward William Lane (1980: 1611) the term refers to a 'place where a martyr had died or is buried', in the case of a vision-site the term exceeds this body-bound meaning. Rather, as a young Egyptian man explained to me, the saint's spirit tires of drifting around the *barzakh* and longs to be anchored in a concrete site. The saint therefore appears in a dream to request a shrine. Outwardly vision-sites resemble other saint shrines: they contain a sarcophagus that is covered with a

---

13 The dream-stories in this paper were collected during my fieldwork in 2003 and 2004. All translations are mine.
14 I am grateful to Samuli Schielke for pointing out to me that a conflicting dream-story circulates with regards to Sheikh Mutwalli Sha'rawi's shrine. Supposedly, the deceased sheikh appeared in a dream to his son Hagg 'Abd al-Rahim who oversaw the construction of the shrine and the organization of the *mulid* and heavily lamented him, telling him that he had done wrong by building a shrine for his father and organizing a *mulid*. Such contradictions are not atypical of Egypt's discursive dream-landscapes but a more encompassing discussion of the underlying politics of dreaming in Egypt would exceed the scope of this paper.

black cloth; visitors circumambulate the shrine, speaking prayers and supplications (*du'a*) to the saint; an annual saint's day celebration (*mulid*) is held at the shrine. But unlike other saint shrines, vision-sites are empty; they do not host the saint's body.

Sayyida Zaynab and Imam al-Husayn each have a number of shrines in Egypt which are dedicated to them; many of these do not lay claim to the presence of their bodies. A famous vision-site in Cairo is also that of Sayyida Ruqayya.[15] While one tradition claims that Sayyida Ruqayya came to Egypt together with her half-sister Sayyida Zaynab, it is generally held that she died and is buried in Damascus. Her shrine in Cairo was built between 1133 and 1153 CE after she had requested it by appearing to the Fatimid ruler al-Hafiz 'Abd al-Magid in a dream. According to Caroline Williams (1985: 44),

that a shrine should have been built for [Sayyida Ruqayya] in Cairo in response to a dream or a vision was not so extraordinary at the time. Supernatural interventions were not uncommon motives for the religious constructions of Islam.

Williams adds that in the twelfth century, and especially in the reign of al-Hafiz, the founding of saint tombs was commonly justified by visions or the miraculous discovery of relics.

A number of historians have remarked upon the phenomenon of vision-sites. In his study of the tomb-centered cult of saints in Egypt between 1200 and 1500 CE, Christopher S. Taylor (1999: 32) notes that large and impressive buildings were erected on the instructions of the saintly dead, as told in dreams, usually without any further corroborating evidence. Rudolf Kriss and Hubert Kriss-Heinrich (1960: 11) confirm that there are many shrines with empty tombs in the Muslim world, and Edward William Lane (1973: 236) observes that "most of the sanctuaries of saints in Egypt are tombs; but there are several which only contain some inconsiderable relic of the person to whom they are dedicated; and there are a few which are mere cenotaphs". Providing a somewhat functionalist interpretation, the Egyptian historian Su'ad Muhammad Mahir (1971: 102f.) links the proliferation of vision-sites to medieval times of hardship and war when believers sought refuge in the Prophet's family and needed more places where they could receive *baraka* and speak supplications. Also Ignaz Goldziher (1971), in his article on saint veneration in Egypt, points to the existence of numerous *Doppelgänger* shrines and argues that authenticity seems to have been of little concern to ordinary believers. In using the term 'authenticity', Goldziher seems to imply a truthful origin, i.e., a

---

15 It is generally believed that Sayyida Ruqayya was the daughter of Imam 'Ali, the fourth caliph and the Prophet's son-in-law, but not Fatima's daughter. Other vision-sites in Cairo include the shrines of Muhammad al-Anwar, Muhammad al-Ga'fari, Rabi'a al-'Adawiyya, and supposedly Sayyida Sukaina.

body that goes with the shrine. He overlooks the possibility that 'ordinary believers' might also be concerned with authenticity but that in their eyes a dream-vision might replace the body's role in authenticating a shrine's location.

This is not to deny that questions of authenticity and orthodoxy are charged political issues in Egypt today. The leading sheikh of the Higher Council of Sufi Affairs, a state institution first established in 1903, was dismissive when I asked him about the phenomenon of vision-sites. He brushed aside the concept with the argument that one can never be sure if the person claiming to have dreamt of a saint is not lying. Such skepticism towards the world of dreams sometimes also manifests itself in a particular kind of materialism which mirrors Goldziher's notion of authenticity as well as the 'new means of manufacturing the experience of the real' described by Timothy Mitchell. When I suggested to the guardians of Sayyida Sukaina's and Sayyida Ruqayya's shrines in Cairo that the shrines might have been built in their particular locations because of dreams, both told me I was wrong and insisted that the two saints are in fact buried in their respective tombs. The shrine here has become a signifier that necessarily indicates a buried body as its signified. The concept of a vision-site does not sit easily with such materialist conceptions of authenticity. A vision-site is seemingly an empty signifier, a token of the imagination. Yet the fact that accounts such as the one about Sidi Gharib circulate among contemporary believers suggests that for them dream-visions are not divorced from the material realm. Dream-visions in such stories figure as a medium of communication, and they inspire actions. As the next section shows, at times they move not only shrines but also dreamers.

Dreams Moving Dreamers: Gifts and Countergifts

Al-Hagga Nura is a pious woman in her seventies who lives in Medinat Nasser, a Cairo suburb, but who rarely leaves her house. One night in July 2004 al-Hagga Nura dreamt that she entered her kitchen and found the sink filled with cooked beans (*ful*). She knew what this meant and the following day she asked her daughter to come over. The latter, in turn, brought me along and the three of us spent hours in al-Hagga Nura's kitchen preparing little plastic bags with cooked beans, sprinkling salt and cumin onto them, wrapping each bag in a leaf of pita bread, and stacking the finished meals in large shopping bags. After completing the preparations, we took a taxi to Sayyida Zaynab's shrine, which sits in the center of Cairo. It is one of the city's most popular shrines.[16]

---

16 Sayyida Zaynab is the daughter of Imam 'Ali and Fatima, and the granddaughter of the Prophet Muhammad.

We entered the women's section, forced our way through the crowd, and began handing out the little bags and bread at random to women sitting on the floor. Someone watching us might have assumed that we were fulfilling the religious obligation to give to the poor, but, whether they knew it or not, the gift that the women in the shrine were receiving was the enactment of an order that had been given in the form of a dream-vision. Al-Hagga Nura had dreamt a dream that requested its own enactment. Her dream-vision had not been of a symbolic nature, but, as both al-Hagga Nura and her daughter insisted, she had dreamt of '*these* beans'.

While al-Hagga Nura explained to me that the beans could be distributed at another shrine as well, some of the women who received our gift that day might have themselves been summoned to Sayyida Zaynab's shrine by a dream. As Nadia Abu Zahra (1997) notes in her ethnography of the shrine, al-Sayyida Zaynab often urges women in dreams to visit her, to eat the food distributed at her shrine, and to keep the vows made to her. During my fieldwork I found as well that people visit shrines for a variety of reasons. Some visit the saints when they are about to get married, when they are sick, before they take an exam, or when they have specific worries and want the saint to intercede on their behalf (*tawassul*). Upper class or Salafi-influenced visitors to the shrines, by contrast, at times were careful to explain to me that they had not come to pray to the saints or to ask them for help, but that they visit out of respect for the saints' exemplarily pious lives. Other visitors in shrines told me that they had come neither to make a request nor to pay their respect but that they had seen the saint in a dream. Dreams, in which a saint visits the dreamer, are considered a special blessing, and stories of such dreams are often introduced with the phrase "I was honored by the vision of ..." (*tasharraft bi-ru'yat ...*). Being a gift, such dreams demand a countergift. As Smith and Haddad (1981: 190) have noted for a historical-textual context, the "interaction of believers and *walis* [saints] is a complex process involving expectation of reward, fear of reprisal for neglect and a highly structured set of particular responsibilities".

When a saint visits a believer by way of a dream, the latter is subsequently expected to visit the saint in his or her shrine. Al-Hagga Nura's example shows that even without a saint appearing in person, a dream can incite a visit to the shrines. What is observable at the shrines might thus in many cases be inspired by non-observable interchanges, spaces and relationships. Such imaginary interactions are not divorced from the material but rather expand its space. Next I turn to an alternative interpretation of dreams in which a saint appears. Sometimes such a dream does not *necessitate* a visit to the saint's shrine but rather *substitutes* for it.

Dreams Leading to Shrines: Night Journeys

'Why walk?' William S. Burroughs asks in his dream book. He continues: "I jump off the iron balcony and swim through the air uptown" (1995: 17). It might be universally true that dreams open up possibilities for movement which are foreclosed to us during our waking life. But such nightly journeys are told, interpreted, valued, and devalued in historically particular ways. According to many of my Egyptian interlocutors, certain dreams can take the dreamers on actual journeys. Within the Islamic tradition an archetypical journey that renders meaningful the believers' own spiritual travels is the Prophet's famous Night Journey (*al-isra wa-l-miraj*). According to the compendia of the tradition, the Prophet Muhammad was asleep one night near the Kaaba in Mecca when he was wakened by the angel Gabriel. Riding on the back of the mythical two-winged horse Buraq, the Prophet and Gabriel flew from Mecca to Jerusalem where they met Abraham, Moses, Jesus and other prophets, and from Jerusalem the journey continued vertically towards the Throne of God. The Prophet passed through all seven heavens and, according to the Qur'an, came 'but two bow-lengths away' from God's presence 'or even nearer'.[17] His bed, it is said, was still warm upon his return to Mecca. Both space and time seem to have been miraculously compressed during this journey. The journey's precise nature, however, is the object of disagreement among Muslim theologians as well as contemporary Egyptians. Whereas according to some the journey was performed both spiritually and physically (as it otherwise would not have been a miracle),[18] others, among them Ibn Baz, the former Grand Mufti of Saudi Arabia, have asserted that it was only a dream. Those adhering to the latter opinion draw on a tradition from 'A'isha, the Prophet's wife, who attested that 'the apostle's body remained where it was but God removed his spirit by night'.[19]

Besides telling me about the Night Journey, my interlocutors in Egypt frequently referred to a Qur'anic verse that reads: 'God takes the souls of those who die, and of those who do not die, in their sleep; then He keeps those ordained for death, and sends the others back'.[20] Based on this verse my inter-

---

17 Qur'an 53:8. All translations from the Qu'ran are Muhammad Asad's.
18 According to miracle narrations in the textual tradition, also living saints sometimes have the ability to appear in two places at once (Gramlich 1987).
19 This hadith is quoted in Ibn Ishaq's biography of the Prophet (Ibn Ishaq 2003: 83).
20 Qur'an 39:42. The Arabic term in this verse is *nafs* (self) and not *ruh* (spirit) but most Egyptians I spoke to understood the verse to refer to the spirit. The *ruh*, of which we know very little according to the Qur'an (17:85), is of divine origin and was passed on to humankind when God breathed His spirit into Adam. According to Egyptian sheikhs and laypeople, the *ruh* is eternal, has no boundaries, and can detach itself from the body during times of sleep.

locutors suggested that also ordinary dreamers' spirits can travel freely while the body is sleeping. According to this understanding, dream-visions take place in a realm which circumvents the conventional restrictions of time and physical space. Whereas Freud (1955: 647) famously called dream interpretation a royal road into the unconscious, for others dreams are themselves roads on which they can travel elsewhere at night. While sound asleep on one's bed in Cairo, one might be circumambulating the Kaaba in Mecca or visiting al-Shadhili's shrine in the south of Egypt.[21] Consider the following dream story told to me by Sharifa, a young upper class woman from Cairo:

One night I was sitting in my room and a person appeared. I didn't see his face. He was wearing a white *gallabiyya*.[22] I saw myself leaving myself; I saw myself with my hair and my body, just like me. I turned and waved bye-bye to myself. Then the person took me to the balcony, and then I was on the street. I don't know how I got from the balcony to the street. I got into my car with him and drove. I don't know where I went, but I found myself in front of a sign saying "The Red Sea". Then there were mountains and people sacrificing animals. There was a big sheikh. We went a few kilometers further, and there was a smaller sheikh. Then we drove back home. I left the car, went back upstairs, and I fell onto myself, like a light blanket—not like a heavy woolen blanket, but something very light. I told Sidi this whole story. I didn't know at all what it was. Never in my life had I known that there are sheikhs at the Red Sea, and I had never even been there.

Sidi is the sheikh of a mystical order to which Sharifa belongs. When she told the sheikh about her dream, he explained that her spirit (*ruh*) had gone to visit Abu Hasan al-Shadhili in Egypt's southern desert, as well as a less famous sheikh buried on the Red Sea coast not too far from al-Shadhili's shrine. The woman had never been to the Red Sea, and it remains ambiguous whether she had actually gone there by way of the vision. Like the Prophet's body during his Night Journey (according to some), her body stayed behind and only her spirit traveled. She speaks of two selves, one waving goodbye to the other, and it seems that she was simultaneously on her bed and at the saint's shrine. According to Sharifa's sheikh, the spirit is not bound by the laws of physicality; it can travel much faster than the body. As the spirit has its own eyes to see and ears to hear, its realm of experience is much wider than that of the body.

As in the previous examples, geographical location in this story is not rendered irrelevant. Sharifa visits two particular shrines, one of which is

---

21 Abu al-Hasan Ali al-Shadhili (d. 1258 CE) was a saint from Morocco who eventually settled in Alexandria. He died in the south of Egypt while on his way to Mecca.
22 A *gallabiyya* is a long dress shirt that is traditionally worn by Egyptian men and women.

marked by an actual sign announcing a nearby geographical landmark ('The Red Sea'). Yet Sharifa's mode of travel exceeds the observable. Also with regards to the Prophet's Night Journey, the question for believers is not *whether* the Prophet truly went to Jerusalem and traveled towards God's Throne, but only *in what form* he did so. Significantly, Ibn Ishaq, the Prophet's first biographer, commented that, "whether [the Prophet] was asleep or awake, it was all true and actually happened" (2003: 183). Dream journeys here offer a fully valid alternative to physical travels.

Shrines Shaping Dreams: Incubation

Whereas some dreams render geographical distances irrelevant, other dreams are shaped by the dreamer's proximity to the saint's *baraka*. Dream-visions seemingly overcome the dreamer but the act of seeing dream-visions can be facilitated through the creation or utilization of spaces which are conducive to dreaming. In addition to its impact upon everyday experiences and popular consciousness (Bourdieu 1977), the construction of material space can thus also affect imaginary dream experiences. Many of my interlocutors told me that bodily practices and the place in which one sleeps can impact the nature of one's dreams. Following the Prophet's tradition, one is more likely to have truthful dream-visions if one sleeps in a state of purity and on one's right side with one's right hand under one's cheek. Dreams of the Prophet or the saints can further consciously be invited through practices such as *dhikr*,[23] by reading specific formulas, or by sleeping in saint shrines. In Morocco in the 1970s, Vincent Crapanzano (1973: 174) observed that pilgrims often tried to sleep in shrines of the Hamadsha saints in the hope that the saints would appear to them and give them instructions. As Elizabeth Sirriyeh (2000: 118) notes, practices expected to result in dreams of the 'holy dead' have a long history in Muslim societies. In contemporary Egypt, too, saint shrines are believed to be places where one is particularly likely to dream of the saints.

Classical orthodox scholars abhorred the practice of sleeping in shrines because of its affinity with the ancient practice of incubation and because of concerns for ritual purity (Fahd 1978).[24] Today sleeping in shrines is often prohibited in line with a broader compartmentalization of social practices and the reorganization of space brought about by modernity's disciplinary power. The

---

23 *Dhikr* here refers to repetitive prayer that has the objective of always being mindful of God. It is a central Sufi ritual for inner purification and divine blessing. Many of my Sufi interlocutors spoke to me of the waking visions or dream-visions they saw after having participated in collective *dhikr* sessions.
24 Incubation here refers to the practice of sleeping in sacred areas with the intention of experiencing a divinely inspired dream or cure. Incubation was famously practiced by members of the Asclepius cult in ancient Greece.

dream's place in the modern order is supposed to be the bedroom, the private sphere, the unconscious; in Ian Hacking's words the 'holy site' for dreams today is the couch (2001: 256). Some of my interlocutors described a sudden need for sleep that overcame them in shrines or the adjacent mosques and then recalled the rude awakenings they faced ("Did you come here to sleep or to pray?!"). Despite these interdictions, I heard a number of dream stories that were framed by the dreamer's locatedness in sacred spaces. Rasha, a middle-aged housewife from Hurghada, remembered the following experience:

There is a sheikh in the direction of Shadhili. His name is Sheikh Malik. We go to visit him every year and spend one or two nights there. The first time I went, I had the following dream: I saw myself in the area in front of the tomb, and I saw a man. He was kind of small, and he was riding on a rock, swinging his arms wildly in circles, like a madman. He was dark like the Nubians or the Sudanese. He seemed to be retarded (*mutakhallif*). When I woke up, I told the people in charge of the shrine about the dream. They said I had seen the sheikh. They recognized him immediately. They said it means the sheikh is content with us.

After Rasha had finished telling her story, her husband added proudly that, while they had gone to visit Sheikh Malik's shrine as a big group, the person who profited most from the visit was his wife. Without any prior knowledge of what the saint looked like, and without knowing during the dream who the madman was that she was seeing, a special bond was established through the dream-vision. According to the underlying dream-model, prior knowledge of the saint's appearance was not necessary as it was not *her* conjuring up his picture, but it was *he* who visited her. By spending the night enveloped in the *baraka* of Sheikh Malik's shrine, the woman had unknowingly facilitated the dream and invited the saint's visit. In this case the physical space of the shrine facilitated an encounter occurring in dream-space.

Underneath the possibility of telling and making sense of such stories lies a different conception of the real and its relationship to physical space. Although her encounter with Sheikh Malik was not observed by others, for Rasha, her husband and the shrine's guardians, this does not mean that it did not occur. In dream-visions the spirits of the dead and the living meet and communicate. Thus, exchanges between saints and believers are not only restricted to the waking world but they take place also in the imaginary realm. As the previous example shows, in some cases visits to saint shrines occur by way of the imagination alone. In Rasha's case, by contrast, the imaginary encounter was itself impacted by her relationship to a specific material space. By traveling to and spending the night in the shrine, Rasha was able to have a dream-vision that she might not have seen if she had not gone on this trip. We have thus come full circle from shrines being built as a result of dreams.

Whereas some shrines are built in their particular location because of dreams, in Rasha's case a dream was facilitated by the material space of a shrine. Just as dreams move shrines, shrines shape dreams.

Conclusion

While talking about the restructuring of a Moroccan village, one of Stefania Pandolfo's informants told her that people in the new village "were so happy to have SPACE! that they didn't realize they were being S P A C E D away" (1997: 64). One of the questions that motivated my fieldwork was whether dreams have been spaced away as well in modern Egypt. At times it seemed, indeed, that in the twenty-first century there was little room for dreams. A seventy-six year old woman from Upper Egypt complained to me that she and all the other inhabitants of her old village were made to move to a new village when the local Phosphate factory shut down. In the new village everything has changed: neighbors don't ask about her anymore; people don't care about each other anymore. And while the woman often used to dream of the saints, the Prophet, and al-Khidr in the old village, in the new village there are no more dreams (*mafish ahlam*).[25] If the right conditions are lacking and if spaces are restructured, can one still see dream-visions? Particularly conducive places for encounters with the saints, according to many of my interlocutors, are the saint shrines themselves. Yet sleeping in shrines is often no longer permitted. Has the disciplinary power of modernity left its mark not only on Egypt's physical landscapes but also on its dreamscapes? As spaces are reordered, mapped, colonized, and compartmentalized, have the possibilities of experiencing dream-visions in these spaces also been altered? Have all dreams been absorbed by the hegemonic order of modernity?

Offering concrete dream-stories as examples, I suggested in this paper that, far from having been erased in modern Egypt, dream-spaces and saintly places figure prominently in believers' everyday lives. Over the course of my fieldwork I came to realize that not only does a multiplicity of spaces for dreams still exist, but also that dreams make necessary a re-imagining of space itself. I accordingly proposed in this paper to think of the dream as a space that interacts with the material space of the saint shrine. This leads to a conception of space which includes both the imaginary and the material, rather than a simple examination of the ways that each half of the dichotomy influences the other. While dream-invitations at times inspire believers to go to mosques and

---

25 The term *hilm* (pl. *ahlam*) in colloquial Egyptian Arabic is sometimes used to encompass all three kinds of dreams, including dream-visions. Al-Khidr is an immortal legendary-mythical figure, who usually appears in green and is associated with a Qur'anic story (18.60-82). He is described as a prophet, an angel or human being and provides guidance to Sufis and travelers.

shrines, believers can also have extensive conversations with Sayyida Nafisa or Sayyida Zaynab without ever leaving their homes. Modernity's disciplinary power has reordered physical space and time, but the saints themselves rarely keep to visiting hours, maps, and timetables when visiting believers in their dreams. The visitational dream thus enables interlocutory possibilities that are foreclosed by physical geographical distance, linear time, and the dividing line that separates the living from the dead. Further, the dream-space parallels the saint shrine in certain ways: Both spaces enable interlocutions and encounters which are less likely to occur in a disenchanted waking world. Both diverge from empty Cartesian abstract space as well as secularized notions of socially-constructed space. To believers they are sacred spaces, and in them miraculous things can happen. At the same time, as other dream-stories in this paper show, social relations and material space can also have an impact on the imaginary sphere. This is not to say that people have dream-visions because they expect to have them or are conditioned to do so through social pressure or economical hardship.[26] Instead, I proposed to expand discussions of the available sphere of social relations to the sacred to include the possibility of having personal relationships with (deceased) saints through the medium of the dream. Likewise, the dream-space itself expands the physical space of the shrine because it allows for people to travel within the dream.

Neither trivializing the material nor reducing everything to it will open up a space for understanding the very interplay between the imaginary and the material. By considering the imaginary as a space that is related to, but not identical with, the social and the material, my goal was in part to complicate straightforward accounts of the modernization of Egypt that allow only for narratives of acceptance or resistance. The dream-spaces and saintly spaces that I have described are neither fully modern nor wholly alternative, representing neither open resistance nor full accommodation. While the disruption of binaries can itself be read as subversive, the framework of modernity/resistance is inadequate to explain the spaces I have described, as my interlocutors themselves do not necessarily conceptualize the shrines and dreams in antagonistic terms. Instead of interpreting saint visitations either as responses to a need for consolation or as acts of resistance, I suggest that we need to take into consideration less easily-observable aspects of the relationships between saints and believers. Interpreting observable religious practice in functionalist terms is reductive as it fails to do justice to the fact that believers often operate within a broader spatial realm. Functionalist interpretations furthermore often miss the 'saint' in the loose triad of dreamer-saint-shrine. Attention to dreams can thus widen our views both of religious prac-

---

26 Also within the Islamic tradition of dream interpretation the category of *hadith nafsi* accounts for dreams that spring from the dreamer's wishes and worries. The focus of this paper, however, is on the dialogical nature of dream-visions.

tice and of space. While never situated outside of modernity, dream-visions are imaginary spaces that expand the order of modernity by effectively rupturing dichotomizations of inner/outer and imaginary/material through their operation as part of a more inclusive conception of space.

References

Aaron, Hughes (2002) "Imagining the Divine: Ghazali on Imagination, Dreams and Dreaming". *Journal of the American Academy of Religion* 70/1, pp. 33-53.

Abu-Lughod, Janet (1965) "Tale of Two Cities: The Origins of Modern Cairo". *Comparative Studies in Society and History* 7/4, pp. 429-457.

Abu-Lughod, Janet (1971) *Cairo: 1001 Years of the City Victorious*, Princeton: Princeton University Press.

Abu-Lughod, Lila (1990) "The romance of resistance: Tracing transformation of power through Bedouin women". *American Ethnologist* 17/1, pp. 41-55.

Abu-Zahra, Nadia (1997) *The Pure and the Powerful: Studies in Contemporary Muslim Society*, Reading: Ithaca Press.

Akkach, Samer (1997) "The World of the Imagination in Ibn 'Arabi's Ontology". *British Journal of Middle Eastern Studies* 24/1, pp. 97-113.

Bourdieu, Pierre (1977) *Outline of a Theory of Practice* (translated by Richard Nice), New York: Cambridge University Press.

Burroughs, Williams S. (1995) *My Education: A Book of Dreams*, New York: Penguin.

Corbin, Henri (1997) *Alone with the Alone. Creative Imagination in the Sufism of Ibn 'Arabi*. Princeton: Princeton University Press.

Crapanzano, Vincent (1973) *The Hamadsha: A Study in Moroccan Ethnopsychiatry*, Berkeley: University of California Press.

Crapanzano, Vincent (1992) *Hermes' Dilemma and Hamlet's Desire: On the Epistemology of Interpretation*, Cambridge: Harvard University Press.

Fahd, Taoufiq (1966) *La divination arabe: Études religieuses, sociologiques et folkloriques sur le milieu natif de l'Islam*, Leiden: E.J. Brill.

Fahd, Taoufic (1978) "istikhara". In: *Encyclopedia of Islam* (Vol. 4), Leiden: E.J. Brill, pp. 259-260.

Foucault, Michel (1984) "Space, Knowledge and Power". In: Paul Rabinow (ed.) *The Foucault Reader*, New York: Pantheon Books, pp. 239-256.

Foucault, Michel (1993) "Dream, Imagination and Existence". In: Michel Foucault/Ludwig Binswanger *Dreams and Existence*, Atlantic Highlands, NJ: Humanities Press, 31-78.

Freud, Sigmund (1955) "The Interpretation of Dreams". In: *Standard Edition of the Complete Psychological Works of Sigmund Freud* (Vol. IV-V), London: Hoghart Press.

Goldziher, Ignaz (1971) "Veneration of Saints in Islam". In: Ignaz Goldziher *Muslim Studies (Muhammedanische Studien)* (edited by S.M. Stern), London: George Allen and Unwin Ltd., pp. 255-341.

Gilsenan, Michael (2000) "Signs of Truth: Enchantment, Modernity and the Dreams of Peasant Women". *Journal of the Royal Anthropological Institute* 6/4, pp. 597-616.

Gramlich, Richard (1987) *Die Wunder der Freunde Gottes: Theologien und Erscheinungsformen des islamischen Heiligenwunders*, Wiesbaden: Franz Steiner Verlag.

Hacking, Ian (2001) "Dreams in Place". *The Journal of Aesthetics and Art Criticism* 59/3, pp. 245-260.

Harvey, David (2006) *Paris: Capital of Modernity*, New York: Routledge.

Hermansen, Marcia (2001) "Dreams and Dreaming in Islam". In: Kelly Bulkeley (ed.) *Dreams: A Reader on Religious, Cultural and Psychological Dimensions of Dreaming*, New York: Palgrave, pp. 73-91.

Ibn Ishaq (2003) *The Life of Muhammad. A Translation of Ishaq's Sirat Rasul Allah* (translated by A. Guillaume), New York: Oxford University Press

Johansen, Julian (1995) *Sufism and Islamic Reform in Egypt: The Battle for Islamic Tradition*, Oxford: Clarendon Press.

Jong, Frederick de (1999) "Opposition to Sufism in Twentieth Century Egypt (1900-1970). A Preliminary Survey". In: Frederick de Jong/Bernd Radtke (eds.) *Islamic Mysticism Contested. Thirteen Centuries of Controversies and Polemics*, Leiden: Brill, pp. 310-323.

Kinberg, Leah (1994) *Ibn Abi al-Dunya: Morality in the Guise of Dreams*, Leiden: Brill.

Kriss, Rudolf/Kriss-Heinrich, Hubert (1960) *Volksglaube im Bereich des Islam. Wallfahrtswesen und Heiligenverehrung* (Vol. 1), Wiesbaden: Otto Harrassowitz.

Lamoreaux, John (2002) *The Early Muslim Tradition of Dream Interpretation,* Albany: State University of New York Press.

Lane, Edward William (1973) *An Account of the Manners and Customs of the Modern Egyptians*, New York: Dover Publications.

Lane, Edward William (1980) *An Arabic-English Lexicon* (Part IV), Beirut: Librairie du Liban.

Lebon, Aymé (1997) "L'Imam al-Shāfi'ī: Entre Justice et Intercession". In: Gilles Broëtsch (ed.) *Droits et Sociétés dans le Monde Arabe. Prespectives socio-anthropologiques* (Collection du Laboratoire de théorie juridique), Marseille: Presses Universitaires D'Aix, pp. 123-149.

Lefebvre, Henri (1991) *The Production of Space*, Malden: Blackwell Publishing.

Mahir, Sa'd Muhammad (1971) *Masajid Misr wa Awliya'uha al-salihun*, Cairo: al-Majlis al-A'la lil-Shu'un al-Islamiyya.

Mahmood, Saba (2005) *Politics of Piety: The Islamic Revival and the Feminist Subject*, Princeton: Princeton University Press.
Mernissi, Fatima (1977) "Women, Saints, and Sanctuaries". Signs 3, pp. 101-112.
Messick, Brinkley (1993) *The Calligraphic State: Textual Domination and History in a Muslim Society*, Berkeley: University of California Press.
Mitchell, Timothy (1988) *Colonising Egypt*, Berkeley: University of California Press.
Moosa, Ebrahim (2005) *Ghazali and the Poetics of the Imagination*, Chapel Hill: University of North Carolina Press.
Mubarak, Ali (1980) *Al-Khitat al-Tawfiqiyya al-jadida li-Misr al-Qahirah wa-muduniha wa-biladiha al-qadimah wa-shahirah*, Cairo: al-Hay'a al-Misriyya al-'Amma lil-Kitab
Pandolfo, Stefania (1997) *Impasse of the Angels: Scenes from a Moroccan Space of Memory*, Chicago: University of Chicago Press.
Schielke, Samuli (2004) "On Snacks and Saints: When Discourses of Rationality and Order Enter the Egyptian Mawlid". In: Georg Stauth (ed.) *On Archeology of Sainthood and Local Spirituality in Islam. Past and Present Crossroads of Events and Ideas* (Yearbook of the Sociology of Islam 5), Bielefeld: transcript, pp. 173-194.
Schimmel, Annemarie (1998) *Die Träume des Kalifen: Träume und ihre Deutung in der islamischen Kultur*, München: Verlag C.H. Beck.
Sirriyeh, Elizabeth (2000) "Dreams of the Holy Dead. Traditional Islamic Oneirocriticism Versus Salafi Scepticism". *Journal of Semitic Studies* 45/1, pp. 115-130.
Smith, Jane I./Haddad, Yvonne (1981) *The Islamic Understanding of Death and Resurrection,* Albany: State University of New York Press.
Taylor, Christopher S. (1999) *In the Vicinity of the Righteous: Ziyara and the Veneration of Muslim Saints in Late Medieval Egypt*, Leiden: Brill.
'Uways, Sayyid (1965), *Malamih al-Mujtama' al-Misri: Zahirat irsal al-rasa'il ila darih al-Imam al-Shafi'i,* Cairo: Al-Hai'a al-Misriyya al-'Ama lil-Kitab.
Williams, Caroline (1985) "The Cult of Alid Saints in the Fatimid Monuments of Cairo Part II: The Mausolea". *Muqarnas 3*, pp. 39-60.
Wright, Gwendolyn (1991) *The Politics of Design in French Colonial Urbanism,* Chicago: University of Chicago Press.

Chapter 3

Remixing Songs, Remaking MULIDS: The Merging Spaces of Dance Music and Saint Festivals in Egypt

Jennifer Peterson

Mulids[1], annual festivals held to commemorate saints, temporarily transform both the physical space and atmosphere of Egyptian urban neighborhoods and villages. With the saint's shrine at their center, public space is restructured to delineate festive grounds, mark frames for ritual practice, and connote the spiritual reach of the saint's presence. The festive time and space of mulids create a unique, ephemeral world, where the 'religious' and 'profane' intersect in manifold ways through a diverse range of spiritual and carnival-like spaces and activities.

At a mulid, groups of pilgrims may erect tents sewn out of plastic wheat sacks and old sheets; others might spread a mat on the ground. Both spaces serve as temporary homes and bases from which to offer 'services' to guests in the way of tea, food, and friendly communality in the deputized hospitality of the saint. Larger tents that are constructed of colorful Arabesque cloth and lit with chandeliers additionally offer *inshad*, Sufi spiritual singing that serves as the musical accompaniment to *dhikr*—a form of standing rhythmic movement meant to facilitate the invocation of God. A practice absolutely essential to mulids, *dhikr* allows some to experience heightened spiritual states of being.

Outside these intimate Sufi 'service' spaces, from the shrine to outlying alleyways, the area's festive space is intermittently strung with colored lights. A fair-like atmosphere unfolds as itinerant vendors spread their wares or set up carts selling toys, trinkets, sweets, snacks, and souvenirs considered to bear the saint's *baraka*, a type of locally-effusive spiritual energy. Carnival workers run swings, shooting booths, and magic shows. Makeshift for-profit cafés are set up, some with stages hosting party bands and singers. DJs work behind large speakers, and youth carve out dance spaces in the streets.

---

1   In the Egyptian colloquial called *mulid* (pl. *mawalid*), taken from the classical Arabic *mawlid*, this literally means a birthday or anniversary and in this context usually marks the anniversary of a saint's death.

The current of dance music these young DJs currently highlight is one called 'mulid', a trend that borrows musically and lyrically from Sufi *inshad*, mixing it with electronic beats and boisterous wedding-party vocal styles. Sometimes hosted in demarcated areas ornamented in ways similar to those of Sufi tents, DJ stations may also distribute a 'service' of cold herbal infusions to mulid-goers dancing, watching, or simply passing by. These mulid DJ spaces thus fuse, whether through physical form, artistic representation, or actual practice, many of the major elements of the mulid experience.

All of these mulid spaces are temporal, creating a time and place set apart from everyday life.[2] Yet mulids are also slowly being marginalized in various spatial, conceptual, and rhetorical ways as modernist and Islamic discourses and policies seek to contain their highly visible and aural forms of festive celebration.[3] Despite their temporality and the pressures being exerted on them, however, this current of 'mulid' dance music has successfully drawn on mulids as a cultural source and enabled representations of them to seep into more mundane social realms such as the production of bootleg cassette tapes, internet forums, public transportation, and the countless weddings celebrated across the country every night. It relocates mulids into social spaces far removed from the physical domain of the saint, extending the very idea of a mulid through time, space, and lived experience into forms and concepts arguably more permanent than those of the mulid itself. And, in the opposite direction, this music current is furthermore contributing to the ever-changing features of actual mulids, offering an alternative 'modern' approach to celebrating these festive occasions and meanwhile reinforcing their social significance.

This study explores how the remixing of Sufi *inshad* has led to a remaking of mulids, by shaping them into cultural metaphors found and used in a variety of social spaces as well as through contributing to an alternative 'modernization' of mulids themselves. In doing so, it follows the trajectory of this music current's developments and examines what meanings are conveyed when its social context is changed from the 'otherworldliness' of the mulid to the 'everydayness' of contemporary Egyptian life.

---

2   See Schielke (2006) for discussion of how the festive experience inverts reality in the context of Egyptian mulids.
3   See Peterson (2005), and, for much greater detail and analysis, Schielke (2006). I would like to point out that the editors of my magazine article made numerous changes prior to publication without my knowledge, including a changed title. The article does not seek to suggest that mulids are 'barely surviving'.

The Places, Times and Spaces of *mulid* Dance Music

Mulid dance music was not developed at mulids themselves, but rather by wedding musicians in low-income urban neighborhoods. Wedding artists first borrowed *inshad* melodies to flavor dance music in 2001, and the distinctive melodic riffs they employed on electric keyboards, ones usually performed on the *ney* and *kawala* reed flutes, were clearly reminiscent of mulids and Sufi *dhikr*. Wedding singer Gamal Al-Sobki then made these nascent dance tracks a hit in 2002 when he sang to them lyrics taken from the mulid milieu ("ya madad"—a form of supplication, "Hayy!"—a name of God chanted when practicing *dhikr*) and others in a traditional Sufi style referring to the Prophet Muhammad as a 'doctor' who heals the spiritually ill. This song, "hanruh al-mulid" (We're going to the mulid), also featured a barked wedding vocal style including salutations to his producers and "all of Al-Mu'asasa" (the cassette tape production and sales center of the sprawling, low-income Shubra Al-Kheima neighborhood). The novelty of this approach was given a marketing boost when his tape *al-mulid* was temporarily banned by the authorities in response to complaints filed by an Islamic preacher who held that some of its lyrics were sacrilegious.[4] Demand for the tape consequently rose, it selling under the table for up to 20 EGP (around 4 USD), nearly seven times its original price.[5] According to Al-Sobky and a magazine article he recalls from

---

[4] The preacher railed against Al-Sobky in his Friday sermons and filed a complaint with the public attorney, leading state security to contact Al-Sobky. The case was dropped when it was confirmed that the tape was recorded 'live', meaning in one shot with all band members performing simultaneously, as opposed to a studied, rehearsed and professionally mixed recording. Under such circumstances, singers can "say what you want" and "nothing is meant by it", according to Al-Sobky (interview in Shubra Al-Kheima, 18 April 2007). The offending lyrics, which were cut from later releases, were, "kalimat habibi al-nabi lazim nidala'ha, wa fi zikra laylat al-nabi halif l-awala'ha, 'ala bab al-kiram da'at da'a wara da'a, wa huwa asl sayidna al-nabi 'amru ma 'al la'a. la'a [...] ha-n'ul la'a, ha-n'ul la'a" ("The word of my beloved the Prophet we must pamper, and on the anniversary of the night of the Prophet I swear I'll burn it up. On the door of the honorable I knocked and knocked, for our lord the Prophet never said no. No. We'll say no, we'll say no.") Offense was apparently taken at this final "We'll say no", as though it were meant as "We'll say no to the Prophet", a statement wholly unacceptable in the Egyptian public sphere. Attention to the song's performance, however, suggests that it was mere execution of a vocal repetition technique not intending to convey this specific understanding.

[5] I bought my copy on the street at a microbus station in the small Delta town of Al-Ibrahimiya for around 3-5 EGP in spring of 2005. My copy, which is counterfeit, has the original lyrics, and is accordingly labeled "ahdath al-munaw'at al-'arabiyya (Up To Date Arabic Types [sic])" to avoid unwanted attention from state security.

the time, it was the best-selling album of the season, outselling Lebanese commercial pop stars Nancy Ajram and George Wasouf.[6]

Like their creators and the urban areas they have been developed in, mulid dance songs are considered *sha'bi* and form a sub-current within a larger class of music referred to by the same term. *Sha'bi* derives from the word *sha'b*, meaning 'people', and is used variously to mean 'populist', 'popular' as in being liked by many, and also 'popular' as in coming from the people, that is, being native, grassroots, and from a 'working-class' socio-economic background. It is this latter definition that applies in the case of *sha'bi* singers and music, although they may also (and often do) enjoy immense popularity (*sha'biyya*) even beyond the *sha'bi* classes. Like its complementary counterpart *baladi*, essentially meaning 'native', 'local', or 'cottage-industry', the term *sha'bi* has both positive and negative connotations. On the negative end of the spectrum, it can imply the unsophisticated, the gauche, the inferior-quality, and the impoverished. Conversely, it is used in positive ways to suggest 'authenticity' and being 'down-to-earth', clever, savvy, and 'street-smart'. Fans and detractors of *sha'bi* music and mulid dance songs apply the entire range of these concepts when appraising them.[7]

Following Al-Sobky's success with *al-mulid*, other *sha'bi* singers began to adopt a 'mulid' style. Mahmoud Al-Leithy, a young up-and-coming *sha'bi* star, produced a *dhikr* dance hit called "qasadt baabak" (I aimed for your door) that borrowed heavily from traditional styles, including that of Sufi *munshid* (*inshad* performer, pl. *munshidin*) 'Arabi Farhan Al-Balbisi, with regard to both its lyrics and melody. This song stormed the so-called microbus circuit and the Nile pleasure cruise scene, at once expressing and reinforcing the sub-genre's popularity in the urban *sha'bi* milieu. Another example is provided by Sa'd Al-Sughayr, a childhood friend of Al-Sobky's and a *sha'bi* superstar (in)famous for his dancing who now performs at 5-star hotel weddings, expensive Pyramids Road nightclubs[8], and in box-office hits.[9] Al-Sughayr produced a mulid song that was featured in the film *lakhmat ra's* (Befuddled) and which reflected and reinforced the popularity of mulid dance songs through commercial mass media, a channel otherwise generally not

---

6   This, and all future references to and quotes by Al-Sobky from interview in Shubra Al-Kheima, 18 April 2007.
7   For more on *sha'bi* culture and music, see Armbrust (1996) and Grippo (2006).
8   Pyramids Road, which leads to the pyramids of Giza, is lined with nightclubs that cater mainly to wealthy visitors from Gulf states and which are notorious for their exploitive atmosphere, all-night belly dancing shows, plentiful hard liquor, and assumed prostitution.
9   Research is needed on the commercially successful yet purely *sha'bi* films produced by Mohamed El-Sobky (of no relation to the *sha'bi* singer Gamal Al-Sobky) and the social tropes they represent and explore.

open to this particular music current.[10] Yet in terms of sheer quantity, most mulid dance songs have been produced either by otherwise little-known *sha'bi* singers, possibly trying to make their break with the mulid style, or largely unidentified DJs who remix this already hybrid sub-genre on their home computers.

Both the fluidity of music as an artistic genre and the relative flexibility of informal *sha'bi* contexts are to be credited for allowing mulid dance songs to take off in the directions they have, both with regard to their musical and lyrical dimensions and to the numerous social spaces they have occupied. Concerning their internal form, the combination of inspiration drawn from mulids, often perceived as 'rural' in origin, and the urban production of dance music is one that works well in the *sha'bi* music genre. *Sha'bi* music often fuses 'rural' musical traditions with 'urban' lyrical concerns, instruments and dance tempos, a characteristic that has facilitated its adoption of mulid motifs. Yet the *sha'bi* framework has also afforded the mulid dance trend the freedom to assume a range of approaches in tone stretching from the earnestly Sufi-oriented to the tongue-in-cheek, boisterous, mocking and naughty, and even the polemical. This range is put into perspective when *sha'bi* mulid songs are compared to the Sufi-inspired and religious songs of mainstream commercial pop stars Mohamed Mounir and Amr Diab, all of which remain staid, relatively slow-paced, and strictly pious in tone. In contrast, and as an example, while the titles of some mulid dance tracks make direct reference to the spiritual mulid context (such as 'mulid of Saint Ali', 'mulid of *dhikr*', and 'mulid of the worshipper and Satan')[11], others flagrantly market themselves as sources of a state of *mazaag*. Literally meaning 'mood' but used in Egyptian colloquial to suggest a heightened sense of pleasure induced or expressed by anything considered well-executed, from music, food and dance to a carefully-constructed stylish outfit or a joyous, carefree attitude, *mazaag* is often associated with states of intoxication.[12] Examples of such titles that boisterously suggest some of the fun-loving aspects of mulids include 'the crazy mulid', 'the mulid is supreme pampering', and 'the "don't awaken pain" mulid'.[13]

In a manner similar to the flexibility granted to the current's musical and lyrical dimensions, the relatively underground nature of the *sha'bi* context

---

10 According to www.egyfilm.com, this film made 4,071,405 EGP in box-office sales (http://www.egyfilm.com/films.php?MovieID=2427).
11 In Arabic, mulid sidi Ali, mulid al-zikr, and mulid al-'abd wa al-shaytan.
12 For more on *mazaag* and the mulid dance trend, see also Peterson (2008). On the related concepts of *tarab* (enchantment/rapture) and *saltana* (which implies being 'reigned' by a state of extreme pleasure), see Racy (1982 and 2003).
13 In Arabic, al-mulid al-magnun, al-mulid al-dala' kullu, and mulid ma tsahush al-muwagi.

and its informal networks has also facilitated the prolific production and wide scale distribution of mulid dance songs, ultimately allowing the current a tangible presence in a variety of mundane, everyday spaces.[14] In terms of accessible production, some mulid songs are recorded at very low cost and quality by a singer accompanying a DJ in an office studio or on the street, while others rely solely on sampling crafted on a home computer. As for distribution, while cassette prices for *sha'bi* music remain low (around 5 EGP), a plethora of even cheaper (3 EGP) bootleg tapes and 'cocktail' compilations make the latest hits, including mulid tracks, easily affordable, and are readily available on the street. Yet as one young DJ told me, mulid songs are essentially an 'MP3' current[15], utilizing digital technology to enter numerous social spaces despite being shunned by the channels sanctioned by the official arts establishments, such as radio, television, and large commercial recording companies. For example, the plummeting costs of computers have made them common in low-income urban and rural areas and homes, and the practice of transferring files between them by removing and re-installing hard drives has contributed to the wide distribution of mulid songs, among others. USB memory sticks, MP3 players, and music-playing cell phones are other increasingly common informal modes of distribution, while compilation CDs can be burned at internet cafés for a modest fee. Arabic-language internet forums are yet another channel for the distribution of *sha'bi* songs, including mulid dance tracks, whereby web forum members and the general public request them, aficionados upload them, and DJs advertise themselves by attaching their names and telephone numbers to the titles of their remixes' music files. The accessibility of the internet has facilitated the distribution of mulid songs even beyond Egypt, with users of one website downloading mulid songs registered as residing in Ethiopia, Germany, Kuwait, Morocco, Palestine, Qatar, Saudi Arabia, and the USA.[16]

Some of the informal, *sha'bi* methods of distributing and promoting mulid songs, of carrying them into social spaces physically and temporally distant from actual mulids, are mobile in themselves. For example, while cell phones that can store and play music files aid distribution in general, ring tones featuring mulid songs also assure the mobility of the dance current and its aural presence in cafés, street corners, workplaces, and all other public and semi-public spaces whenever they receive an incoming call. Mulid songs have also found a space in various forms of transportation, both those used for getting around in practical terms and those employed for fun outings. A cheap and semi-informal mode of public transportation that primarily services *sha'bi*

---

14 On the mulid dance trend and *sha'bi* uses of technology, see also Peterson (2008).
15 Interview with DJ 'Alaa' in Al-Sayyida Nafisa, 17 July 2007.
16 This was www.tzbeets.com, accessed in April 2007.

neighborhoods, microbuses (mini-vans) and their cassette players have long been considered an important means of distribution for *sha'bi* songs in general. Yet *tuk-tuks*, which are unlicensed three-wheeled motorcycle carriages serving crowded *sha'bi* quarters as informal public transportation, are now assuming this role even more so than microbuses. Usually driven by teenagers and featuring a carnival-like atmosphere with decorative lighting, ornamentation, large speakers, and a thrillingly dangerous ride, they often blast the latest mulid dance hit. In a similar vein, colorfully lit-up motorized pleasure boats that boast significant dance floor space and powerful speakers act as mobile barometers of the moment's most popular music as they noisily cruise up and down the Nile, often blaring mulid songs. Mulid tracks are also loudly featured in the highly ornamented horse carriages that take outing-goers for a ride along Cairo's Nile promenade.

While these dance songs have brought musical references to mulids into a variety of relatively everyday spaces such as internet forums, cell phone ring tones, public transportation, and evening outings, their extensive reach into these various social spaces has also allowed for their development into an independent metaphor representing boisterous fun as expressed by *sha'bi* youth culture. It is, further, a marker of their popularity that mulid dance songs have inspired a transfer of their name to other semiotic spaces in the world of *sha'bi* music, used as a label for products other than themselves. Some highly popular *sha'bi* songs, such as Emad Ba'rour's 2006 version of the song "al-'aynab" (Grape), are occasionally titled mulid songs on compilation tapes and internet forums (hence, "mulid al-'aynab") although they are not in fact mulid songs in that they do not employ *inshad* melodies or incorporate lyrical references to mulids. This practice is also applied to *sha'bi* hits from movie soundtracks, resulting in titles consisting of "*mulid*+movie title", an adoption that can be interpreted as both affirmation of and marketing for their supposed party-atmosphere inducing quality. Yet this metaphorical development has gone even further in the titling of entire compilation tapes "such-and-such mulid" although they might have only one, or even no mulid songs listed. The covers of such party 'cocktails' invariably feature photos of belly dancers and small cutouts of the popular *sha'bi* singers whose songs are included on the tape. On the one hand, producers have explained this use of the term 'mulid' as a gimmick meant to draw attention to potential purchasers.[17] Indeed, titles such as "mulid of who doesn't pay can watch", "mulid of the stoned" and "mulid of Al-Ahly" (a soccer team)[18] are eye-catching, and maybe particularly so to *sha'bi* youth. On the other hand, however, 'mulid' has in this con-

---

17 Conversations with Gamal, a producer of bootleg cassette tapes in Imbaba, and Abdel Megid Al-Mahdi, producer of Abdu Company tapes in Imbaba, March and April 2007.
18 In Arabic, mulid illi ma-yidfa'sh yitfarrag, mulid al-mastul, and mulid al-ahly.

text become almost synonymous with both 'raucous fun' and 'cocktail compilation', implying a somewhat chaotic mixed bag of delights offering something for everyone, much like in actual mulid festivities.

'Mulid' has hence come to mean more than just the carnival-like celebration of a saint or a particular strand of dance music. After having been condensed into musical representation, mulids, in their new social space of *sha'bi* music, have been re-packaged into a concept suggesting chaotic and boisterous fun, noisy expressions of joy, a wild party-like atmosphere—an experience that bootleg cassette customers are offered to try on their own terms, at the time and in the place of their choosing. Just as various aspects of mulids have entered the Egyptian cultural consciousness at large through, for example, a metaphor for chaos, 'it was a mulid missing the saint'[19], and representations of sweetly quaint folkloric celebration, as in the much-loved puppet operetta "al-layla al-kabira" (The big night)[20], mulid dance songs have now established a cultural representation of mulids as mind-bending fun and a musical means to accessing the out-of-the-ordinary, even in the everyday.

Yet while mulid songs have been traveling through *sha'bi* networks into various mundane social spaces and become cultural metaphors for the ultimate *mazaag* in *sha'bi* youth culture, they have also traveled from their origins in the *sha'bi* wedding milieu back to the source of their inspiration, mulids themselves. Mulids have always featured various forms of popular music entertainment, and in recent years the mulid dance current has created a strong presence for itself in this mulid context, affirming the role of youth in a mulid's more secular celebrations and highlighting their contributions both physically and aurally. At rural mulids, this may be confined to the loud playing of mulid songs by cassette vendors and as accompaniment to rides, such as bumper cars or a Ferris wheel, in the amusement area. At the 2007 mulid of Abu Hatiba held in the Delta village of Al-Sids[21], however, these songs in fact aurally competed with that of the *sayyita*, a Sufi performer whose songs are woven into the narration of a morality tale, and whose truck-bed stage was in close proximity to the amusement area. Moreover, the performance of this *sayyita*, in addition to being remarkable because she was the first woman to have taken on this public spiritual role at this particular mulid, contained some musical and lyrical borrowings from the *sha'bi* mulid current itself. Here, *sha'bi* dance variations inspired by the mulid context were contributing to the re-shaping of the performance of Sufi *inshad* itself.

---

19 In Arabic, mulid wa-sahbu ghayib.
20 Written by Salah Jahin, composed by Sayyid Makkawi, and performed by the Cairo Puppet Theater, cassette tape recording produced by Sono Cairo, 1972.
21 Al-Sids is located in Al-Sharqiyya governorate, and the finale night was held on Thursday, 12 July 2007.

Perhaps more readily striking, however, are the DJ stations proliferating at many Cairene mulids. The flexibility and affordability of DJs is contributing to their increasing popularity and partial replacement of live bands (which now also play live versions of mulid dance tracks), while the rise of the mulid current has resulted in it virtually monopolizing the play lists of these mulid DJ stations. The dominant presence of such youth culture was tangibly felt, by way of example, at the 2007 mulids of Fatima Al-Nabiwiyya, where at least seven different DJ stations dotted all the paths leading to the shrine, and Sayyida Sakina, where the four DJ stations outnumbered both the popular bands and Sufi *dhikr* spaces (two each).[22] The area alongside the mosque and shrine of Sayyida Sakina, the spatial and spiritual heart of the mulid, was marked by two DJ stations that towered along the mosque walls with eight to ten large speakers stacked upon tables and a DJ perching atop one of them, framed by the mosque's strings of flashing lights. A party-like atmosphere was created as the DJs shouted into microphones to encourage youth to dance, and others sprayed foam and created flame jets by igniting aerosol sprays. Here, mulid dance songs and their spatial theater were not simply representing select aspects of mulids, they were remaking them, spatially, aurally, and in terms of social meaning. Martin Stokes aptly describes this power of music and its use as a negotiation of social space and its ultimate transformation:

Music and dance [...] do not simply 'reflect'. Rather, they provide the means by which the hierarchies of place are negotiated and transformed. Music does not then simply provide a marker in a prestructured social space, but the means by which this space can be transformed. (Stokes 1994: 24)

Even as many of the youth who attend mulids to dance and joke with their friends consider the spiritual intent of mulid celebrations invalid and a form of *bid'a* (innovation discouraged in Islamic law), or perhaps outdated folk custom, their active contribution to mulids in the form of DJ dance areas legitimizes and reinforces the role of mulids as a space for the enactment of fun.[23] Various forms of modernist discourse and policy are seeking to limit and control the mulid in numerous ways including their relative spatial, temporal and aural marginalization[24], and yet in the case of mulid DJ stations, the 'modernity' of the latest youth culture practices are reshaping the mulid according to a different logic, one that is as chaotic and loud (and yet, 'modern') as the 'traditional' mulid is typically perceived. While these youth may refute some of the spiritual beliefs and activities related to mulids, their dance-oriented

---

22 The finale night of the mulid of Fatima Al-Nabawiyya was Monday, 23 April 2007, and that of the mulid of Sayyida Sakina was Wednesday, 30 May 2007.
23 On cultural and religious debates around mulids, see Schielke (2006).
24 Ibid. Also, see Peterson (2005) and Schielke (2004).

participation reinforces some of the other, more secular (and ever modernizing) elements of frenzied carnival-like fun at the mulid. And in doing so, they also reaffirm a sense of local identity connected through time and place to the mulid event, by using the opportunity it provides to celebrate the *sha'bi* culture of themselves, their neighborhoods, and ultimately their mulids, through proudly performing *sha'bi* dance, to *sha'bi* music, in an area they have staked out in possibly the most quintessentially *sha'bi* space there is—the street.

Farah: Expressing Joy at Weddings and *mulids*

Mulid songs have carved out a tangible presence in various everyday spaces and metaphors, in urban outings, and even at mulids themselves, where they help to reinforce *sha'bi* identity and heighten the mulid's focus on fun. Yet, why is it that mulids in particular are being drawn on in the production of *sha'bi* youth culture, and why did urban wedding musicians choose saint festivals as material to begin with? To answer these questions, it may be useful to examine how mulid songs are used as actual music tracks, and in what kinds of social contexts this use produces meaning. As Virginia Danielson points out,

'Music *use*' [...] 'is no less part of "social practice" than is production' (1990, p. 139). Assuming that musical meaning is co-produced by listeners and that, as Middleton argues, 'acts of "consumption" are essential, constitutive parts of the "material circuits" through which musical practice exists—listening, too must be considered a productive force' (1990, p.92). This is salient in the Arab world where historic definitions of song include the listener as a principle constituent of the process of performance. (1996: 300)[25]

Egyptian 'listeners' typically use mulid songs in two ways—by dancing, and by watching dancing, interacting with and encouraging the dance performance by clapping in time. This is true to the extent that the above statement could be modified to "listening *and dancing*, too must be considered a productive force" and that "definitions of song include the listener, *dancer, and dance spectator* as principle constituents of the process of performance." Ramy, a 19-year-old dance enthusiast from the *sha'bi* neighborhood of Al-Sayyida Zeinab, stresses the essential dance factor of mulid songs thus: "Mulid songs in general are not listened to. It would be noise pollution if you listened to

---

25 Danielson's reference, a source I was unable to locate, was Middleton, Richard (1990) *Studying Popular Music*, Milton Keynes: Open University Press.

them. They are only danced to. If I'm sitting here and you play a mulid song for me, I won't be able to listen to it. I can dance to it, but not listen."[26]

Mulid songs are thus meant to be danced to, and Egyptians readily do so. On a comic home-made video spoof that circulated on cell phones in 2007, their love of dancing is exemplified as both uncontrollable and more representative of nationhood than nationalism itself. The clip shows a spy, hooded and kneeling on the ground before his two weapon-wielding executioners. A statement is made declaring that he has betrayed his country and been sentenced to death, but when the popular *sha'bi* song "*al-'aynab*" starts playing, all three dance together joyously, spontaneously tossing hood, shackles and weapons aside.

Given their dance prerogative, mulid songs are most commonly used in contexts of social dance, which in Egypt are manifold. Mulid songs are danced to at social events that range from the street-side grand opening party of a small business (such as a cell phone store or butcher shop) or a short pleasure cruise on the Nile, to a picnic outdoors or even a simple gathering of friends in a private home, dancing to entertain one another. The communal context is essential, as stressed by *sha'bi* singer Gamal Al-Sobky who says, "There's no such thing as someone who sits alone and dances. Dancing needs *lamm* (close gathering together)." Also essential, yet perhaps a product of this dancing as much as a contributor to it, is a sense of joy. As Al-Sobky further explains, "if you want *haysa*, you have to listen to *sha'bi*." *Haysa* means a loud and raucous time, considered equivalent to an experience of fun and the expression of joy. It is also considered an ingredient essential to the success of many forms of Egyptian celebration, which range from store openings to birthday parties (including the 'birthday' marking the first seven days of an infant's life, *al-subu'*), and the various stages of wedding celebrations. Mulid songs are thus widely used in celebratory atmospheres in which people dance (or encourage dancing by enthusiastically watching and clapping) as a medium of communally enacting joy, and particularly so, but by no means exclusively, in *sha'bi* contexts. (*Al-subu'* and birthday parties, for example, are often relatively quiet and contained indoor affairs, yet in some *sha'bi* neighborhoods they may be held in the street with *haysa* provided by a DJ and mulid songs, flashing lights, and refreshments ranging from soda and cake to beer and hash).

Just as mulid songs developed in the wedding milieu, then, the most common context they are found in is the wedding party, Egypt's ubiquitous, and arguably most socially significant, communal context for celebrating, dancing, and expressing joy. Mulid songs feature in the celebratory atmos-

---

[26] Interview with Ramy 'Al-'Aqil' ('the rational'—so called because he's 'crazy') in Al-Sayyida Zeinab, 27 April 2007.

phere of engagement and wedding events ranging from back-alley affairs in unplanned housing districts to five-star hotel receptions to rural village weddings.[27] And it is important to note that in Egypt most weddings are indeed parties. Rather than the white lace motif, pink roses, and harp music associated with American weddings, for example, Egyptian weddings typically feature disco lights, dry ice, bright, primary colors, and dancing crowds. Muslim marriage rituals are usually performed separately, often far in advance of the wedding that socially marks and sanctions the marital bond, and typically in the privacy of the immediate family. The wedding, in contrast, is a highly inclusive event that is often open to the public in the way of a street party. It is officiated only by DJs or other MCs and lacks speeches or other textual narrative, the entire event being orchestrated by loud music and various shouts of encouragement to dance or clap, from the moment the bride and groom arrive and until they leave.[28] Mulid dance music, then, both draws on and facilitates a collective experience of clamorous joy that is considered essential to Egyptian weddings and intrinsic of their structure. A shopkeeper explains its musical and connotative connection to Egyptian wedding party atmosphere in the following terms:

This is mulid music. You can only hear it here [at the mulid] and at weddings. At any other time and place it has no meaning; you won't be able to listen to it. These songs are full of raucousness (*haysa*), uproar (*dawsha*), and clamor (*dawda'*). Weddings (*afrah*) need things with lots of raucous clamor—slow songs won't work. And it needs to be loud to suit the *sha'bi* environment.[29]

This focus on celebratory joy and its public expression is reflected in the Egyptian colloquial term for an engagement or wedding party—*farah* (pl. *afrah*) literally means 'joy'. The concept and enactment of *farah* is perhaps most obviously associated with weddings due to their weighty social significance and everyday pervasiveness among Egypt's family-oriented populace

---

27 On the topic of mulids, music, and weddings, it also should be noted that traditional, ritual-based Sufi *inshad*, used by listeners in the form of the rhythmic movement accompanying *dhikr*, is performed by famous *munshidin* at certain weddings, mostly in Upper Egypt or those held by migrant Upper Egyptians in Cairo.

28 This framework and orchestration was even the case at a dance-free Islamic wedding I attended (in Shubra, 9 July 2007), where DJs blasted Islamic wedding songs mainly sung in chorus to the accompaniment of Islamically-condoned frame drums.

29 Grocer on Al-Tabbana Street in the historic, *sha'bi* neighborhood of Al-Darb Al-Ahmar, and whose shop faced a DJ station during the mulid of Fatima Al-Nabawiyya, 23 April 2007.

of an estimated 80 million.[30] Given the crowded population and the high percentage of marrying-aged youth, as well as the many highly visible and loudly celebrated public customs associated with weddings (such as transporting the couple's new furniture, picking up the bride from the beauty parlor, touring the city to take photos at scenic sites, wedding processions, etc.) various aspects of weddings and their effusive joy are casually encountered on a daily basis. Yet, through the wedding-oriented development and use of mulid dance songs, the Egyptian *farah* draws on another event in which the concept and enactment of joy is arguably just as essential—the mulid. Even as a spiritual occasion, Sufis convey a feeling of joy at the mulid as being part of the love that is felt, expressed and shared in the realm of the beloved—the saints, the Prophet, and God. Even the toil associated with offering 'services' of food, refreshments, and spiritual-social gathering spaces can be framed by a concept of joy, as expressed by a Sufi tent sponsor who told me that while she never even washes a teacup in her own home, at the mulid she scrubs the very mats and is happy (*farhana*) as she does so. She says that she sits for hours on a low stool cooking in huge pots, but that her body never aches because she is happy, doing it out of love.[31] For other mulid-goers, joy experienced at the mulid is part of having fun and celebrating a change of scenery, of exploiting an opportunity to let one's hair down and enjoy the mulid's party-like atmosphere.[32]

The concept of joy is so entrenched in both the practices of celebrating weddings and participating in mulids that the word *farah* actually crosses semantic boundaries in their respective contexts. The teenaged dancer Ramy, for example, made several slips of the tongue when telling me about his mulid experience, saying things such as "Then we went to another *farah* (wedding)" when he meant another DJ station. And in fact, within the mulid context, *farah* is commonly used to mean both 'an experience of joy' and a type of metaphorical mulid 'wedding' celebration. Both of these meanings are implied in the following quote by a Sufi woman at a mulid as she explains her opinion of the loud dance music played by a nearby band and highly audible in her mosque-side tent:

This is a *farah* and the people act out their joy (*bi-yifrahu*) each in their own way. That girl dressed up in trendy pants is not in mulid dress but rather like that for a wedding or holiday ('*eid*). See how that boy is walking down the street, clapping his

---

30 July 2007 population estimate according to the CIA World Factbook, accessed online at https://www.cia.gov/library/publications/the-world-factbook/print/eg.html on 24 July 2007.
31 Hagga Ragaa', who sponsored a small Sufi service tent beside the mosque at the 2007 mulid of Fatima Al-Nabawiyya, 22 April 2007.
32 See Schielke (2006) for discussion of the concepts of love and fun at mulids.

hands? People eat more than they should, dance about, wave their arms, laugh hysterically as though visiting with a dear old friend. That music is part of the *farah*, and those playing it must be happy (*farhanin*).[33]

With regard to the first meaning of *farah* in the mulid context, that of 'joy', it applies as readily to the spiritual framework as it does to the carnival funmaking. To Sufis, love of the saint is so powerful and pervasive that it touches all those welcomed in his or her presence, and this love is held to be a source of joy that can be experienced in manifold ways. Sufism's inclination towards tolerance allows for the embracing of seemingly disparate manifestations of joy, while the conception of joy as being contextualized by and/or compatible with spirituality also conforms to a general cultural sense that there is no inherent contradiction between being pious and making people happy. Acting with a religious purpose can also seek to bring people joy, as illustrated in a conversation with young men who sponsored a DJ station at an ironer's shop during the 2007 mulid of Fatima Al-Nabawiyya. When I asked why they offered the 'service' of cold herbal infusions and a DJ station with loud speakers, they responded with "To make the people happy (*'ashaan nifrah al-nas*)" in the same breath as "For Fatima Al-Nabawiyya." When I further asked why they wanted to make the people happy, I was given the response, "The people are choked (*makhnuqa*); the people are in poor shape (*ta'bana*). We want to make them happy. Muslims love to make people happy."[34]

As for the other meaning of *farah* as a 'wedding', this too is pertinent in both the Sufi and more festival-like contexts of mulids. With regard to the latter, mulids are compared to weddings and major religious holidays (*a'yyad*, sg. *'eid*) because each are exceptionally special, joyous occasions that occur relatively rarely, either once a year or, in the case of weddings from the perspective of those marrying, typically once in a lifetime. Their being long anticipated and set apart from the everyday heightens the uniqueness of their festive atmosphere and the joy felt and expressed in their celebration.[35] In the Sufi context, as a celebration marking the anniversary of a saint's death and union with God, the wedding is in fact an apt metaphor. And accordingly, many of the symbolic traditions practiced at mulids are also essential ele-

---

33 Hagga Ragaa', see footnote 22.
34 Sayyid Al-Gazzar, Abu Haroun, Hassan Ali, Okal, and Obeida each contributed 35 EGP to host the DJ event and prepared hibiscus and tamarind infusions to distribute to guests at their site a block away from the shrine of Fatima Al-Nabawiyya, 23 April 2007. This was the second year they had hosted this 'service'.
35 A more concrete connection between weddings and mulids is the fact that some musicians and *sha'bi* singers perform in both. See Puig (2006) and Van Nieuwkerk (1996).

ments of wedding rituals—both share forms of the henna celebration[36] the night before; the opening *zeffa*, or procession; and the *sabahiyya*, the morning-after reception. Moreover, female saints are often referred to as *'arusa*, bride, during their mulids, and their tombs are sometimes re-draped on the occasion with white tulle and silver sequins reminiscent of bridal gowns.[37]

The similarities between mulids and weddings with regard to their physical form and practice do not end here, however. In terms of spatial and temporal dimensions, both are night events, and at a glance, their ornamentation is strikingly similar with flashing colored lights, beaded chandeliers, and colorful tent awnings, to the point that when sighting them from a distance, it is not always immediately clear which kind of celebration they are.[38] More immediately pertinent to the mulid dance current, however, is the critical role of rhythmic bodily movement in each. In the spiritual context of mulids, *inshad* is typically used as musical accompaniment for and an aural catalyst of *dhikr*, a communally performed ritual that nonetheless fosters an individual bodily and spiritual experience. This form of standing, swaying movement is an absolutely key element in mulids. In parallel, and as explained by Ramy above, mulid dance music, which draws from this very *inshad*, is an art form that is essentially danced to, and dancing to mulid songs and others is generally indispensable at weddings. While the style of dance particular to mulid songs differs greatly from the movement of *dhikr* in its complex combination of varied moves and focus on sensational performance, the inevitability of its practice when mulid songs are played is reminiscent of the intrinsic relationship of *dhikr* to *inshad*.

Given the many conceptual, metaphorical, and material similarities between weddings and mulids, it should not be surprising that the words *farah* and 'mulid' cross semantic boundaries in both directions. In addition to mulids being termed *afrah*, the word 'mulid' has, since the rise of the mulid dance trend, also become a term of reference for large weddings with an extreme party atmosphere, ones that create a 'mood', in the words of *sha'bi* singer Gamal Al-Sobky. Such events, like the engagement party of Al-

---

36 The henna party is a type of warm-up to the actual wedding, and can be held separately or jointly for the bride and groom. Music is played and danced to, and prepared henna is displayed in a cooking tin and filled with lit candles; attendees may dye their hands with a piece of it.
37 The wedding analogy is also applied in Egypt to elements of the healing zar ritual.
38 Mulids and weddings also share various aspects of their ornamentation with those of other celebratory occasions and even funerals, as well as official events such as lectures and seminars, in addition to being used as cover-up for construction sites. The most commonly shared decorative element is brightly-colored Arabesque tent cloth.

Sobky's younger brother, do in fact resemble mulids in certain ways.[39] The all-night male-only segment of this event was essentially a huge street-side makeshift cafe (including a staff of waiters in uniform) covering an entire block and featuring a *sha'bi* band hosting numerous popular singers. While guests got stoned, snacked on treats, and ordered beer and water pipes, seemingly independent entrepreneurs made the rounds of the street space selling tea, fenugreek infusions, cigarettes, papers, lighters, trays of roasted seeds and peanuts, tissues, and flower garlands. While some of these items are sold by itinerant vendors or available from makeshift cafés at mulids, more significant was the similar atmosphere of public festivity, of an ephemeral world complete with all the actors and other means necessary to facilitate an experience of joy. It was more than a typical engagement party; it was a kind of outdoor festival—a mulid, as the newly-coined metaphor frames it.

Given the manifold similarities and overlaps between mulids and weddings on a number of levels, then, what is it that clearly differentiates them? Other than their distinct purposes—commemorating a saint and celebrating a marriage—the two forms of celebration are most markedly separated by a spiritual divide. The mulid, despite its many 'secular' aspects, is fundamentally an event with a spiritual origin and purpose, and many of its participants recognize the commemorated saint's *baraka*, spiritual energy, as one that affects all aspects of the occasion. Even though most youth I spoke with for this study were generally skeptical of the concept of *baraka*, one young DJ conceded that proximity to the shrine ensures that even DJ-sponsored dance events at mulids remain free of problems.[40] Yet this concept of *baraka* remains local and material—it is not transferred musically or lyrically through *inshad*, or, consequently, mulid dance songs. *Baraka* is not to be found at weddings, even those hosting Sufi *munshidin*.[41] Instead, the force that connects these two kinds of events remains that of pure joy, one that is perhaps heightened by the marvel of encountering the out-of-the-ordinary in spaces otherwise construed as the everyday.

---

39 Ahmed Al-Sobky's engagement party was held in Shubra Al-Kheima on 30 April 2007.

40 Interview with DJ 'Alaa' in Al-Sayyida Nafisa, 17 July 2007.

41 This point was strongly affirmed by Sayyid Imam, a musician and singer with years of experience in each of the fields of the zar healing ritual, Sufi *inshad* at both mulids and international festivals, and weddings and other venues for *sha'bi* music, and who stressed that *baraka* and weddings have no relation to each other (Interview in Al-Muqattam, 18 July 2007).

Mulid Music with a Message

But are mulid songs only about expressing joy, only popular because they "have a good beat and you can dance to it"?[42] And does their failure to transmit baraka or the mulid's spirituality mean that they exist outside of a religious framework or are devoid of any mulid characteristics other than that of fun? On the contrary, the songs of Mahmoud Al-Leithy, one of the mulid current's most popular singers, provide an example of a moral-driven and heritage-inspired style he describes as part of his vision for producing music with a message (*al-fann al-haadif*).[43]

Al-Leithy was raised in the mulid milieu, being related to performers in the old Al-'Akif Circus. He tells of traveling mulid circuits across Egypt with his dagger-throwing and gymnast aunts and uncles, and of being taught *madih*, lyrical praise of the Prophet, by his grandfather. By age 10 he was singing on stages at mulids, briefly taking over from the performing *munshid*, a context he still describes as "the most beautiful thing in the world. The best speech that comes out, the most sincere, is that singing [...]. [When singing in this context] I'm happier than all the people present".[44]

Al-Leithy went on to become a *sha'bi* wedding singer, and after Gamal Al-Sobky introduced the *nabatshi*[45] wedding salutation style to *dhikr* melodies, he decided to sing Sufi lyrics to them in a manner that would make people dance. His idea was to make *madih* chic (*madih mitshayyak*). Al-Leithy produced a *sha'bi* dance version of *dhikr*, to which he sang lyrics taken from Sufi *inshad* and others used to frame traditional epic ballads, and the individual track, "*qasadt baabak*" (I aimed for your door) was a huge success. According to Al-Leithy, the album it was included on, *'asforayn*, sold a million copies.

Although certain aspects of marketing to the musical fashion of the moment (and of honoring his *sha'bi* producers) can be found in Al-Leithy's work, the Sufi-, tradition-, and moral-inspired content of his songs rings true to both his upbringing in the mulid milieu and to his own self-proclaimed religious and artistic orientations. Al-Leithy is often described by fans of *sha'bi* music as 'respectable' and 'polite', and he describes himself, in addition to being a *sha'bi* singer, as one who sings *madih*[46], saying that he learnt his art

---

42 Amber von Tussle in the 1988 John Waters film *Hairspray*.
43 On Mahmoud Al-Leithy and moral content in mulid dance songs, see also Peterson (2008).
44 This and all further references from interview in Imbaba, 25 April 2007.
45 The *nabatshi* is the master of ceremonies who collects gifts of cash and loudly greets and praises those who give as thanks and recognition.
46 The reason Al-Leithy says that he *must* have a *kawala* reed flute in his band is that he sings *madih*.

from *al-shuyukh* (sg. *shaykh*, here meaning *munshid*). And in addition to his songs being widely played and danced to at mulid DJ stations, Al-Leithy continues to attend mulids in person, where he says he is dragged by fans from one popular band stage to the next, performing his moral-imbued mulid hits live.

His second album, *Ya rabb* (Oh Lord), includes, in addition to the religious-oriented title track and others of a moral nature, a song called "*al-anbiya'*" (The prophets) that names and briefly describes 25 different prophets in a romantic, tender tone. A track that DJs say is much in demand at weddings, it is one example of the approach Al-Leithy characterizes as music with a message, his goal being to teach the younger generation about its religion through a medium it enjoys and relates to. Al-Leithy says that his next song will address the five obligatory daily prayers and their spiritual benefits to Muslims, and that he also plans to sing about the Companions of the Prophet. In the coming months he further intends to produce his first video clip, extending his music with a message to a wider audience and possibly bringing mulid musical and lyrical borrowings, via *sha'bi* dance tracks, to the world of television at last.[47]

It is among street-smart youth often preoccupied with reaching or creating a state of *mazaag* that Al-Leithy's morally-driven and tradition-inspired mulid songs have been such a huge success. In contrast to how religious rock music might be received in an American context, for example, the moral content of Al-Leithy's songs is not considered a kill-joy force, just as acting with a religious intent is not seen as incompatible with facilitating the fun enactment of joy. Even as the 'sacred' and 'profane' do not form a dichotomy in mulids, the boisterous fun-making character of most mulid dance music (and the fact that it does not carry *baraka* or spirituality) does not preclude its existence within a larger cultural context in which religion, even at times of merry-making, remains a dominant and unquestioned force.

The actual use of mulid songs sheds some light on how they function within an overarching religious framework. At weddings, mulids, and in other celebratory contexts, DJs typically open their musical event with recorded recitation of the Qur'an, often followed by a popular religious song whose lyrics consist solely of the 99 names of God.[48] At weddings, this is often followed by Western trance dance music and then a slow romantic song, while at mulids, the transition is immediately made to mulid dance tracks. Another way of defining the DJ's aural space as Muslim is the use of a microphone to shout things like "If you love the Prophet, raise your hand!" (whereupon everyone, including those smoking hash, does). Out of respect for the power of

---

47 On video clips and al-fann al-hadif, see Kubala (2005).
48 Called "'asmaa' allah al-Husna" this song has been recorded by numerous young popular singers including Hisham Abbas and Hamada Hilal.

religious utterances, DJs also turn off their music when the call to prayer is sounded and sometimes leave it off until nearby worshippers have completed their prayers. A final example of the respectful co-existence between the *mazaag*-focused mulid dance current and a larger religious cultural framework is provided by the case of a mulid DJ station that conceded shared aural and physical space to a *munshid* when he was ready to perform, even sharing its speaker system with him.[49]

With the exception of the controversy around Gamal Al-Sobky's first mulid song, there has been no religious outcry over the mulid dance current. Although the dance songs do not transport *baraka* or a sense of spirituality from the source of their inspiration, the mulid, their youthful boisterousness is not seen as counter to religion or as overstepping the boundaries of Muslim sensibilities. Rather, while sanctioned by the permissibility of 'religion' and 'joyous fun' commingling, their actual use and practice takes place within an unquestioned overarching Islamic cultural framework that is reinforced by the DJs and dancing youth themselves. This religious cultural umbrella is one that, on the one hand, allows for the moral songs of Al-Leithy to gain popularity among youth, and, on the other, sanctions the force of joy, spurred on by the informality of *sha'bi* culture, to carry various notions of the mulid into ever more 'secular' social spaces.

Conclusion

A block away from her shrine in Cairo's historic *sha'bi* neighborhood of Al-Darb Al-Ahmar, celebration of Fatima Al-Nabawiyya's 2007 mulid was still going strong following the dawn call to prayer.[50] People of all kinds passed through on their way to and from the shrine and mulid center. Men created spaces in front of their daytime shops to smoke water pipes, drink tea, and observe the late night activity. Families gathered on the wrought-iron balconies of dilapidated Ottoman-era homes to watch the scenes below, and rained hard candies upon street-side revelers. Without prior arrangement, a live band suddenly hosted the popular singer Mahmoud Al-Leithy, and he performed his *sha'bi* dance version of Sufi *dhikr*. Those present at the space's makeshift café clapped in time, while teenager Ramy spontaneously danced on the stage in his unique, eye-catching style. Around the corner, an ironer's shop blasted electronic 'mulid' music from large speakers while a group of teenage boys, some enthusiastically ripping off their shirts, danced energetically. Matronly figures watched on from the street margins, as did a Sufi dervish dressed in

---

49 This occurred at the mulid of Al-Rifa'i, whose finale night was on 28 June 2007. The *munshid* was 'Adel Al-'Askari.
50 The finale night was on Monday, 23 April, and the dawn prayer time was at 4.47 am.

layers of filthy, oversized *gallabiyyas*.[51] Eventually he rose to interact with the youth through dance, sliding his head and arms from side to side, keeping in time with the rhythm and in sync with the teenager facing him.

Here, at the height of the mulid's post-dawn climax, *sha'bi* dance versions of Sufi *inshad* provided the soundtrack as various dimensions of the mulid met on one street corner. Dancing youth, an itinerant dervish, and families all came together to communally celebrate in an inclusive atmosphere of fun. Those seeking a celebration of local identity, the release of youthful energy, spiritual closeness to the saint and God, or reinforcement of fame, were all drawn together by the joyful mulid dance songs that musically, and through their actual use, combined various essential elements of the mulid experience.

The successful integration of this dance music in the mulid's festive space, as well as its wide-reaching popularity in other social arenas beyond the saint's domain, affirms that the mulid, despite the various pressures placed on it, remains both a dynamic and productive cultural source and an animated social occasion. Music, with its fluid yet powerful nature, is at once able to represent aspects of the mulid, freeing them from the physical and temporal constraints of the saint's domain to enter other social spaces, and to augment the mulid by reaffirming its significance to local *sha'bi* culture and stressing its spiritually legitimized enactment of fun.

Although materially and conceptually centered around a shrine and embodying the various physical and social characteristics of its local place, the mulid is essentially an ephemeral event, a 'happening' of sorts that creates a form of festive space. Because it is a socially constructed space, the mulid can be restructured in other social locales that both outlive the original mulid's temporality and overstep the bounds of its limited geography. It is the *experience* of a mulid that can be, if not relived, reconfigured and applied to other experiences removed from the actual time and place of the mulid event. Although a particular mulid may only take place once a year, and the scope of its celebration may be increasingly restricted by the authorities, various aspects of its fun-loving joy and *sha'bi* identity can be, through their musical representation and dance-based re-enactment, expressed and experienced throughout the year in an untold number of other spaces and places.

It is also as this state of exemplified *haysa* that the musical representation of mulids re-enters the mulid event itself, highlighting its cultural dynamism and celebrating its provision of a framework for merry-making. Through its condensed musical metaphors and the spectacular performance of its dance forms, *sha'bi* mulid songs reshape the festive space of mulids, heightening their focus on the experience of fun. The remixing of Sufi *inshad*, then, in ad-

---

51 A *gallabiyya* (pl. *gallalib*) is a traditional form of dress for Egyptian men, essentially a full-length, tapered tunic/gown.

dition to reconfiguring the conception of mulids at celebratory events throughout the Egyptian social sphere, also contributes to the remaking of mulids themselves. Young DJs and their dancing audiences, the every embodiment of 'modern' fun-making, serve as cultural actors interpreting and remaking mulids as events that are at once relevant to *sha'bi* youth culture and increasingly expressive of unbridled joy.

References

Armbrust, Walter (1996) *Mass Culture and Modernism in Egypt*, Cambridge: Cambridge University Press.
Danielson, Virginia (1996) "New Nightingales of the Nile: Popular Music in Egypt Since the 1970s". *Popular Music* 15/3, pp. 299-312.
Grippo, James R. (2006) "The Fool Sings a Hero's Song: Shaaban Abdel Rahim, Egyptian Shaabi, and the Video Clip Phenomenon". *Transnational Broadcasting Studies* 16.
Kubala, Patricia (2005) "The Other Face of the Video Clip: Sami Yusef and the Call for al-Fann al-Hadif". *Transnational Broadcasting Studies* 14, pp. 38-47.
Peterson, Jennifer (2005) "On the Margins: Facing Religious and Official Disapproval, Mulids Barely Survive". *Cairo Magazine*, 10-16 March, pp. 14-19.
Peterson, Jennifer (2008) "Sampling Folklore: The 'Re-Popularization' of Sufi *inshad* in Egyptian Dance Music", *Arab Media and Society* 4/January 2008 (online at http://www.arabmediasociety.com/?article=580).
Puig, Nicolas (2006) "Egypt's Pop-Music Clashes and the 'World Crossing' Destinies of Muhammad 'Ali Street Musicians". In: Diane Singerman/Paul Amar (eds.) *Cairo Cosmopolitan: Politics, Culture, and Urban Space in the New Globalized Middle East*, Cairo: The American University in Cairo Press, pp. 513-536.
Racy, Ali Jihad (1982) "Musical Aesthetics in Present-Day Cairo". *Ethnomusicology* 26/3, pp. 391-406.
Racy, A.J. (2003) *Making Music in the Arab World: The Culture and Artistry of Tarab*, Cambridge: Cambridge University Press.
Schielke, Samuli (2004) "On Snacks and Saints: When Discourses of Order and Rationality Enter the Egyptian *Mawlid*". In: Georg Stauth (ed.), *On Archeology of Sainthood and Local Spirituality in Islam. Past and Present Crossroads of Events and Ideas* (Yearbook of the Sociology of Islam 5), Bielefeld: transcript, pp.173-194.
Schielke, Samuli (2006) *Snacks and Saints: Mawlid Festivals and the Politics of Festivity, Piety and Modernity in Contemporary Egypt*, (Ph.D. dissertation), University of Amsterdam

Stokes, Martin (1994) "Introduction: Ethnicity, Identity and Music". In: Martin Stokes (ed.) *Ethnicity, Identity and Music: The Musical Construction of Place*, Oxford: Berg Publishers , pp. 1-28.

Van Nieuwkerk, Karin (1996) "*'A Trade Like Any Other': Female Singers and Dancers in Egypt*, Cairo: The American University in Cairo Press.

Filmography

Hairspray (1988) John Waters. New York: New Line Cinema.
lakhmat ra's (2006) Ahmed Al-Badri. Cairo: Al-Sobky Film.

Select Discography

Gamal Al-Sobky (2002) *al-mulid*. Shubra: Al-Imam for Artistic Production and Distribution.
Mahmoud Al-Leithy (2007) *ya rabb*. Imbaba: Sawt Al-Tarab for Acoustics.
Mahmoud Al-Leithy (2005) *'asforayn*. Imbaba: Sawt Al-Tarab for Acoustics.
mulid al-kharbana al-gadid (2007). Imbaba: Abdu Company.

Chapter 4

Notes on Locality, Connectedness, and Saintliness

Armando Salvatore

The Place of Saintliness within the Sociology of Islam

This is the second issue of the *Yearbook of the Sociology of Islam* to be dedicated to saintliness with regard to 'locality', a fact that witnesses the strategic importance of this topic for the overall project of the sociology of Islam. The thematic link between saintliness and locality stimulates some reflection on the founding paradigm of such a sociology, on what is specifically sociological about it, or also on whether a clearer opening to anthropology might enrich the project. This is not just a special theme, but a topical question that embraces the core issue of the 'ambiguous positioning of Islam in the global construction of society', as we read in the flap page presentation of the *Yearbook of the Sociology of Islam*. A discussion of the special theme of saintliness and locality might reveal a fundamental ambiguity concerning how sociology positions Islam within its purview.

One main potential of the overall project of the sociology of Islam lies in the fact that the study of phenomena related to Islam might lead to revise basic categories and relocate fundamental antinomies within social theory at large. The project can include a more radical, yet situated, critique of the classics of social thought than it has been possible thus far though various 'immanent' critiques of modernity and modern society. Such critiques, like the work of Michel Foucault, revealed the power formations on which modernity rests, and in this way strengthened modernity's own capacity of theoretical regeneration via nourishing the spiral of challenges and transgressions internal to its own logic.

Many ambiguities of social theory are inherent in how sociology itself was constituted in Europe by instituting a strategic link between religion and modernity, also through the influence of studies on Islam. Notably in the work of Max Weber, modernity appears as the completion of the semi-rationalizing spirit of religious traditions, whereby reformers and modernists within those traditions play the role of the midwives of modern social worlds (cf. Turner 1974). Yet the study of Muslim saints (as in volume 5 of the *Yearbook*) has already triggered off a more basic interrogation: can an archaeology of Muslim saintliness question the sociologically received character of the inherent link between religion and modernity? Wouldn't rather the study of Muslim saintliness help resituate the tension and ambivalent relation between religion and modernity and so show in a clearer way the extent to which the ambiguous positioning of Islam in global society is not primarily due to alleged rationalizing deficits of Islamic traditions? Can this ambiguous positioning be instead related to Islam's ongoing role of a counterexample and/or background screen to the spiraling antinomies inherent in the functioning of global, Western-centered modernity? Would then the way be open for a more productive use of the sociology of Islam for deflating the binary logic on which those antinomies of modernity have been based? Could such a deflation of the tension restitute a more lucid look at how religious traditions, their carriers and contesters, ingrain into the economic and political structures of the modern world? Can this operation ultimately facilitate a more sober but also more nuanced view of the autochthonous modernizers: the 'modernists', the 'reformers', the *salafis*? (cf. Salvatore 2001; Schielke 2004).

Moving in this direction, it is possible to propose a different reading of the issue of saintliness and locality. We cannot indulge in this brief note in any definitional game about what 'saintliness' is essentially about. If sought, such a definition can emerge through the overlapping topics of the contributions to this volume as well as to volume 5 of the *Yearbook* or can be searched in the work of scholars who singularly tried to provide such a definition (e.g. Cornell 1998: xvii-xxiv). The reason why saintliness is preferred to 'sainthood' or 'saintship' is due to the fact that the latter terms' morphology appears quite immediately oriented to institutionalization processes, or better canonization of saints, notably as available within the Catholic tradition. Local rooting or localization as found in the making of Muslim saintliness cannot be considered an exact counterpart to canonization, though some authors do not consider this difference an obstacle to a unified definition (Ib.). The main emphasis here lies on what is not or not easily definable with regard to saintliness. Therefore I can suggest a reading of saintliness coming into the purview of inherited sociological categories as a syndrome of reconciliation of what is sociologically irreconcilable and not even susceptible to be reduced to a classic sociological antinomy like between individual and society, movement and institution, rationality and authenticity, abstract rational systems vs. local accretions: it is the syndrome inherent in the ongoing and unsolvable tension between relations and locations, between the networks and the movements attending to the construction and reproduction of saintliness and the corresponding sites of accumulation of material riches and symbolic power, between the self-sufficiency of the enactment of a drama of suffering and redemption, of meditation and play (the dimension of immanence and selfness), on the one hand, and the inherent dispersion of the game itself, the impossibility to contain it into a unity of place, staging and ritual orchestration (its dimension of transcendence and otherness), on the other, between the fluidity of saintly charisma intended as patterns of connectedness and the apparent but often misleading solidity of sacredness as the provider of stability to the dynamics of settled groups. In this perspective, saintliness should be decoupled from sacredness, although the two concepts appear often as conflated, like in volume 5 of the *Yearbook*.

The perspective here adopted concerns the universe of binary oppositions developed within social theory, the mother of which is the dichotomy between tradition and modernity. This is not to deny that a social scientist might in good faith try to apply social theory concepts to explain social phenomena related to Islam. Yet the aporias that result from their use might lead us either to pragmatically revise, or at least to question some binary concepts stemming from the ambiguities and antinomies inherent in the development and self-understanding of Western social science. In this way, the scope of a sociology of Islam would not be restorative vis-à-vis the problem of the universal applicability of social science concepts, but rather genealogical, through locating the conceptual and also historical junctures where tensions emerge and strictures are created. The goal would not be to produce new or better concepts, but to show how aporias arise and contribute to construct and stabilize relations, both internal to societies and between them. In this perspective, the ambivalence mentioned in the presentation of the *Yearbook* project appears not related to Islam's positioning in global society, but ingrained in the dynamics, contradictions and conflicts of global society itself. The study of Islam from a social theory perspective might help to understand them better.

Connectedness vs. Locality?

I will refer to one chapter of volume 5 of the *Yearbook* in order to understand how saintliness might reflect a syndrome of reconciliation between connectedness and locality. Saintliness might then appear as resistant to a rationalizing path of a Weberian type. My argument questions the euro-christianocentric dimension of notions that are prominent in the European classics of sociology, like internalization, extraordinariness, habitual intellectualization, the nexus between 'calling' and 'office,' eruption and routinization, virtuoso religion, and, last but not least, charisma: the ultimate matrix of power and agency where all contradictions in the conceptual chain are recollected and redeemed.

Patrick Franke's study of Khidr, the 'Man in Green' of both Islamic and pre-Islamic lore, can be taken as an example, since it tackles a root figure of Muslim saintliness by direct reference to the sacralization of places (Franke 2004). In volume 5 of the *Yearbook* Franke analyzed in particular how Khidr, a prototypical character of Islamic saintliness who appears and disappears at different places and through various epochs, is widely evoked in narratives that are intended to sacralize a certain place, for constructing its territorialization or more precisely *Landnahme*, the 'taking possession of the land' in the 'theo-political' sense elucidated by Mircea Eliade. Khidr intervenes in several narratives concerning the institution of such major sacred places of Islam like the Kaaba, the Dome of the Rock, and the Aya Sofia. This seems at first glance to institute a close relation of saintliness to locality, or rather to its legitimization. Nonetheless Khidr is at the cusp of the system itself of saintliness, intended as the capacity to create grace and distribute blessings first of all through caring for the concrete other who is the reflection of the abstract, absolute Other: the poor and the weak, the *alter* to *ego* who are closest to *Alter*, i.e. God. Khidr is like the backup system of the entire network of Muslim saints. As shown by Franke, many key saints, often founders of the most important orders (*turuq*), are narratively related to Khidr and his authority. In today's Cairo, one of the biggest metropolises of the world, several devotees, including Sufi sheikhs, claim to have met Khidr during critical moments of their lives. Khidr is known as the sheikh of those who have no sheikh and pre-exists all of them. He connects and relates. He works as a primeval hyperlink of what human society needs above anything else, i.e. the almost self-referential care for the integrity of the social bond and the capacity to act in the world, as represented, in its most critical situations, by the care for the needs of the neediest.

On one hand, Khidr exists to visit places and then to escape, transcend them. He can justify their sacralization, in modern parlance, by showing that in a universalistic religious tradition the local can only be an instantiation of the global, by literally running through the globe, disappearing here and reappearing there. The legitimization of locality is therefore as much needed for the politics of instituting local networks as it is impossible to justify in purely local terms. It needs a transcending imagination de-personalizing local links, before they are re-personalized through historical saints rooted in their environment. On the other hand, neither prophet nor angel, Khidr is a perfect *wali* ('friend' of God, therefore saint), so perfect that he is unlike any other *wali*, while he endorses the biography and legitimizes the authority of many of them. He is the symbol itself of what in principle needs no symbolization since it is a pure eruption of practice and blessing, reflected in the factual normativity of the social bond, whenever there be need. E.g. Franke mentions that ambulance services in Turkey today are sometimes still called 'Khidr-Service' (Francke 2004: 26). Khidr is not properly a presence but rather the making-present of what is necessarily absent, the satisfaction of a legitimate need. This situation corresponds to the idea itself of grace or blessing. He is the absent convivial guest to which one offers a meal. He witnesses the necessity of an absence, and the presence of a necessity. He completes relations in what they can never be completed: in the attainment of perfect, symmetrical reciprocity. If there were perfect reciprocity, there would be no social poor, i.e. those made poor by imperfections or failures in rules of reciprocity. Yet Khidr does not personify the injunction itself of giving to the poor: he immediately fills the gap through the sheer evocation of his presence, yet to vanish again and make the gap painfully felt by those who remain.

In the Introduction to *Yearbook* 5 it is stated that "Max Weber transformed the idea of the 'primitive magician' and his charismatic qualities being the *Ursprung* (origin) of professional man into a genealogy of the human character, office and institutional governance in modernity" (Stauth 2004: 8). Yet in Weber's analysis the type of dynamics through which the charisma of institutional governance is distinguished from a charisma of eruption, effervescence and transformation is rigidly wrapped into a dichotomy opposing a supposedly 'authentic' or 'intrinsic' force of charisma to its routinization into an institutional form crystallizing in 'office.' Weber was conscious that prophecy was the main example, probably the pinnacle of such a charismatic breakthrough. This did not lead him to paying enough attention to the dimension of care for the social bond inherent in the eruption, since this dimension would rather be assigned to the moment of institutional routinization that follows the eruptive momentum. Thus the caring or reforming dimension of the breakthrough is conceptually diluted in the theoretical grid of dichotomizing social processes. In my view, the same fallacy is present if we lay too much emphasis on a primeval location as an autonomous factor in the institutionalization of saintly networks. This is like putting the cart before the horse and constructing a primeval sacredness tight to a *genius loci* or even a charisma of the place, laying an undue emphasis on the inertial continuity of the *locus* and its irreducibility to the painful reconstruction of connectedness across localities and via relations and networks. An 'inner impetus' of charisma and its sacredness is so transferred from persons to places. The question is evaded concerning how relations are formed by virtue of just such 'charisma.' In an interpretive context influenced by the Weberian concept of charisma, the significance of location risks to be played out against relation and connectedness. The machine of ritual consumption reposing on the locus might then become an anti-systemic, yet equally functional reflection of the modern—national and global—disciplinary systems of power. Here we see both the danger of a dualism and the possible seeds for a fruitful reframing of the basic tensions underlying modern antinomies, in order to understand them no longer as antinomies but as contingent and ambivalently relational tensions. We could then focus on relations and locations as two spheres in mutual tension, whose reconciliation might be facilitated by a focus on 'saintliness' as the relational dimension of 'spirituality' that can't evade the dynamics of places, yet builds its authority by connecting and ultimately transcending them: this is also the pattern of formation and operation of Sufi *turuq*. This alternative approach might facilitate overcoming any excess of emphasis either on charismatic rupture or on ritual per se. It could also help performing preparatory steps for giving a dignified burial to the time honored, but sociologically abused notion of charisma.

In parallel, we could de-emphasize what in Weberian terms is defined as a 'substantive' or 'value oriented' rationality, a traditional type of rationality seen as rooted in 'religion'. In this context one cannot neglect that some strands of older Orientalist scholarship were important precursors of the identification of such a rationality also by reference to saintliness in Islam. They even added to it a vivid functionalist coloring. As reminded by Georg Stauth in the Introduction to *Yearbook 5*:

from the perspective of the founders of modern Islamology, such as Goldziher, C.H. Becker and Snouck Hurgronje, Islamic mysticism was considered as filling the function of closing the gap between law, theology and individual piety. Accordingly, Sufism was labeled as being secondary to the dominant conception of religion (Stauth 2004: 10).

An important Muslim scholar and intellectual like Fazlur Rahman started to challenge the classic Orientalist view by showing that Islam would not be what it is today—not least in terms of its diffusion, mobilization, and integration of popular classes—without the key contribution of Sufism (Rahman 1979 [1966]). In this sense, the scholarly association between saintliness and Sufism and thus the functionalization of Muslim saintliness as the factor 'closing a gap' and thus a deficit of rationalization in the Islamic system of knowledge production should be questioned. It is also sociologically relevant to show that Sufism has been re-evaluated as a coincidental source of both socio-religious movements of an Ikhwani type, and of modes of state governance and discipline (Eickelman/Salvatore 2002). But the main issue here is how to situate the 'substantive rationality' carried by Sufism in a modern context, where another type of rationality purportedly prevails, based on science and productivity. Again, relations are probably key, if we do not reduce them to a mere social infrastructure for distributing power, wealth, and prestige which can flexibly fit into different types of rationality systems.

Relations are at the origin of the idea of charisma, before it became an overloaded concept denoting the subjective possession of immaterial sources of power susceptible to accumulation and even territorialization. The Greek idea of *charis* ('grace'), from which charisma originates, denotes the type of situation that makes relations possible, starting from a situation of asymmetry between ego and alter (Szakolczai 2006). Unlike Weber's sociological, personalized understanding of charisma, but also unlike its Catholic supernatural-institutional formation, *charis* is a genuinely relational concept. As suggested by Szakolczai, there are two possibilities to build relations between *ego* and *alter*, either by violence (see the political theory of Hobbes), or by gift (see the anthropology of Malinowski, Polanyi, and Mauss). In the latter case, a third person appears necessary, and this is where *charis* or grace starts to take form. Wherever grace is not instantly produced by the relation itself, it is bestowed by a god or a saint. The enigma of how relations can be formed should be solved by reference to the new type of tensional power generated by the triadic frame whereby *ego* can connect to *alter* via a special *Alter* who is both internal and external to the relation. It is not the case of a charisma being located in *Alter* or appropriated by whoever is close to him (like the *wali Allah*, the 'friend of God'), it is rather the case of *charis*, the classic name for the triadic framework, that generates the tensional power.

The specific reasons why social theory neglected the *charis* of a triadic construction of relation (Salvatore 2007: 54-67) in favor of the charisma of persons and institutions or to the sacredness of rituals and places, are too complex to ascertain in a brief note. At large, this twist corresponds to the way the modern institutions of Western states happened to function and be legitimized, relying on structures of governance depending on leadership patterns and on representative and monumental seats of office carriers. Yet via the above mentioned interventions of Khidr precisely the opposite happens: the instituted law, the *nomos,* is created through a kind of displacement, of escape from the sacred locus. This movement is the source of all innovative reform, of all 'heterodox' movements, and Sufism as the engine of saintliness is no exception. In a well-known episode of the Qur'an, in the surah of the cave (18: 60-82) this is exemplified by the way an enigmatic character that the several commentators have identified with Khidr (Omar 1993) teaches Moses a lesson, by taking decisions that do not make sense on the basis of the law of Moses but prove to be wise and fair, especially from the viewpoint of the weakest actors involved. It would be tempting to explain this pattern as the way through which saintly charisma supplies to law what it lacks, a sense for the place and circumstances. Yet this reading would be still confined within the limits of the above mentioned functionalist approach, where Weber and islamologists found a common terrain. At a more careful scrutiny, if we adopt the triadic scheme of *charis*, we see that the story of Khidr and Moses show that law can only be practicable if it adheres to the social bond and is able to face its fragility and unpredictability. Real law is not the product of a routinization of charisma but is co-essential with the social bond, instituted ever and again in the framework of the tensional power of the triadic scheme. Saintliness is prior to any distinction between a charisma of eruption and transformation and its institutionalization. Therefore it is also inherently translocal.

Khidr and Moses move through three different places and situations to which they are strangers, in order to reinstitute the social bond. The human and normative resources found in the locus are not enough to preserve and promote human community in it, yet purportedly universal law is also limited, if a sense for the specificity of any situation is not complemented by translocal knowledge and movement.

This approach can be related to Marcel Mauss' valorization of connectedness, expanding on the perspective of transcendent mediation and situating it into a wider context of social practice (Salvatore 2007: 33-45). The inclusion of the fellow human being into a given community of salvation was an expansion of the primordially Hobbesian *ego-alter* dyadic relationship. This relationship happened to be buffered by cosmological myth and holistic visions, the undifferentiated collectivity of Mauss's *mana*, the force that humans see as intrinsic to things (Tarot 1993: 565-67). At a further stage, it solidified into the pattern of I-Thou connectedness mediated by a transcendent God. The new triad replaced primordial forms of the contract as gift. This rupture with archaic religion and its intrinsic model of sociality marked the reconstruction of the social bond within the triadic scheme of *ego-alter-Alter*/God, whereby now God is explicitly recognized as the transcendent *Alter*. The breakthrough disengages agents from their dependence on the mediating capacity of objects as gifts. It thus transposes the 'it' of things into the 'It' of divine transcendence. The Weberian vision of charisma as first personalized and then diluted into routine practices contrasts with this view, and can be interpreted as the ultimate outcome of a long trajectory of post-Protestant secularization of sociality that focuses on the inwardness of subjects and misrecognizes the relational and 'spontaneous' (*charis*-like) dynamics of both breakthroughs and crystallizations. This Weberian vision privileges the machine of modernity as the routinization of an ethic of 'office' and reads a metamorphosed charisma originating in prophet 'calling' backwards into it. This is not a wrong genealogy or an anachronism, it is rather an appropriative self-genealogy of hegemonic Western views, whose hegemony did not outlive long the time of their formulations. It cannot account for the deployment of global modernity and the role of religion in it during the last half century.

An important revision of the Weberian paradigm, which saw the light around half a century ago, was the Axial Age theory, usually associated with the name of Karl Jaspers (see volume 7 of the *Yearbook*). It is probably symptomatic that in this theoretical framework the notion of charisma was not subject to critique or revision, but rather swept under the carpet, although this approach, from the time of Jaspers to its sociological reformulation linked to the work of Shmuel N. Eisenstadt, seems to lay a strong emphasis on the momentums of constitution of the reflexive social bond. Concerning the Western civilizational area, the patterns of axial transformations crystallized in the prophetic role, but a reflective elaboration on the constitution of the social bond and on its religious dimension was equally present in the Greek 'axis', revealed by key concepts like the already mentioned *charis* and *phronesis*. The latter is the 'spontaneous' reason of Eraclitus and Sophocles, the *protosophia* or inherent wisdom of the common speakers, the lips of reason or the reason of the lips. It denotes a type of knowledge oriented to action that was later trivialized into the modern 'common sense' of pragmatic reason, via a metamorphosis of the previous standardization performed by Aristotle (Salvatore 2007). Yet in classic Greek philosophy *phronesis* is a virtue that transcends a purely pragmatic accommodation of means to ends and constitutes a singular model of rational action-*cum*-communication. It provides the only possible mediation between the *xenon* and the *idion*, the common and the singular, the public and the private: *phronesis* is the spoken *logos*, uttered via human lips to the extent it is understood by other. In Aristotelian terms, the ultimate Other authorizing the *logos* transcends the human *ego-alter* dyad. *Phronesis*, that some contemporary social theorists like Bourdieu have trivialized into a notion of practical reason sustaining the 'logic of practice' consisting in following a rule (Salvatore 2007: 93-94), presupposes a mediation, a third element, and therefore a triad, via the orientation of the agent to a *telos*, the cusp of the triangle without which the directionality of action would not be able to sustain the practical judgment. Such notions like *charis* and *phronesis* seem to have impregnated the logic of reasoning and action both in a Western and in an Islamic context and have also provided visions of 'connective justice' among human beings. The sociology of Islam could make better use of them, instead of insisting in twisting Weberian concepts to suit a changed world where a Western civilizational and discursive hegemony cannot be taken for granted any more.

The 'secular machine of modernity' does not suppress all axial differences, which are as much due to varieties among and tensions within cultural traditions as to differences in the positioning and repositioning of different localities on a global scale. The question should then be asked whether a reframing of saintliness as accommodating a notion of spirituality through the lenses of a deepening global governance can suppress the politics of grace and gift based on the asymmetry of connectedness, a type of micropolitics of the social bond that is often in tension, but can also be compatible with traditional and modern policies of regulated violence.

As stressed by Georg Stauth:

since the genealogy of modernity is so intrinsically linked with asceticism and the religious roots of modern dialectics of inwardness and power construction, we need to understand why the Islamic adherence to saintliness would reject any ultimate dialectic (sic) between inwardness and externality (Stauth 2004: 20).

Here a crucial question is raised, on which the whole project of the *Yearbook of the Sociology of Islam*, as also illustrated in a seminal essay in volume 1 of the *Yearbook* (Stauth 1998), dangerously hinges: whether the categories of Weber's sociology of religion along with their dichotomous perspective are *at all* feasible for the Sociology of Islam. This Weberian perspective might even presuppose a political theology of the subject that effects, at will, delocalization and re-localization:

Modernity supposes the transgression of collective norms into individuality, of ethical inclinations into knowledge and of wisdom into individual action, in other words the ever more self-responsible methodization of everyday life. The question that may be asked in this context is whether 'saints' and 'Sufis' open up a specific modern way of individuation and an alternative to Western individualism (Stauth 2004: 20).

Categories like 'individuality,' 'rationalization' or 'methodization' might be too much entrenched in a view of the self-reforming subject and too little bent on a relational perspective on action: charisma being the point of highest vulnerability of this perspective on hyper-subjectivation. Accepting that modernity is strictly associated with an individually willed and managed methodization of life does not require that the issue of saintliness, which implies individualization and methodization to some degree, should be incorporated by default into an issue of modernity—*unless* one follows a strictly genealogical perspective that clarifies the extent to which such Sufi practices delineate a parallel *and* different way of being in the modern world which puts into question the categories of modernity inherited from Weberian sociology.

Against this Weberian background, saintliness might be given a chance to be reconstructed as a syndrome of interaction and connectedness, where locality plays a role, yet within, and as a specification of, the translocal dimension of connectedness as *charis* and the rational dimension of action as *phronesis*. One should not miss the chance, within the Sociology of Islam, to be more critical of the idea that at whatever historical stage, it is always an external power formation that takes over the governing of the ritual staging, so that saintliness cannot exert any control of the stage of human connectedness and only becomes essential, naked, sublimated individuality. According to this view, individuality is first severed from connectedness and then docked again to the impersonal mechanisms of regulation and disciplining imposed by the agents of modernization. This severance is facilitated by the discourse of modern individualism, whose latest stage is the sacredness of life and of human rights. Neither should we reduce this operation to a purely post-Protestant syndrome. The arch-Catholic Louis Massignon has an important place in the genealogy of the dialectic between the inwardness of the self and the externality of power. A methodically oriented genealogy might prevent twisting the Massignonian approach into a self-affirmative logic.

The archaeological digging into the Islamic machinery of saintliness could then show that this construction does not match any dialectic of inwardness and externality comparable with its post-Protestant, Weberian (or Habermasian) brand. Not by chance the Sufi and saint Hallaj (857-922), Massignon's hero of spiritual selfhood, lost his radical battle for affirming a convergence between God and the self, and was executed. Nonetheless, his execution was authorized by Ibn Dawud Ispahani (d. 910), the author of the most celebrated Arab commentary, in rhapsodic form, of Plato's theory of love (*kitab al-zuhra*). He interpreted love as a divine madness (*junun ilahi*) that is simply there, unexplainable, neither to be praised nor to be condemned, since it is an unsolved perennial tension between lover and Beloved, the self and God. Here relational tension stops short of reaching a convergence (*tashbih*) at the level of inwardness. The Hallajian dialectic between lover and Beloved was identified as the dangerous entry into the *shirk* (associating other divinities to the only God) of a trinitarian scheme, replacing connectedness with a charismatic type of personalization that would signify the almost Hegelian solution (*Aufhebung*) to the dialectic of inwardness and externality or even the psychoanalytic normalization of divine *eros* (Corbin 1964: 275-83).

At the end, the issue concerns, again, the modalities—and limits—of rooting individuality and inwardness in new, modern forms of power. Are Nietzschean resentment and Foucauldian microphysics of power immediately 'applicable' to the global politics of Islam or are they first and foremost the reflex of North-Western European exceptionalism? (Stauth 2005; Salvatore 2007: 28-32). Isn't the ambivalent relation of Western culture to its axial, spiritual sources and their purported authenticity a smoking screen preventing an understanding of the complex workings of civilizing traditions? Isn't such a power-culture syndrome the main marker of a peculiar, globalizing, 'continuously unfolding,' yet not therefore universal 'secular machine of modernity'? (Stauth 2004: 10). No doubt the issue of saintliness—particularly as related to Sufism—is ever more embedded in a 'battlefield of east-west philosophy and cultural globalization', yet it cannot be explained—and sociologically valorized—by this 'embeddedness' alone.

References

Corbin, Henri (1964) *Histoire de la philosophie islamique*, Paris: Gallimard.
Cornell, Vincent (1998) *Realm of the Saint: Power and Authority in Moroccan Sufism*, Austin, TX: University of Texas Press.
Eickelman, Dale F./Salvatore, Armando (2002) "The Public Sphere and Muslim Identities". *European Journal of Sociology* 43/1, pp. 92-115.

Franke, Patrick (2004) "Khidr in Istanbul: Observations on the Symbolic Construction of Sacred Spaces in Traditional Islam". In: Georg Stauth (ed.) *On Archeology of Sainthood and Local Spirituality in Islam. Past and Present Crossroads of Events and Ideas* (Yearbook of the Sociology of Islam 5), Bielefeld: transcript, pp. 36-56.

Omar, Irfan (1993) "Khidr in the Islamic Tradition". *The Muslim World* 83/3-4, pp. 279-294.

Rahman, Fazlur (1979)[1966] *Islam*, Chicago and London: University of Chicago Press.

Salvatore, Armando (2001) "Introduction: The Problem of the Ingraining of Civilizing Traditions into Social Governance". In: Armando Salvatore (ed.) *Muslim Traditions and Modern Techniques of Power* (Yearbook of the Sociology of Islam 3), Hamburg and New Brunswick, NJ: Lit and Transaction, pp. 9-42.

Salvatore, Armando (2007) *The Public Sphere: Liberal Modernity, Catholicism, Islam*, New York: Palgrave Macmillan.

Schielke, Samuli (2004) "On Snacks and Saints: When Discourses of Order and Rationality enter the Egyptian Mawlid". In: Georg Stauth (ed.) *On Archeology of Sainthood and Local Spirituality in Islam. Past and Present Crossroads of Events and Ideas* (Yearbook of the Sociology of Islam 5), Bielefeld: transcript, pp. 173-194.

Stauth, Georg (1998) "Islam and Modernity: The Long Shadow of Max Weber" In: Georg Stauth (ed.) *Islam. Motor or Challenge of Modernity* (Yearbook of the Sociology of Islam 1), Hamburg and New Brunswick, NJ: Lit and Transaction, pp. 163-186.

Stauth, Georg (2004) "Introduction: Muslim Saints and Modernity". In: Georg Stauth (ed.) *On Archeology of Sainthood and Local Spirituality in Islam. Past and Present Crossroads of Events and Ideas* (Yearbook of the Sociology of Islam 5), Bielefeld: transcript, pp. 7-23

Stauth, Georg (2005) "Resentment, Religious Institutions, Modern Dialogue: Europe and the Non-European". In: Sigrid Nökel/Levent Tezcan (eds.) *Islam and the New Europe: Continuities, Changes, Confrontations* (Yearbook of the Sociology of Islam 6), Bielefeld: transcript, pp. 114-126.

Szakolczai, Arpad (2006) "Global Ages, Ecumenic Empires and Prophetic Religions". In: Johann P. Arnason/Armando Salvatore/Georg Stauth (eds.) *Islam in Process: Historical and Civilizational Perspectives* (Yearbook of the Sociology of Islam 7), Bielefeld: transcript, pp. 68-94.

Tarot, Camille (1993) *De Durkheim à Mauss: l'invention du symbolique*, Paris: Découverte.

Turner, Bryan S. (1974) *Weber and Islam: A Critical Study*, London: Routledge and Kegan Paul.

Part 2: Contested Places

Chapter 5

Saints (*awliya'*), Public Places and Modernity in Egypt

Ahmed A. Zayed

Introduction

Places close to the shrines of saints (*awliya'*) in Egypt are seen in this paper as public places that are continuously changing in relation to the surrounding structural context. Such gradual transformations can manifest themselves in the complete disappearance of this saint's public place itself or its being turned into a public trading and consumer center. Such transformations are undoubtedly linked to the broader framework of Egyptian society, however in many cases the veneration of the saints at their places often appears to resist all these changes.

I am not inclined here to see change in pure terms of proceeding from a traditional system to a modern one, as conventional theories of modernization would suggest, but wish to perceive this as the creation of a type of peripheral or counterfeit modernity, a thesis which I have already developed elsewhere (Zayed 2006). I assume that peripheral societies develop their specific modernities, which are culturally and structurally eclectic and politically authoritarian, however well equipped with all ingredients of modern consumer societies. In this type traditions co-exist alongside modern structures, and we find modern and traditional forms in a permanent process of interaction leading to a 'third culture' which is neither modern nor traditional. In its process of structuration, the 'third culture' or the 'third society' adapts itself to and copes with wider global and local contexts in contradicting ways. History is not made through accumulative actions and strategies, but through the accumulation of sporadic responses that end in the building up of new contradicted modes of social morphologies and social actions. Looking from the angle of these structural determinants, I assume that the places surrounding the shrines of saints quite strongly reflect such a third type of modernity, specifically where they continue to exist for ages and are entangled in processes of transforming their functions in relation to the society in which they exist. It may be anticipated that the 'traditional' and the 'modern' systems, engaged in a continuous dialogue and permanently reacting to each other, will be found here.

Modernity demolishes public places surrounding the shrines of saints and/or transforms them in such a way that the place reflects all of these contradictions of modernity in the periphery, including the veneration of saints in rural Egypt.

In this context clarification of what I mean by public places is needed. Public places are known as interactive, democratic, and meaningful places; they are open places receiving all groups, protecting the rights of all individuals involved in the reaction thereto, granting them the liberty of action, giving them both power of action and power of momentary ownership of the place or claiming its possession. Thus, a public place is transformed into a place, in which an individual behaves more freely, and he is tinctured by the deeds of individuals participating in the public or group activities. The salient feature of a public place is that it is a place owned by all people, a place in which individuals learn how to behave together (Carr et al. 1992: 19-20).

This definition brings to light two main characteristics of a public place: i.e. the relative absence of private interest and the domination of public or group activities. However, we might object to the definition on the grounds that a public place also provides an opportunity for the pursuit of private interests. Therefore, it cannot be defined purely in terms of public activities and a wider definition of the public place based on the experience of the human beings using the public place should be developed. The public place is a place where a number of people interact without necessarily knowing each other and at the same time participate in both group and private activities. According to this definition, public places are places which accommodate multiple types of interactions, extending from the pursuit of private interests to public interaction and representation, thus, all in all, a diverse range of an individual's local experiences (Smithsimon 1999).

While taking this into account, I wish to place the focus in this paper on the cultural nature of public places. In fact, there is a physical aspect of place involved that affects the social nature of the place. This is where we have to regard its nature as a cultural place which embodies the reproduction of different forms of social interaction and of the actions of individuals or groups.

This is where we must be aware of the fact that, although public places, as I see it, the saints places in Egypt entail certain characteristics of society, however, they are not merely a microcopy of it. The forms of interaction here are different from institutionally bound forms of interaction in society. Moreover, constraints and social control are weaker here than in places of institutionalized social interaction. In the saints' public places, there is a space for open forms of interaction and more liberal behavior than is known at other public places in society. The place also provides an opportunity for the mixing of different degrees and types of status, roles, and symbols. This may not be a general rule for all public places surrounding the shrines of saints. There is a hierarchy of shrines and spatial order around them that narrows or widens the restrictions, class distinctions, and different levels of behavioural constraints. Shrines and the public places linked to them can be arenas or stages of power, status, and class representations; equally they can be places of very intensive liberal interaction. This local diversification of saints' places can be complemented by looking to the diversity of festivals or other occasions involving the meeting of individuals or groups in the place. For example, on the occasion of the celebration of the Prophet's birthday (*mawlid an-nabi*), the place does not accommodate status, class, and power-based privileges. It may even reshape such privileges differently, regardless of the place's local nature. Accordingly, public places can be looked at as localities which materialize some aspects of public sphere. Eisenstadt argued that Muslim societies had developed autonomous and vibrant public spheres that play in important role in the control of the moral order of the community in contrast to their "limited autonomous access to policymaking" (Eisenstadt 2006: 310-311). Public places, especially those surrounding the holy shrines of saints, open horizons for different groups, sects, and/or organizations to interact and to express themselves freely apart from any political and social restrictions. Thus, they constitute venues for interaction and representation for the different groups of such 'autonomous public spheres'.

Finally, an explanation for the neighborhood of saints' shrines as archaeological sites might shed light on the historical role of local public places as cultural places. Al-Gawhary argues that such vicinity indicates that the graves of the *awliya'* were originally built on the rubble of ancient temples or sacred sanctuaries (al-Gawhary 1988: 109-112). By the same token George Stauth argues that Egypt was perceived in the religious mind "as the power of the past, combining broader concepts of Goddess with strong local ritual and symbolic practices […] that ends in reinventing the powers of ancient gods" (Stauth 2006: 163) and a continuous accumulation of cultural heritage. What made such accumulation possible is the cultural and social functions of the public places. They are not conceived as mere physical spaces, but as cultural spaces. Certainly, this affiliation of shrines with archaeological sites reflects historical transformations in the use of a place. The antiquities, mosques, and shrines contained in a place indicate the historical importance of the place and its relations with other places, and also tells us of the local society in relation to different historically and currently interacting cultures. Throughout history, such places might have been used as trading centers, as stations on the route of entertainment caravans (mostly by gypsies), and as venues by Sufi orders for their rituals. In this way it is obvious that these places have been points of cultural blending throughout history. They might have been used as cultural transit points, as places of interaction between villages and towns, expanding their relations and mixing experiences. Some of them even changed from being pure places to village centers, and furthermore contributed to the transformation of villages into towns or even cities.

This paper attempts to cast light on the transformations that occur in places surrounding the shrines of saints in Egypt by considering them as public places and specifically analyzing the influences of modernity on them. The main questions to be addressed here are: how had the traditional mind built a sacred image for such places? How were they transformed into spiritual and cultural places? How were such images structured in the traditional society? What are the modes of transformation of such places and images in modern Egypt? And how is the modern life of Egyptians reproduced in the festivals and rituals related to saints in different parts of Egypt. I shall begin to answer these questions by demonstrating the nature of the relation between saints and their burial places, laying particular emphasis on the holy nature of such places and the way in which both the place and the saint (*wali*) establish their own reputation. I will then go one step further to describe the role of these places in traditional society. After this I will explain changes undergone by such places in modern Egypt. In treating each of these points, I shall depend on qualitative data collected recently from different saintly places in Egypt.

Specificity of the Place: The Making of a Domain

Hobsbawm claims that traditions could be created or even invented through processes affected by the political claims of the organized social and political movements, and/or by unofficial groups with no definite political objectives (Hobsbawm 1993: 263-307). In this perspective the tradition connected with saints (*awliya'*) and their miracles (*karamat*) could be considered as an invented tradition. Several studies have emphasized this fact. In his study on saints of the Atlas, Gellner referred to the inventive processes connected with the making of a saint (*wali*), endowing him with extraordinary faculties enabling him to impose his authority on a tribe (Gellner 1969). Works published in Egypt emphasized that saints are locally invented, in locations where people attribute certain stories to a man and thus identify him as a saint who performed exceptional deeds or miracles. These stories may even be developed when he is alive and they continue up to his death, whereupon new stories about the miracles he performed during his burial are narrated. All these narratives manifest the *wali*'s extraordinary faculties and thereby shape the images of the saint in the minds of individuals and in the general memory of the populace (al-Gawhary 1988; 'Uthman 1981; Mustafa/Ibrahim 2004).

Accordingly, public places around the graves of saints are similar objects of invention. It is through the narrations about *wali* that special sanctity is endowed to a place and that rites are performed in the place. Narratives about the miracles performed by the saint and about the rites performed in the place reproduce the image of the place as a 'cultural space' in which the pity of the saint marks the frontiers of the space. To begin, it should be said that the place surrounding the saint's grave is sometimes called *haram al-wali* (the saint's sanctuary); that is to say, it is inviolable. Such terminology not only symbolizes the relation between the place and the *wali*'s grave, but it also endows it with a certain sanctity. It is often reported that the *wali* himself might choose his own burial place. Thus the place and all land associated it easily ends up being subject to the orders of the saint rather than remaining in full possession of its owner. It is only through the *wali* that they might continue to benefit from it. It is the *wali* who chooses the ground on which he walks, lives or sits while he is alive; in the same way, he chooses his burial place. He has a supreme freedom to live his life as he likes and to be buried in any place he selects. A variety of stories have been collected on the ways in which saints choose their burial sites:

1. It is often reported that some other greater *wali* or a group of important *awliya'* take possession of the people escorting the deceased (new) *wali* to his final resting place. It is the spirit of the great *awliya'* that makes the coffin fly to the burial place.
2. On order of these (greater) *awliya'*, the body of a deceased *wali* might refuse to move from one place to another one. If he wants to stay in his place, he must be buried here, as is the case of Sidi Musa Ghanim (Abu Lamuna) at Minyat Samanud, in the district of Aga, Daqahliyya Governorate, and Sidi Khamis Gubbarah, in al-Shuhada', Minufiyya Governorate.
3. The *wali* may have traveled from afar to his burial place, he first chooses his place, and may wish to wander further after his burial. There are various narratives about *awliya'* who came through the Nile or by sea and settled in a place on the sea shore or river bank until their death and then were buried in another chosen place. Of these *awliya'* are Sheikh Al-Awwam, at the town of Marsa Matrouh; and Sidi Muhammad Al-Iraqi (Kafr Ruzqan, in the Tala District, Minufiyya Governorate).
4. There are different rituals involved in the choice of the burial place, such as by hurling a stick or a piece of stone so that the place where the stick or stone lands will be his burial place. There is a story about Sidi Muhammad Al-Murshidi (Mutubis District, Kafr al-Shaykh Governorate) who came to this area from Morocco escorted by as-Sayyid Ahmad Al-Badawi. It is told that a difference of opinion occurred between him and Ahmad Al-Badawi about the site on which the shrine was to be built. Finally, the difference was resolved by Sidi al-Murshidi who held a piece of green palm branch (a twig recently taken out of a palm tree) and threw it in the air. The mosque was to be built on the site on which the thrown

stick fell and settled. The stick actually fell down on the place now containing both the mosque and shrine of Sidi al-Murshidi at a site which once was on the shore of Lake Burullus. Sheikh Murshidi was later known as the 'man of the palm branch'.

5. The body of a deceased saint or *wali* may be moved either by the *wali*'s will and action or by the will of certain persons who visited his shrine in their dreams and were ordered to undertake that mission for him. A good example of this is the story about Sidi Abdallah Ibn Salam: "his corpse, after being killed, flew in the air and came to the graveyard in Daqahliyya Governorate, and every drop of his blood falling down on a place turns that place into a blessed one whereupon a shrine for him is constructed." This narration symbolizes the saint's supernatural power which makes him capable of expropriating land anywhere for his benefit. All land is his and nobody can prevent him from being buried wherever he wants. One drop of his blood is even sufficient to make a place a blessed one. It also explains why so many of his shrines exist in the Daqahliyya Province.

Dreams and visions intermingle with reality, in that certain people wake up with visions requesting them to build a shrine for a certain saint. This occurred in the case of such famous saints as Al-Husain Ibn Ali, al-Sayyida Zainab, the Seven Girls (Sab'a Banat), and al-Sayyid Al-Badawi who have numerous shrines at different places around Egypt. The place chosen by the *wali* and/or the people 'who dream' is not just a place for the tomb but it turns into domain protected and safeguarded by the *wali*. Once chosen nobody can claim it. The will of the *wali* must be realized, even by force. Let us consider the following three stories narrated in three different places:

1. In a story about the saint Sidi Ali al-Yatim (in the village of Kafr Abu Gum'a, Qalyubiyya Governorate), we found that his shrine is located on cultivated land because he was a Bedouin and liked seclusion in open fields. People in the village say that the *wali*'s body is spread in all the grass covering the area, and that he lives under the grass with forty others.

2. In another story about the saint Sheikh Muhammad Hasabu in the village of Tarabumba, in the city of Damanhour (Buhayra governorate), people mention that "he used to sit under a tree close to the cemetery in an open area. After his death, he was buried in an ordinary cemetery but he appeared to one of his sons in a dream and told him that his grave was under the tree where he used to sit. This tree and this place were owned by one of the wealthy people. Thus, the saint's children did not want to bring out the subject. However, the *wali* insisted on appearing to them and telling them to look out for his grave under the tree. They did so and transported the body from the cemetery to the place under the tree and this

tree became a blessed one, and the whole place became a blessed place".
3. In a similar story, Sheikh Talha al-Tilmisany, in Kafr al-Shaykh City, "used to move from country to country till he settled in the area where he wanted to be buried and said that this was his place at present and ever after. The story mentions that when he settled in this place, he had a horse that landed on a piece of land owned by the King of Sakha nearby and ate from it, thus the king sent forces to drive Sidi Talha away. Forces came through the sea and were surprised to see Sidi Talha himself walking on the water, pointing at them to stop the ship. The force could not move the ship (as if they have been frozen) and so they went to summon the king who went to see the truth of it. Sheikh Talha came out to the King of Sakha walking on the water and indicating once again with his hand, so the ship stopped again and could not move. The King asked the Sheikh what he wanted and the Sheikh replied that he wanted this area to himself so the king responded to his request".

These three stories may well illustrate how saints create their own places. In the first story, the saint's body is spread in the fields, thus, preventing farmers from trespassing over the land. The idea the saint being spread over the land represents a symbol of the extension of his strength, despite the fact that the saint's shrine is small and built of clay. Also he keeps forty people with him. They are also saints and they guard the domain against any violation (can I dare to say that they constitute a hidden army to help in times of crisis). In the second story there is conflict between the worldly power of the land owner who owns the place of the tree and the relative weakness of the saint. The conflict ends to the advantage of the saint. In the third story, the conflict is turned into an open conflict between the temporal power (of the 'king') and the spiritual power (of the saint). We notice here that the use of the word 'king' is rather metaphorical and the story teller wants to confirm the strength of this worldly power. The word 'king' is invented because rulers of districts have never been called kings in Egypt. The story ends with the victory of the spiritual power. The saint wins over horses and swords with his magic powers. As soon as he appears walking on water the war ends. The story develops a symbolic relationship between the worldly civil power and the spiritual power, stressing the winning of the latter by means of the supernatural. This symbolizes the potential strength of ordinary people against the governor and the nature of their relationships to men of power. There is here an ambiguous wish to resist, however combined with a disability to indulge in an open conflict. The helplessness of the weak compels them to look out to the world of magic to find their own power.

Once the saint occupies an area, it is considered 'sacred' also in the sense of being 'protected'. At the same time ever more stories are recycled about miracles that happened in the place, defending the sanctity of the saint and his place. In the case of Sidi Hassan Abu Raytayn in the village of Bani Walims (Minya Governorate) a thief attempting to steal wheat from the field surrounding the sheikh's shrine, was kept stuck to the ground until the owner of the wheat woke up, forgave the thief, and released him.

Sometimes the holiness of a place relates to a tree, a well, or a lake, based on their symbolic power which identifies them as sources of magic or blessing. The sycamore tree and the prickly pear trees that surround the famous shrine of Sheikh Abu Mandur in Rashid (Rosetta, north of the Delta) bestow blessings on the place and provide a picnic site for the visitors. A tree can also be considered a source of healing as in the case of the tree near the shrine of Sheikh al-Gharib in the village of Bani 'Amir in the al-Adwa district (al-Minya Governorate). People come here to seek the blessings of the sheikh and request healing or release from distress by hammering a nail in its trunk or by hanging something on it. The same is reported about the wells found near some of the saints's shrines, for example the well near Sheikh Abu Mandur's shrine, in whose water the sick bathe, the well in the Church of the Virgin Mary in Mostorod (Helwan, Cairo) and the lake near Sheikh Abu Ghunayma's shrine in the village of Sakola (al-Minya governorate) where people bathe in search of healing or the resolution of their problems. It is believed in these cases that the tree or the waters of a well or a pond are inhabited by the spirit of the *wali* and thus transmit his strength and blessings.

We have pointed out previously that a strong relation exists between miracles (*karamat*) and local conflicts where the saint is linked to a sort of separate sphere which is dominated by the world of saints (*awaliya*) and confronts the world of the real. This is certainly linked to the process of creating a public sphere around the saint's shrine. This creation of a public sphere around the shrine could be considered as related to people's desire to create within the realm of the saint's personal space (a specific domain) a space full of common freedom and culture, as opposed to the different world of the everyday bound to authority and legal restrictions. Truly the first world is also a world of power where authority, status, and power are included, and influence cannot be disputed. However, it is a world by people's choice which they create in their imagination, co-existing with real power as though it were a reality in itself and beyond discussion. However, the continuation of such an imaginative world as a public sphere owned by the people should also be seen in relation to modern society, the state, the mass culture and one could suggest that the greater the scale of these these influences, which are often viewed in local contexts as a type of authoritarianism of modernity, the more people escape to their personal caves, and the more they produce daily life utopias relating them to the disputes over real human existence and the life of the saints. It may also be suggested that the greater the pressure of modern institutional hierarchy, the greater is the inclination of people, who live on the periphery, to create autonomous domains and to recognize and dispute territories and frontiers. The mythical culture and the rituals and actions related to that culture is only one example of such domains. It is only the most important because of its historical roots.

Awliya's Squares in Traditional Society

In traditional village society, when a *wali*'s shrine was located in a central spacious place, it was used as a public place, even though that it could be privately owned by one of the families that traced their descent to the *wali*. It was used by everyone for a variety of activities. It gave people an opportunity to reveal personal behavioral attitudes and representations which otherwise would not have been accessible to them due to social rules and class hierarchies. Here, the villagers were able to meet strangers, the poor among them could meet rich people, the weak could meet the strong. The place opened up for interaction which social constraints would otherwise have prevented. This open communication between different social classes at the place parallels that between life and death, or, in other words, between the life of people in the place and the shrine of their *wali*, a dead human being, who sorts out matters and rules them while they seek his blessing. They enjoy being close to him and celebrating his anniversary, and he is believed to protect them and guard the place for them. For them he is the weak, poor, and humble man who became powerful owing to his spiritual and then supernatural ability to perform miracles (*karamat*). He is believed now to possess the place, allowing them to use it. This public place allows for everything and even for behavior which otherwise may not be socially acceptable. It seems that people derive their freedom from the saint, using him to build a relationship with the other world and an experience of being close to it.

This ideal picture of the relationship between the people and their *wali*'s shrine is of course a more common and pure case in traditional village societies, as the example of Sheikh Hassan Abu Raitain in one of the al-Minya villages shows. The *wali*'s shrine is located on a small hill surrounded by the village's cemetery (*kum*) which was surrounded by wide open place (*gurn*) which reached to the river banks of Bahr Yusif. The location remained unchanged until the mid 1970s.

It was a place that saw strangers, especially in between village wanderers, like cattle traders, entertainers and gypsies. Of course the place was used by local cattle traders too. They took the place in order to tie their cattle before selling it. As for camel traders, they usually came from far away villages. Sometimes they came in caravans from the desert. Every year, people in the village talked about the caravan that would arrive soon. It consisted of camels which were led and ridden by strangers from Morocco or from Sudan moving to the village from the Western Desert. These traders took the area surrounding the wali's shrine as a place to settle for a week or two before moving to another village. Concerning entertainers, they were swing owners, moving from village to village especially after the harvest, when people were free and had time and money for fun. Among the people who would periodically frequent the shrine were gypsies who settled with tents for a month or two near the Wali. Of course, not knowing from where they make their living, people were suspicious that the gypsies could steal. However, they normally would not do it in the village they settled. In the night the place becomes a ground for children and youth to play. One of the most popular games played in this place is *turnaza*. Similar to hockey, it is played with a ball made of twisted strings and hooked rods from palm branches. However in the times of the harvest and at the festival of the Prophet's birthday, the place was differently used.

In the harvest season, from the beginning of summer in May and continuing till the end of July, peasants brought their principal crops, broad beans, clover and wheat to the area near the shrine in the belief that the *wali* guards their crops.

In the days of the anniversary of Sidi Hasan Abu Raytayn, which starts on the first day of the Islamic month Rabi' al-Awwal, that is, shortly before the Prophet's birthday festival, people set up market stands to sell sweets, peanuts, and tea and tables for playing cards. The stands are called *farsh* and consist of two or three benches and a table to display the goods. The roof of the kiosk consists of palm branches or corn reeds supported on four wooden columns. There are about ten of these stands. The festival continues until the night of the 12th of Rabi' al-Awwal when the 'great night' (*al-layla al-kabira*) is celebrated. The market stands are more or less empty in the morning and at noon, but from the afternoon until the evening they are crowded with people: some eat peanuts and sweets, others play cards, and some buy peanuts and sweets, either as souvenirs to bring home from the festival, or for female relatives who spend the festival in tents further away from the center of the celebrations. Youths invite one another to eat sweets and peanuts. Family relations influence the choice of market stands people frequent: young people from a certain family prefer the *farsh* belonging to some of their relatives, although this is not a general rule. Swings are set up to children and professional entertainers attract the visitors to shooting stands, circus performances, and tests of strength—in a popular attraction known as 'train' or 'cannon' young men push heavy iron weights on a rail. If the contestant manages to give the weights enough speed, they hit a firecracker at the upper end of the rail. The weights can be adjusted depending on the strength of the contestant.

Meanwhile, the servants of the shrine prepare it by cleaning it, giving it a fresh coat of paint, and placing a large flag fixed on a tall thick column of wood that marks the beginning of the celebration in the middle of the square facing the shrine. At the beginning of the festival, the servants of the shrine invite a group of drummers from a nearby village called al-Garnus. The drummers, three or four of them, belong to a Sufi brotherhood associated with Sheikh Abu Shuk of al-Garnus. They are joined by the professional drummers from the village. Together they form a procession that passes through the village on each of the twelve days of the festival, carrying flags of Sheikh Abu Shuk and Sheikh Abu Raytayn. They all participate in celebrating the days of the anniversary. In the morning, the drummers come out with the two flags carried by two of Sheikh's servants or their children. They start their tour around the village houses, stopping by each one to recite loudly the *Fatiha*, the opening Sura of the *Qur'an*, so that the house owners give them a small present in cash or seeds (depending on the family's financial means), known as *al-'ada*, i.e. '(the Sheikh's) habit'.

This procession ends in the afternoon at the Sheikh's shrine where people gather to celebrate or begin another procession. There is a reason for this: the young people compete in parading with the flag around the village to the rhythm of drum beats. This is called 'touring the flags'. Women stand further away, observing their children and encouraging them with waves. The young men not only carry out this process just to be blessed, but also to show off their pride and strength. Each one who waves with a flag, pays a piaster or more to be collected and added to the total income of the celebration.

The villagers call the group that tours around the village with drums and flags *al-zawiya*, meaning literally 'corner', but in this context referring to a Sufi group's meeting place where the group performs its rituals and, indirectly, the group itself. Many people donate a meal to this *zawiya* at lunch or dinner throughout the days of the celebration to the extent that members of the *zawiya* are unable to attend every invitation for dinner or lunch. Therefore members of the *zawiya* often accept the invitations without eating.

Every evening, a *dhikr* (a rhythmic, dance-like meditation on Qur'anic verses and poetic praises of the Prophet) is performed in front of the shrine. It is led by the only Sufi order present in the village, the Bayyumiyya order, which has spread in the village since the early 1970s. Prior to this, *dhikr*s were organized by the followers of Sheikh Abu Shuk who were experienced in this. This could be the reason for the continued privileged position of the *dhikr*s in celebration. The donations collected during the festival are divided by three among the 'servants' (*khadim*, pl. *khuddam*) of the sheikh of the village, the followers of the main sheikh in al-Garnus village, and the followers of Abu Shuk.

The 'great night', the last and most crowded night of celebration, marks the end of the festival; it is the night of the prophet's birthday when people delay their work to attend the nocturnal celebration. The celebration begins in the afternoon when the *khalifa*, dressed in white and riding a camel which is also covered with a fresh blanket, leads a procession around the village. The *khalifa*, literally 'successor' is the local representative of the larger Bayyumiya order and a descendant of the Prophet Muhammad. Men on the left and right of the *khalifa* carry flags, and others in front of him beat the drums. After him come children and youths who ride richly decorated donkeys and camels. After the procession of the *khalifa*, the smaller flag processions continue until the evening. On the square facing the shrine, a *dhikr* begins, amplified by loudspeakers. At the end of the great night, a sheikh recites religious supplications and finally receives money from people asking for God's protection, saying "Mr. so and so". His chorus follows by saying, "Oh, may God protect him" or "Oh, may God have mercy upon him", each according to the situation until dawn. Each person or household seeks protection or mercy for their dead family members through this chorus. Women sit behind and receive gifts of peanuts and sweets. Trade flourishes on this night as everybody buys peanuts and sweets for their houses. The celebration lasts until the morning when everything comes to an end and the days and nights return to their normal course.

Undoubtedly, this is an ideal description of the celebration, for the village could be in anguish for the death of a village nobleman, youth, or a large number of men. In such a year, there is no festival at all, or there could be one but on a more restricted level than that described here. Importantly, the festival is influenced by the general economic and societal situation.

The celebration manifests different patterns of symbolic exchange and power representation. Openness is the key characteristic of these patterns: while various groups and authorities participate in the celebration, none of them has exclusive power over the site. The festival is open for the various celebrations of different groups of people. The square surrounding the *wali*'s shrine functions in a traditional society as a public place in which interactions of different types take place. It is the place through which villagers interact with foreign traders and entertainers, accommodate outsiders such as gypsies, prepare their crops for storage, and gather to celebrate a religious occasion.

Modernity and Transformation of the Place

Many observers, both in Egypt and abroad, expected that modernity disrupts and totally destroys the quietude of a traditional place like the saint's square in the village. Modernity, which we shall deal with here, is a peripheral, or counterfeit modernity. In other words, it is a type of modernity that is not established on an internal foundation, but depends on the random and irrational transference from Western modernity which spread through colonization, mass media and communications around the world. As a result, this type of modernity is characterized by its dependence on induced modernization, irrational selection, and consumerism (Zayed 2006: 72). This kind of modernity does not obliterate traditionalism totally or even boycott it, but instead copes with, transforms, and uses tradition in different ways. Of course, this was also the case with the high modernity in Western industrial nations in the 20th century. But while the high Western modernity, along with the nationalist project of developmental modernity in Third World countries, have been built on a strong (even if often imagined) dichotomy of modernity and tradition, peripheral modernity, both as an ideology and as a social practice, gives up much of the dichotomizing nature of high modernity in favor of an idiosyncratic mixture of different forms of power and social organization.

In the following I explore the impact of modernity on the surrounding places of saints (*awliya'*), and the manifestations of peripheral modernity in these places. Before getting into the subject, let us relate some narratives by supporters of the saints that relate to the impact of modernity:

1. First narrative: "The place is the shrine of Sheikh Hasanayn in the city of al-Mansura, Daqahliya. The shrine is inside a small mosque which is near to a larger one. Both mosques are located in a big square called Sheikh Hasanayn Square. In the framework of a project to renew both of them, it was decided to demolish them. (In Egypt 'renewing' usually means the demolition of an old building and its replacement by a new one). The larger mosque had already been destroyed and so is part of the smaller one. When the contractor decided to move the grave of the *wali* from the small mosque using a tractor, the *wali* defended himself against this violation (because he does not want to leave his simple and small room). As a result, the tractor broke down, and the same happened to other three tractors. Besides, seven workers got sick while demolishing the mosque and were taken to hospital."

2. In a second narrative, we will relate an anecdote told by a servant of the shrine of Yusuf Abd as-Salam Ga'far also known as Sidi Yusuf in San al-Hagar village, Sharqiya Governorate: "The young people of this village gathered to prevent the servant from celebrating the festival of the *wali*, considering it a novelty with no religious ground and an event in which non-religious acts occur. As a result, the festival was stopped for four years. This harmed the financial benefits of the servant who depended on the annual income from the festival. Thus, he sought the assistance of the Sufi leaders who came to the village and persuaded the protestors to allow the resumption of the festival. The leaders' request was granted on the condition that no immoral conduct should be allowed during the festival."

3. The third narrative tells about Sidi Shibl al-Aswad and his seven sisters and/or brothers (*sab'a banat, sab'a ihwat*) in Al-Shuhada', a city in the Minufiyya Governorate. The story revolves around the saint's rescuing of a drug dealer from the police: "The latter had been caught and in his possession was an amount of drugs inside a box. During his arrest, the dealer raised his hands and said, 'Help! Sheikh Shibl, I seek your help'. When the policemen opened the box, they found nothing but some snakes. So, they released him. Soon after his release, the drugs were back inside the box". Such stories of the saint rescuing a follower from hands of the police are common, although, unlike this narrative, they often end with the saint personally punishing the wrongdoer after demonstrating his superiority towards the power of the state.

The three aforementioned stories show significant testimonials of the experience of peripheral modernity—in alliance with Salafi reformism—in Egypt as well as the clashes and contradictions resulting from it. In the first story, the traditional attitude triumphs over modern technology and even destroys it. Technology can be made use of in several fields, yet when it clashes with religious beliefs (we must remember that while it is easy for an outside observer to label them 'popular ones', for those who hold them they are a part of correct Islamic creed), such beliefs emerge victorious. Therefore, technology should co-exist with such beliefs and allow them to remain. It is not an exaggeration to say that in the conflict between modernity and traditions, traditions come out victorious. Moreover, modern forms may have only superficial existence that do not run deep in any way.

The second story is common story also found elsewhere in Egypt. There have been clashes between groups of young Salafis (a radical Islamic reformist movement strongly opposed to saints and Sufism) and the servants of some shrines in some villages in various locations. The Salafis believe that the practices and beliefs of the *khuddam*, i.e. the servants of the saint, such as visiting the graves of *awliya'*, the existence of a *wali*'s grave beside a mosque, and the celebration of festivals for *awliya'* contradict the principles of the Sunna doctrine. According to some studies, these clashes have a historical dimension since there have always been conflicts between a purist doctrine and Sufism, between orthodox religious scholars and Sufis. Sometimes, such conflicts ended with contriving conspiracies and arresting Sufists (Mustafa/'Abbas 2004: 200). Some attributed this historical enmity to the popularity and proliferation of Sufis, for they take control of people's hearts who like their way of practicing religion, a fact which some purist scholars of the Scripture consider as a danger against the true religious creeds (al-Tawil 1964: 174). Recent studies do point out, however, that this theory is strongly exaggerated and anachronistic, projecting a modern conflict on pre-modern times. While there has always been conflict between more purist and exclusive, and more inclusive and ecstatic currents within Sunni Islam, Sufism and scholarly orthodoxy have nevertheless been very close throughout centuries, and the Islamic al-Azhar University contains a significant and powerful Sufi faction to the present day. The implicit enmity between purity and ecstasy has, however, changed over time to become more explicit and clear. Since the emergence of modernity in late 19th century, there has been a pronounced and strong antagonism between Sufis supporters of Salafi reformism. Although both claim to represent the true orthodox Islam, it is worth noting that the project of modernity in Egypt has shown much more sympathy for the Salafi reformist claim. The material collected from Delta villages displays some glaring examples of this conflict between some Salafi groups and the Sufis (especially the servants of the saints' shrines). Material from other villages in Egypt demonstrated that these conflicts are widespread and, in some villages, the success of the Salafis in proselytizing their doctrine (which claims that saints-day festivals are an un-Islamic and novelty) has reached an extent whereby some *awliya'* festivals have been stopped or are only being celebrated on a small scale.

What we encounter here are two attitudes reflecting two forms of religion; namely, the Salafi religious movement and Sufism. We are not referring here to the view of 'folk' religion as the alleged opposite of 'formal' religion, which has long prevailed in both Egyptian and foreign literature (Uwais 1965; Gellner 1981). In this case, both sides claim to represent true, correct religion. What we have here is a conflict between a traditional mystical practice of Islam and novel form of religion, that is, the strict Salafi form of Islam. (I consider this form of Islam as an integrated part of peripheral modernity.) This conflict is a modern one which did not feature previously in traditional society. We have already referred to this conflict by saying that while conflicts between purist and ecstatic approaches have a long history, they were largely latent. The emergence of contemporary conditions have brought these differences to the surface and sometimes turn them into an open source of conflict. One of the most important of these conditions is the prevalence of an affinity with fundamentalism among the youth. The spread of this attitude was boosted by the intensive migration to the Gulf countries from the 1970s. Many of the migrants were influenced by the Wahhabi doctrine (named after its founder Sheikh Muhammad ibn Abd al-Wahhab), which prevails in much of the Arabian Peninsula. One of the key objectives of the Wahhabi and other similar doctrines is to fight what their supporters believe to be novelties and superstitions. Wahhabis and Salafis believe that visiting the graves of the dead and resorting to the intermediation of saints are pre-Islamic customs which started to spread in Muslim societies from the 8th century after Higra (Mostafa 1989: 305). Holding to a very strict interpretation of monotheism, Wahhabis and Salafis believe that any kind of devotion to saints is outright polytheism that renders its practitioner an unbeliever.

In the third story we find the *wali* coping with the requirements of the modern age in a thrilling and astonishing manner. In this story, the *wali* does not stand beside a victim of injustice, protect someone from falling in danger, prevent a robber away from stealing, protect a cow from falling into water, bring back a lost child or causes a sick person to recover from pain—as he may do in many other stories—but the *wali* safeguards a drug trafficker. Narcotics and their criminalization are a feature of the modern society. Police forces that find narcotics and arrest their traffickers are one of modern society's apparatuses. In the first story we have a *wali* who refuses to be moved from his place and resists urban reconstruction and here we have another *wali* who condones the protection of a narcotics trafficker, that is to say, ensures the protection of a legally deviant person. One could wonder why the *wali* helps a trafficker against the police instead of helping the police to catch the drug trafficker. The saint's assistance is telling of the deep distrust of many Egyptians towards their police force and the competing forms of authority and power in peripheral modernity. Resorting to the help of saint appears as something like a resistance mechanism against the state as represented here by policemen. Helping the drug trafficker is thus not framed in terms of law and deviation, but of the saint standing up for his people against the state apparatus.

Let us move on now to study the effect of modernity on the use of public places surrounding the shrines of *awliya'*. The first of these effects was the disappearance of the place altogether, or at least the reduction of its size. This took place as a result of the spread of modern buildings in such locations. In the 1980s and 1990s, Huge expansion of the villages and cities took place in the 1980s and 1990s as a result of the free market economy and the increase of migration ratios making previously unseen amounts of capital available for the construction of houses. Together with rapid population growth, this led to a dramatic expansion of the geographic area of villages, towns, and cities and random slum expansions which spread in every direction. This urban expansion has often devoured the areas surrounding the shrines of *awliya'* unless they are protected by legal prohibitions, such as the existence of archeological monuments on these sites. Local authorities often participate themselves in such building operations by making use of open spaces to build schools, local administration centers, or youth centers.

An example of such a development can be found at the shrine of Sidi 'Awwad in Qalyub City District (Qalyubiyya Governorate) which is located near a main road and a railway line. The area surrounding the shrine used to be free from buildings until a mosque was built beside the shrine. This was accompanied by an urban development that resulted in the shrine being surrounded by residential buildings and shops. The area, moreover, witnessed the construction of schools and administrative buildings (e.g. the local administration of the city and district of Qalyub, telephone exchange, and a post office). Another example is the aforementioned shrine of Sheikh Hasan Abu Raytayn where the once spacious place around it has become crowded with buildings. Unable find a place in front of the shrine to celebrate the sheikh's *mulid* celebration, people have moved to celebrate it in the streets leading to the shrine. Sometimes, a shrine that was originally far away from a village becomes surrounded by new buildings, especially if a mosque is built beside it. We can see this in the case of the Nur al-Sabah shrine in the city of Tanta, capital of the Gharbiyya governorate. The construction of a mosque beside the shrine led to the construction of a road leading to the mosque which, in turn, was followed by houses and a large governmental building lining the two sides of the road. Almost the same thing occurred with the shrine of Sidi Abu al-Naga al-Ansari in the town of Fuwa, Kafr al-Shaykh governorate where a bank branch, a car parking area, and a market were built beside the shrine.

There are several manifestations of the state's interference in affairs concerning *awliya'* and the mosques containing their shrines. Such state interference reflects forms of induced modernization:

The inclusion of saints' shrines in tourism development plans as happened with the graves of the Sab'a Banat (seven girls) in Al-Bahnasa village, Al-Minya governorate. There, the site containing the graves of the seven girls was developed as a tourist site. Accordingly, an iron fence was constructed around each grave and painted green. Each grave was covered with a green cloth. The area surrounding the graves was cleaned in order to make it suitable for tourism.

A. Interference in the processes of collecting money at the shrines: visitors often come to the shrine of a saint to make a vow to God and leave a sum of money at a box next to the shrine. The income from these vows is significant, at major shrines in particular. These shrines have been under direct state control since the nationalization of the *awqaf* (religous foundations) in the 1960s, and the Ministry of Awqaf organizes the collection and distribution of the donations, keeping a lion's share for itself.

B. Interference in the organization of the annual *mulid* (pl. *mawalid*) festivals at the shrines: While large *mulids* of national significance have always been organized and policed by the government to a significant degree, festivals of local and regional importance were organized largely autonomously by Sufi orders and local notables. In recent decades, however, state interference in all *mulids* has increased, be it through the distribution of locations for market stands and Sufi *dhikr*s, through the restriction of the movement of the public at the festival or through an intensive security presence.

C. One of the most important forms of state power at the shrines is urban reconstruction at the *wali*'s shrine. In this case, the area is redeveloped to appear in a modern form. For example, the shrine of Sidi Muhammad al-Murshidi in the village of Minyat al-Murshid, Kafr al-Shaykh governorate: the shrine and a small mosque overlooked an anchorage for boats in Lake Burullus. When the old mosque was demolished and replaced by a new one, the canal connecting the village to the lake was filled up with earth, and the land adjoining the berth was reclaimed. The new mosque was built in the standard style that has come to replace historic mosques in almost all of Egypt's villages and small towns. The shrine, dating back to 13th century and unlike the mosque an architectural site under supervision of the Ministry of Antiquities, is the only historical structure remaining. Both the shrine and the mosque overlook the new 'Sidi al-Murshidi Square'.

D. Interference may come from civil society and from the Sufi orders themselves with the help of governmental bodies as occurred in the case of the square of the shrine of Sidi 'Izz ad-Din Madi Abu al-Aza'im (Itay al-Barud, al-Buhayra governorate). The shrine is located inside a large mosque which also functions as the local center of the Azmiya Sufi order. A civil organization allied to the Azmiya order built a hospital—as an annex to the mosque—for the town's inhabitants and for the needy from neighboring villages. The new mosque complex also houses a kindergarden and a pharmacy and hosts private tutoring classes for school children. Thus, the place has changed from a religious shrine to a both religious and civil shrine. Just as the traditional square in front of the shrine is open for all kinds of people and activities, the new shrine complex is also open to functions other than those deemed purely religious. However, in a distinctively modern manner, the variety of functions is clearly limited to those deemed in line with the reformist Sufi creed of the Azmiya, a group whose members largely originate from the urban middle classes. As multifunctional as the new shrine may be, it has no space for the genuine openness of the traditional shrine.

E. Finally, the traditional organization of saints-day festivals (*mawalid*) has been effected by societal and economic changes. The *mulid* festival, celebrated annually at the shrine of the *wali*, provides a space for various economic, social, cultural, and artistic practices. It is also a place where Sufi groups gather to meet, mobilize their supporters, and display their identity to the visitors (M. El-Gawhary 1988; F. Mostafa 1980). Until early 20th century, major *mulids* (especially the *mulid* of as-Sayyid Ahmad al-Badawi in Tanta) constituted the country's most important markets.

With the growth of the modern economy, mulids have largely lost their importance as markets. However the cafes, amusements, and the trade in toys, souvenirs, sweets, and religious commodities continue to have enormous economic significance for towns that host major *mulids*. This trade demonstrates the many changes that have taken place in the traditional organization of festivals. Rather than unchanging traces of traditional culture, *mulids* today are in many ways thoroughly modern and infiltrated by the culture of consumerism. The first of such manifestations of change to emerge was the appearance of modern cafés in the public places around the shrines of *awliya'*. Previously, the tea-maker used to appear only at the festival (*mawlid*) in villages or sit in a remote place of the square in towns and cities to make tea for people sitting around him on ground. Some tea makers still run their business in this way. Next to the tea makers, however, there appeared modern cafés with chairs, tables, glass cups, and glittering lights. Another manifestation of modern consumerism is the development of simple shops in the districts around important saints' shrines into modern shopping centers with radiant facades and modern commodities. For example, the shops selling sweets around the shrine of as-Sayyid al-Badawi in Tanta are no longer small shops selling products made inside the shop, but have become part of a major industry with central distribution and a network of branches. Even the small trade of travelling vendors is connected to the global economy with the vendors selling incense made in India and rosaries made in China. With the availability of electric light, loudspeakers, and brightly colored textiles, the sound and appearance of the *mulid* have changed: Sufi *dhikr*s have turned into concerts with audiences reaching the thousands, the *mulid* is illuminated by a striking display of colorful lights, and Sufi processions appear to have become more radiant and splendid through the glittering colors of turbans and banners. The forms of entertainment have become more diverse, and new games have appeared. Thus, while certain places diminish and disappear due to urban expansion, other places undergo radical transformation under the influence of modern urban development. Their functions are also transformed, reflecting the general outlook of modernity prevailing in the society.

Conclusion

In this paper I have attempted to open new horizons for the study of Egyptian saints (*awliya'*) and their miracles (*karamat*). I propose that we go beyond the conventional way of looking at saints as established in Egyptian folkloric and ethnographic studies. A peripheral structure of modernity exists in Egypt that is largely linked to the re-creation of saint veneration and beliefs, re-inventing the world of saints and guarding it throughout all transformations of the social context over the years. I concentrated my analysis on the areas surrounding the saints' shrines as public places. There is a significant difference, however, in the nature of the 'publicness' found in these areas in traditional and peripheral modern societies. While the traditional square of the saint's shrine was most importantly characterized by the openness it enjoyed due to the *baraka* of the saint, the modern public space of the saint's square is in many ways more contested and fragmented due to ideological and religious contestation, urban expansion, modern economics, and state attempts to impose fences, police surveillance, and other physical restrictions on the use of the space. I have shown some aspects which are instrumental to the way in which these places have been transformed from the setting of traditional culture to places where saint veneration and communal culture and new forms of state and consumer culture overlap. I hope that this analysis will prompt further research incorporating this view of the continuity of the relationship between the spiritual power and the surrounding temporal powers, the role that popular beliefs play in shaping modern public ideology, and the problems and contradictions related to the construction of a modern society. There can be no doubt that we must consider the contradicting modes of the formation of modern material and cultural life in peripheral societies.

References

al-Gawhary, Muhammad (1988) *'Ilm al-folklor* (Vol.2), *Dirasat al-mu'taqadat al-sha'biya*, Alexandria: Dar al-ma'rifa al-jami'iya.

al-Tawil, Tawfiq, (1946) *al-Tasawwuf fi Misr fi al-'asr al-uthmani*, Cairo: al-Adab Bookshop.

Carr, Stephen/Francis, Marc/Rivlin, Leanne/Stone, Andrew (1992) *Public Space*. Cambridge: Cambridge University Press.

Gellner, Ernest (1969) *Saints of Atlas*, New York: The University of Chicago Press.

Gellner, Ernest (1981) *Muslim Society*, Cambridce: Cambridge University Press.

Hobsbawm, Eric (1983) "Mass-Producing Traditions: Europe 1870-1914". In: Eric Hobsbawm/Terence Ranger (eds) *The Invention of Tradition*, Cambridge: Cambridge University Press, pp. 263-307.

Eisenstadt, Shmuel N. (2006) "Public Spheres and Political Dynamics in Historical and Modern Muslim Societies". In: Georg Stauth/Armando Salvatore (eds.) *Islam in Process. Historical and Civilizational Prespectives* (Yearbook of Sociology of Islam 7), Bielefeld: transcript.

Mustafa, Faruq (1980) *al-Mawalid: dirasa li-l-'adat wa-t-taqalid al-sha'biya fi Misr*, Cairo: al-Hay'a al-misriya al-'amma li-l-kitab.

Mustafa, Faruq/Muhammad, 'Abbas (2004) *Sina'at al-wali: Dirasa anthropolojiya fi al-sahra' al-gharbiya*, Cairo: Center for Social Research and Studies, Cairo University.

Mustafa, Faruq (1989) "al-Shaykh Muhammad Ibn 'Abd al-Wahhab wa-l-usul". *Bulletin of the Faculty of Arts* 37.

Smithsimom, Greg (1999) *The Death of Public Space? Histories of Jewish and Puerto Rican Neighborhoods Tell A Different Story*. Online document: www.columbia.edu/-gs228/writing/histps.htm.

Stauth, Georg (2006) "'Abdallah b. Salam: Egypt, Late Antiquity and Islamic Sainthood". In: Georg Stauth/Armando Salvatore (eds.) *Islam in Process. Historical and Civilizational Prespectives* (Yearbook of Sociology of Islam 7), Bielefeld: transcript.

'Uthman, Su'ad (1981) *Al-Nazaria El-Wazifia fi El-Torath El-Shabi: Dirasa Maydoniya Li-Takrim El-Awalyaa Fi El-Mogtamaa El-Marsi* (M.A. thesis), 'Ayn Shams University.

'Uthman, Su'ad (1982) "Child Saint" [Al-Tifl Al-Wali]. In: M. al-Gawhary (ed.) *Egyptian Yearbook of Sociology*, Cairo: Dar al-Ma'arif.

'Uways, Sayyid (1965) *Zahirat irsal ar-rasa'il ila darih al-imam al-Shafi'i*, Cairo: Center for Social and Criminological Research.

Zayed, Ahmed (2006) *Tanaqudat El-Hadatha Fi Misr*, Cairo : Maktabat al-Usra.

Chapter 6

Islam on both Sides: Religion and Locality in Western Burkina Faso

Katja Werthmann

Introduction

Although the history of Islam in West Africa has been studied by historians for a long time, anthropologists have tended to focus on the non-Islamic, 'traditional' elements of West African cultures (Launay 2006; Şaul 2006). A closer look at these cultures, however, reveals that Islamic elements seem to have been incorporated ever since Islam made its first inroads into the West African Sahel and Savannah zones more than thousand years ago. Instead of maintaining a dichotomy between Islam and non-Islam, Mahir Şaul (2006: 8) suggests regarding Islam as a "major ingredient of West Africa's historical heritage" that has created a shared 'canvas of meanings' through exchanges between West Africa, the Mediterranean, Europe, and the Middle East. Islam has had a profound influence on West African cultures, even where conversion did not take place.

Before the 19th century, Muslims rarely were politically dominant. A political division of labor between rulers and warriors, shrine priests, and Muslim advisors and mediators was a common feature throughout West Africa. Through their command of literacy, Muslims acted as secretaries, diplomats, and counselors at the courts of rulers. Conversion to Islam was not a one-way street; depending on the historical and local circumstances Muslim groups became non-Muslims and then Muslims again over the centuries, with some Islamic elements retained in local religious practice. Populations who never adopted Islam as a whole incorporated Islamic elements into local religion (Şaul 1997). On the other side, Muslims in some regions practiced masking traditions on the occasion of Islamic holidays. "People keep debating the Islamic or non-Islamic origin of certain practices, in which their own collective identities now hang. From a historical perspective, both sides of the divide are saturated with Islamic elements" (Şaul 2006: 23).

This paper is about two cases of 'Islam on both sides' in present-day Burkina Faso.[1] It compares the sacrificial site of Dafra and the Muslim village of Darsalamy, both in the vicinity of Bobo-Dioulasso. Bobo-Dioulasso is Burkina Faso's second-largest city, its population of an estimated half million is predominantly Muslim, and the *lingua franca* is Jula.[2] In terms of cultural history, Bobo-Dioulasso has much more in common with the Mande-speaking areas of the neighboring countries Mali, Côte d'Ivoire, and Guinea than with the Moose (Mossi) areas which make up much of present-day Burkina Faso.

Dafra and Darsalamy are closely connected with the history of Bobo-Dioulasso and the history of Islamization of this region. At an initial glance, these two places seem to epitomize the difference between non-Islam and Islam. Dafra is seen by many Muslims as a quintessentially pagan place, but stories of the origin of Dafra told by Muslims and non-Muslims alike say that a Muslim saint discovered it. Darsalamy, on the other hand, was intentionally founded by Muslims in order to create a place where pagan practices are forbidden. The comparison of these two localities shows that they do not correspond to a clear dichotomy between Islam and 'paganism', but instead represent two points on a continuum of more or less Islam in Burkina Faso.

The Spread of Islam in Burkina Faso

In contrast with the neighboring polities of ancient Ghana, Mali and Songhai to the West, and the Sokoto caliphate to the east, the Islamization of what is today Burkina Faso began relatively late. Before the 19th century, and in some parts until well into the 20th century, many areas were predominantly inhabited by populations who were religiously non-Muslim, economically farmers and herders, and politically organized in largely autonomous units of localized kin groups, even if nominally part of overarching political hierarchies. Muslim traders probably came to the Volta region from at least the 16th century, but Muslims did not attain positions of political superiority. Although some rulers converted to Islam, and Muslims held important positions at rulers' courts (Kouanda 1989), the Moose (Mossi) polities were credited as be-

---

1   Fieldwork was carried out in 2006 and 2007 in the framework of the multidisciplinary research program SFB 295 'Cultural and linguistic contacts' at the University of Mainz, funded by the Deutsche Forschungsgemeinschaft (DFG). I thank Lamine Sanogo (CNRST) for taking me to Bobo-Dioulasso in March 2006, Lassina Sanon for introducing me to some of the old-established Muslim families, Alimatou Konaté for her cooperation and friendship, Bruno Doti Sanou (CAD) and Mahir Şaul for their comments on an earlier version, and all those who kindly agreed to be interviewed. This paper presents work in progress and may contain shortcomings yet to be corrected by further research.
2   The Jula spoken in Bobo-Dioulasso is very close to the standard Bambara/ Bamanankan of Mali.

ing 'bulwarks' against Islam until the beginning of French colonial rule (Clark 1982: 59; Levtzion 1968: 163-172). Only a small portion of what is today the northernmost part of Burkina Faso mainly inhabited by Tuareg and Fulbe populations fell under the influence of the *jihad* movements of the 19th century, and the Fulbe polity of Liptako became an emirate of the Sokoto caliphate (Kouanda 1995: 236; Pelzer et al. 2004: 265-269).The *jihad* movements also had repercussions on the upper Mouhoun where Mahmoud and Moktar Karantao tried to establish a Muslim polity around Ouahabou in the mid-19th century. In contrast with the neighboring West African regions, Sufi orders such as the Tijaniyya or the Qadiriyya were almost absent in Burkina Faso until the colonial period (Otayek 1988: 107).

Around 1960, the percentage of Muslims in what was then Upper Volta was estimated as 20-25 percent (Clark 1982: 214). During the 1980s, this figure rose to 40 percent, and currently there are around 50-60 percent Muslims[3]. Since the colonial period, Muslims founded several associations such as the *Communauté des Musulmans au Burkina Faso* (CMBF), *Mouvement Sunnite du Burkina Faso* (MSBF), *Association Islamique de la Tijaniyya de Burkina Faso* (AITBF), *Association des Elèves et Etudiants Musulmans du Burkina Faso* (AEEMBF), *Centre d'Études, de Recherches et de Formation Islamiques* (CERFI). Most of these associations have recently been united under the umbrella of the *Fédération des Associations Islamiques du Burkina* (FIAB) which was created in 2005.[4] Rivalries exist both between these associations and among members of one and the same association (Kouanda 1998).

Burkina Faso is a laic state. "There is no official state religion, and the Government neither subsidizes nor favors any particular religion. The practice of a particular faith is not known to confer any advantage or disadvantage in the political arena, the civil service, the military, or the private sector" (International Religious Freedom Report 2005 Bureau of Democracy, Human Rights, and Labor, US Department of State).[5] Both Muslim and Christian feasts such as Eid al-Adha or Easter Monday are national holidays. Although individual politicians may support or sympathize with specific religious institutions or associations, or the other way around, the state by and large does not interfere in religious affairs. To date, religion has rarely been a cause of conflicts. When conflicts occur, it is within religious communities, such as for instances the clashes between Wahhabites and other Muslims in the 1970s,

---

3 https://www.cia.gov/library/publications/the-world-factbook/geos/uv.html (last download August 8, 2007).
4 http://www.hebdo.bf/actualite2/hebdo349-350/societe_federation349.htm (last download June 4, 2007).
5 http://www.state.gov/g/drl/rls/irf/2005/51451.htm (last download August 8, 2007).

rather than between Christians and Muslims (cf. Fourchard 2002: 243). The cohabitation between Muslims, Christians, and adherents of local religions has been mostly peaceful, partly because many families in Burkina Faso are multi-religious. Conversions occur rather pragmatically, and individuals can convert more than once from one religion to the other (Langewiesche 2003, 2005).[6]

Scholars, Traders, and Warriors

As in other West African regions, the spread of Islam in the Volta area was a concomitant of long-distance trade. Mande-speaking Muslim traders and craftsmen who came to be known as Jula[7] slowly made their way from further west. Some of these Muslims settled down in agrarian, segmentary communities and adopted local religions over the course of several generations (Levtzion 1968: 143; Wilks 2000: 101). Others settled in separate villages or town wards where they built mosques and founded Qur'anic schools for their own and other people's children.

Since Muslims in the Volta region lived in *dar al-harb* (land of the unbelievers), they needed legitimization for trading with unbelievers—an activity viewed with disdain by some North African Muslim jurists (Wilks 2000: 95). This legitimization was provided by Al-Hajj Salim Suwari, a 15th or 16th century scholar from the Sahelian town of Ja (Dia) who established "a pedagogical tradition that survives to this day despite the pressures of modernism" (Wilks 2000: 97; see also Wilks 1968: 177-180; Wilks 1989: 98-100). According to Suwari's teachings, the Jula developed a 'praxis of coexistence' (Wilks 2000: 98) with unbelievers which was rooted in the conviction that conversion to Islam could not be enforced, and that submission to non-Muslim rulers was acceptable as long as Muslims could keep their faith.

The Jula, notably those groups carrying the patronymic Saganogo,[8] were instrumental in the spread of Islam in the area between the Middle Niger and

---

6 For Islam in Burkina Faso since the colonial period, see also Cissé (1998); Deniel (1970); Koné-Dao (2005); Otayek (1988, 1993); Skinner (1966); Traoré (2005).
7 Alternatively Dyula, Dioula, Juula.
8 Other pronunciations and spellings: Sanogo, Saghanogho, Saghanughu. For the history of this patronymic, see Rey (1998). In conversations and in the literature, patronymic groups are frequently represented as one family or kin group, but individuals and groups adopted Jula patronymics at different times and for a variety of reasons which were not always connected with conversion to Islam, e.g. to facilitate marriage and war alliances; to show allegiance to a local ruler; to adopt one's master's name when being a slave; to become traders and thus Muslims; as a 'nom de guerre'; under colonial pressure; or simply as a nickname after having traveled to the Mande-speaking regions.

the forests of the Guinea Coast (Wilks 2000: 101).[9] The history of Islam in Bobo-Dioulasso is closely related with the history of Kong (Kpɔn), a major center for trade and Islamic learning in present-day Côte d'Ivoire, c. 250 km south of Bobo-Dioulasso. Those Saganogo who eventually settled in Bobo-Dioulasso were descendants of Muhammad al-Mustafa Saganogo, an important scholar who had twelve sons. Two of them, Ibrahim and Seydou, moved to Bobo-Dioulasso in 1177/1764 (alternatively 1168/1754 or 1188/1774[10]) at the request of warriors carrying the patronymic Watara[11] who needed the social and spiritual services of the Saganogo scholars. These consisted not only in providing religious advice, but in settling conflicts and mediating between different interest groups. Until today, the Saganogo act as 'maîtres de pardon' for the Watara (Quimby 1972: 53).

Bobo-Dioulasso, or Sya in pre-colonial times, was a trading center along the axis that linked Djenné in present-day Mali to Beghu in present-day Ghana, with connections to other trading centers such as Bondoukou, Bouna, Kong, and Salaga, in present-day Côte d'Ivoire and Ghana (Fourchard 2002: 31). The town of Sya emerged from several settlements of Bobo-speaking groups along the banks of the streams We (Houet) and Sanyon. Sya's inhabitants are the result of the merging of different groups, among them those known as Bobo-Jula or Zara.[12]

The Muslim scholars Seydou and Ibrahim Saganogo accompanied a group of Watara warriors from Kong.[13] The Saganogo settled in the quarter of Farakan where they built a mosque whose first Imam was Seydou. Another mosque was built later in the quarter of Kombougou where the Watara resided. As in other West African towns, there was a division of labor between the warriors who protected the trade routes and captured people as slaves, and the Muslim specialists who provided the warriors and traders with spiritual protection (Fourchard 2002: 34-35; cf. Green 1986; Launay 1982). Until the end of the 19th century, Islam in Sya was restricted to the families of the Saganogo *karamɔgɔw* ('the people who teach', from ar. *qara'a* 'read'), other groups of foreign traders such as the Dafing, and some converts among the

---

9 In contrast with Muslims east of the Mouhoun (Black Volta) who became politically and culturally integrated into the existing polities such as Dagomba, Gonja, or Wala, the Jula Muslims west of the Mouhoun retained their linguistic and cultural identity (Levtzion 1968: xxv).
10 Traoré (1996: 245); Wilks (1968: 175) and field research in Bobo-Dioulasso 2006/07.
11 On the history of the Watara and the Watara 'war houses', see Şaul (1998, 2003).
12 As elsewhere in Africa, collective identities in pre-colonial times did not necessarily correspond with what came to be referred as 'ethnic' today (Lentz 1995).
13 Jula scholars stood in defined relationships with, or 'belonged' to, their respective Watara allies (Quimby 1972: 42).

Watara and local families. It was only during colonial rule that Islam became the religion of the majority of the inhabitants of Sya (Fourchard 2002: 219). In 1904 Sya was officially renamed Bobo-Dioulasso.

Alliances and Rivalry:
Relationships between the Sanou, Watara and Saganogo

A tourist in Bobo-Dioulasso will inevitably visit the 'quartier touristique Kibidoué'.[14] It is one of the oldest parts of Bobo-Dioulasso and characterized by compounds built of mud connected by a multitude of small passageways. In this part of town, the visitor is led to two houses said to be the 'first houses' of the respective communities. In front of one of the first houses is a board that says 'Sya-kourou. La maison et l'autel du premier ancêtre Bobo-Madarê'. In the courtyard, there is a huge shrine in the form of an ovoid mound of earth. The other first house has a board saying: 'Konsasso. La maison du premier ancêtre Bobo du Sya'.[15] The existence of these two 'first houses' reflects the complex processes of population movements, the emergence of 'ethnic' identities, and claims to firstcomership in western Burkina Faso. 'Bobo-Madare' is an umbrella term for groups known as Bobo or Bobo-Fing in the literature.[16] Guy Le Moal (1999) thinks that the groups known as Bobo today emerged from clans of sedentary farmers with various origins. The other group called Bobo is better known as Bobo-Jula or Zara. According to Le Moal (1999: 17-18), the Zara ancestors came from the Mande-speaking areas between the end of the 16th and beginning of the 18th century and specialized in trade and warfare.[17] They were later called Bobo-Jula by the Watara of Kong. The Zara, or at least some Zara families, first allied with the Watara, but later became their rivals for trade routes and political authority.

---

14 Bobo Dioulasso, Plan Touristique, IGB Ouagadougou 1990.
15 In fact, every ancient quarter has its 'first house', i.e. the house of the founding family which contains important cult objects and is the venue for specific celebrations.
16 For a discussion of 'Bobo' as an ethnonym, see Le Moal (1960).
17 For a reconstruction of the history of the Zara, see Le Moal (1999: 17-25). Sanou (2005: 51) situates the immigration of the Zara between the 11th and the 16th century. Traoré (1993: 10) differentiates between 1) 'Zara de souche', the ancestors from Mande, 2) Zara who married Bobo women, and 3) Bobo who converted to Islam and thus became Zara. Zara is used as a self-reference of the groups more widely known as Bobo-Jula, but the name Zara may not be known by other inhabitants of Bobo-Dioulasso, even if born and bred there. Today, the Zara families of Bobo-Dioulasso carry the patronymic Sanou/Sanon. Relations between the Watara and the Sanou predated the arrival of Watara in Bobo-Dioulasso (Kodjo 2006; Le Moal 1999: 21, n. 58; Rey 1998: 143; Şaul 1998: 548).

A legend repeatedly cited in the literature[18] and told in Bobo-Dioulasso has it that the ancestor of the Bobo-Jula/Zara was a Muslim who settled in Bobo-Dioulasso among the local non-Muslims. When he made the pilgrimage to Mecca, he entrusted his children to his Bobo hosts. During his long absence, the children gave up Islam and practiced the religious cults of their hosts. Underneath a small shrine in the first house of the Bobo-Jula/Zara there are said to be buried a Qur'an, a staff, or a prayer mat of this ancestor.[19] The majority of the Bobo-Jula/Zara remained non-Muslims until well into the colonial period.

There was, however, one Bobo-Jula/Zara who became an important figure in the history of Islam in Bobo-Dioulasso: Sakidi Sanou. According to what seems to be a fairly standardized version of his biography,[20] he was the son of a wood carver named Kiétré Traoré. Kiétré was a pagan but became friends with a Saganogo scholar named Seydou Babema. Babema was a grandson of Seydou, one of the two Saganogo brothers who first came to Bobo-Dioulasso. Kiétré converted to Islam and took the name Mahama. When Kiétré's wife died in childbirth,[21] he gave the child to Seydou Babema who entrusted it to his wife Makossara.[22] The child, Sakidi, was raised by Seydou Babema and Makossara and later became a pupil in Seydou's Qur'anic school. When he was old enough to be inititated into the Bobo mask cult, his non-Muslim relatives claimed him back, but Seydou refused. He arranged for Sakidi to be sent to a renowned Muslim scholar in Dia, Abubakar Karabinta. Sakidi's return to Bobo-Dioulasso coincided with mounting tensions between the Watara and

---

18 Rey (1998: 143); Traoré (1984: 20-21); Traoré (1993: 14); Traoré (1996: 199); Wilks (1968: 193).
19 Cf. Person (1968: 145) who found similar stories: "On nous raconte souvent dans la zone préforestière comment les descendants d'un Ladyi célèbre ont transformé le Coran que leur ancêtre, acheté à la Mecque, en 'fétiche' sur lequel ils sacrifiaient très régulièrement." See also Levtzion (1968: 144). Rey (1998) sees this legend as a condensed version of what also happened in other West African regions during a time when Islam was not yet permanently rooted. According to Rey, the reversion to local religion was a result of Suwari's and other scholars' exit of Dia after Askia Muhammad came to power in Songhai. Their retreat led to a general decline of Islam in Dia and in other Muslim centers.
20 Interview with Imam Siaka Sanou and others, 28.10.2006; Interview with Imam Mohammed Kassamba-Diaby, 4.11.2006; Interview with Ali 'Mossi' Moulaye, 14.11.2006; Interview with Mohammed Sabti Saganogo; 15.11.2006; Interview with Fajabi Saganogo, 23.3.2007; see also Person (1975: 1903, n. 53); Traoré (1984: 72-75), Traoré (1993), Traoré (1996: 640).
21 According to one document in the possession of Mohammed Sabti Saganogo and written by Elhaj Muhammad Fodé Mory Saganogo aka Marhaba, Sakidi was born in 1245/1829. Traoré (1993) gives 1840 as Sakidi's year of birth, Doti-Sanou and Sanou (1994: 126) between 1820 and 1830.
22 The fact that Babema's real name was also Seydou is probably the reason why these two persons are frequently confused in stories about Sakidi.

the Zara. Sakidi wanted to construct a Friday mosque but was not given permission. It was only after he and other Muslims had helped the Zara and Watara warriors against their enemy Tieba of Sikasso that he was given a piece of land for the mosque which was built in 1292/1875[23] in what is now the quarter of Dioulassoba.[24] The relationship between Sakidi and the warlord Samori Touré is said to have spared the town from being sacked in 1897. Sakidi also tried to act as mediator between the people of Bobo-Dioulasso and the French troups in the same year, but was killed in the course of the attack on the town. He was buried in his mosque, and is today venerated as a saint.

Sakidi is an important figure for the history of Islam in Bobo-Dioulasso because he personifies the historical alliance between the Watara and Saganogo on the one hand and their Zara hosts on the other. Sakidi also stands for the transfer of religious authority from the Saganogo to the Zara. Although he never became Imam himself, the building of the Friday mosque epitomizes a shift in the pattern of religious leadership, because the Imamate eventually came into the hands of the Zara.[25] To the present day, the Imam of the mosque of Dioulassoba is considered as 'grand Imam', although other Friday mosques have been built since then.

Darsalamy: A Saintly Place

Darsalamy is a settlement 15 km south of Bobo-Dioulasso that was founded around the mid-19th century by Muslim Jula scholars from Bobo-Dioulasso.[26] One particular incident is cited as the reason for their emigration: a pupil of one Saganogo scholar was flogged by a Bobo mask and thereby lost an eye.[27] This incident epitomized the mounting tensions between the Saganogo scholars and their Watara allies and Zara hosts, who—even if nominally Muslims—would not give up certain habits and customs such as drinking sorghum

---

23 Interview with Mohammed Sabti Saganogo 11.11.2006; according to others either in 1880 or after the war against Tieba of Sikasso which was in 1893.
24 Dioulassoba/Sya comprises the ancient quarters or villages of Kibidoué and Tiguihɔn (Sanou 2005: 61).
25 Since there was no 'central mosque' before that built by Sakidi, it seems unlikely that the Zara were Imams before that time, as claimed by Griffeth (1971: 173).
26 Exact dates are notoriously hard to come by in African history, even where written sources exist. According to Mohammed Sabti Saganogo, who relies on documents by Al-Hajj Marhaba Saganogo, Darsalamy was founded in 1266/1849; according to Balaji Saganogo from Loto 40 years before the arrival of Samori, which would be 1857; according to Traoré (1996: 785) and to Griffeth (1971: 174) in the middle or the latter half of the 19th century respectively.
27 Traoré (1984: 79-80); Traoré (1996: 639), interview with Baflémory Saganogo, Darsalamy, 31.1.2007; interview with Balaji Usman Saganogo, Loto, 16.3.2007.

beer, masking traditions, or the dances of *kurubi* and *jɔmɛnɛ*[28]. *Kurubi* is danced by Jula girls and young women in the 14th and 27th night (*laylat al-qadr*) of Ramadan. *Jɔmɛnɛ* is danced by Bobo-Jula/Zara girls and women on the day of the Muslim New Year (Ashura, 10th day of Muharram). These dancers were practically naked in pre-colonial times, and they still appear naked to present-day Muslims who do not consider a bra as a top and a cloth and some strings of pearls tied around the waist as decent clothing.

Darsalamy is one of the few settlements in Burkina Faso that were intentionally created or renamed in order to stress Muslim identity and piety. Other examples are Ouahabou near Boromo which was conquered and renamed by the Karantao during their attempt to wage *jihad* against the local populations in the mid-19th century (Kouanda 2000), and Ramatoulaye near Ouahigouya which was founded by one important figure of the Hamalliya/Hamawiyya in the early 20th century (Dassetto/Laurent 2006). The Muslims from Bobo-Dioulasso who went to settle in Darsalamy wanted to have a saintly, or 'pure', place (*yɔrɔ sanyiani*; 'ville saine et sainte', Kouanda 2000: 259), away from non-Muslim customs. "Darsalami became a place of refuge for learned Muslims, a center where judicial appeals were argued before clerical courts, and a school center" (Griffeth 1971: 174).

Today, Darsalamy is one of the few places in Burkina Faso where there are tombs of Muslim saints. Among them are the tombs of the founders, but also tombs of ordinary persons who were not considered as someone special during their life-time. Tombs are not normally marked. Old graves may only be discovered when holes are dug for new ones by accident. In Darsalamy, a horse stepped on an old grave several years ago. The ground caved in, and people discovered that the corpse of a woman who was buried there, and whose name was not even remembered, had not decayed. As in other parts of the Muslim world, this is considered as a sign of saintliness and, since then, the grave has been surrounded by an enclosure, pilgrims come to visit, and prominent Muslims, such as the late patriarch of the Saganogo in Bobo-Dioulasso, Al-Hajj Abdulkadir Asséou (died 10.1.2007), ask that their families be buried next to it. However, there is no unanimous opinion concerning these practices. Some scholars explicitly asked that their graves not be marked to prevent the emergence of a cult.

There are several versions of the foundation of Darsalamy, but those I have heard so far agree that the founder was Bassaraba Saganogo, a grand-son of one of the two Saganogo brothers, who came to Bobo-Dioulasso from Kong. Other Muslim families such as the Barro, Coulibaly, Diané, Diarra, Fo-

---

28 Other spellings: Djombele, Jombele, Zɔmɛlɛ. For the *kurubi*, see Bauer (2005: 345-377); Quimby (1972: 75, 1979); Traoré (1996: 706). "Le *Jõmènè* est chez les Bobo-jula ce qu'est le *Kurubi* chez les Mandé-jula" (Traoré 1996: 703; see also Sanou 1993).

fana, Kassamba-Diaby, Sesuma, Sissé, Touré, and Traoré joined them. Since the Barro do not specialize in Islamic scholarship, the Saganogo offered them the village headmanship (*dugutigiya*).[29]

The foundation of Darsalamy must be set in the historical context of the *jihads* that marked West Africa during the 18th and 19th century. The tolerance for pagan practices and non-Muslim rulers which for centuries had characterized the Jula scholars' attitude vis-à-vis unbelievers came under strain in the second half of the 19th century. In particular the new doctrines by the West African *jihad* leader Al-Hajj Umar Tall, according to which paganism had to be fought, not tolerated, created a dilemma for the Saganogo scholars whose philosophy rejected conversion by force (Traoré 1996: 690-691, 785). In contrast with the previous 'revolutionary' *jihads* which had primarily aimed at reforming Islam within the societies of the respective *jihad* leaders, Umar Tall's was an 'imperial' *jihad* aimed at imposing Islam on the lands east of the Fulbe *Dar al-Islam*, but also included attacks on Muslim polities such as Masina (Robinson 1985: 3-4, 323).[30] Umar Tall also was a major figure of the West African Tijaniyya whereas most of the Saganogo scholars belonged to the Qadiriyya. This situation probably led to diverging opinions among the Jula Muslims in Bobo-Dioulasso about how to position themselves. In any case, even before the creation of Darsalamy, there had been differences between the descendants of Ibrahim and Seydou which led to the relocation of Seydou's descendants from Farakan to Kombougou.

During the same period, there was a mounting rivalry between the Saganogo, the Watara, and the Zara about commercial and political interests. According to Traoré (1996: 784), the Zara who started resenting the Watara dominance suspected the Saganogo of 'connivance' with the Watara. In fact, spiritual and other support was exactly what the Watara had always expected of the Saganogo. The Zara's claim for political leadership meant that the Muslims could come under non-Muslim rule. Although this had not been a problem for the Jula in previous centuries, it became unacceptable in the historical context of the *jihad* period. Eventually, the circumstances made it difficult for the Saganogo to cohabit with their non-Muslim hosts. Rather than engaging in combat against paganism, a part of the Saganogo left Bobo-

---

29 Interviews with Ali and Bakoba Diané (Darsalamy), Bafaga Diané (Kotédougou), Baflémory Saganogo (Darsalamy), Balaji Saganogo (Loto), and Mohammed Sabti Saganogo (Bobo-Dioulasso) in 2007.
30 Umar's most spectacular achievement was the conquest of Segu in 1861. After the conquest, he sent a message to Kong demanding its rulers to submit. A delegation from Kong went to Umar and asked him to spare the city. To the relief of the people of Kong, Umar died shortly thereafter in battle (Binger 1892: 341; Robinson 1985: 300). According to a popular account, Umar Tall stayed with Ibrahim Saganogo in Bobo-Dioulasso for some time on his way to Mecca between 1810 and 1820, but Robinson (1985: 96) considers this as a legend.

Dioulasso and founded the village of Darsalamy. The name Darsalamy, 'land of peace', is significant in itself, because, in contrast to the old-established pattern of Jula scholars following the Watara warriors to new settlements, no Watara preceded or accompanied them this time.

The episode cited as the reason for leaving Bobo-Dioulasso—the Qur'anic student who was injured by a Bobo mask, see above—was probably only the last, or the most memorable, in a serious of similar events that preceded the move-out. This episode points to two different, but related aspects concerning the relationship between Muslims and non-Muslims. On the one hand, Muslim scholars felt offended by the disrespect of their non-Muslim neighbors. On the other hand, they were also afraid that their children—many of whom obviously had the habit of watching the mask dances—might become non-Muslims (as had the children of the Zara ancestor). A third reason for the relocation to Darsalamy was brought up by a present-day Saganogo scholar:[31] some of the Saganogo, especially those considered as great *marabouts*, needed a more quiet place for practicing *khalwa* (spiritual retreat), away from the crowds and noises of town life, and from their religious and social obligations to attend name-giving-ceremonies, funerals, and the like. The relocation to Darsalamy thus led to a concentration of *marabouts* in a small place.

The combined spiritual powers of these Muslim scholars are reputed to have influenced some decisive historical moments. When the inhabitants of Bobo-Dioulasso were at war with Tieba of Sikasso (in present-day Mali) at the end of the 19th century, it was with the help of the Saganogo *marabouts* that an albino or a female *jinn* was transformed into Tieba's favorite wife and managed to poison him with food. In the colonial period, when the Watara were *chefs de canton*, one Watara was refused a woman of the Saganogo in Darsalamy on the grounds that she was already married.[32] As a revenge, he managed to have forced labor imposed on the Muslim scholars and made them build a road. This was highly offensive for the scholars because in Jula society manual labor was normally done by slaves or social minors. The Saganogo scholars united their spiritual forces and made the French remove the power of the hands of the Watara and give it to the Zara of Bobo-Dioulasso. Stories like these stress the political agency of the Saganogo although they never were officially political leaders. They also illustrate once more the shifting loyalties between Watara, Zara, and Saganogo that until today have repercussions in local politics.

Khalwa is also one of the means to obtain solutions for the problems of people who consult the scholars. Until today, Darsalamy is more a village than a town, but it is a place with a veritable 'prayer economy' (Soares 2005).

---

31 Interview with Mohammed Sabti Saganogo, 29.8.2007.
32 This represented not only an inappropriate request but an outright affront. Traditionally the Watara gave wives to the Saganogo and never the other way around.

Until recently, the main source of revenues seems to have been spiritual services by a number of *marabouts* who were visited by people from all over the region. Darsalamy has a train station which only a few years ago was closed after the privatization of the national railway company RAN. Whenever passengers got off the train, they were immediately surrounded by local guides who offered to take them to one of the local scholars who provide spiritual services. Obviously, religious and commercial interests have merged in the creation of Darsalamy.

The emigration to Darsalamy was not an exodus. From the existing literature, one may get the impression that all the Saganogo from Bobo-Dioulasso left for Darsalamy. In fact, it was only one branch that left and was later joined by others, many of whom came directly from Kong after the (in)famous warlord Samori Touré had destroyed the town in 1897. The move-out of a part of the Saganogo does not necessarily reflect a complete breach with the Watara and the Zara. There were and are close relations and a constant stream of visits between Bobo-Dioulasso and Darsalamy, especially on the occasion of Islamic holidays. The relocation of Bassaraba and his followers instead reflected internal divisions which may have been articulated, among others, in terms of religious differences. According to one interview partner, it was primarily the Saganogo who were allied with one particular Watara family or 'house'[33] who would not agree to tolerate pagan customs any longer. Those Saganogo who stayed in Bobo-Dioulasso kept acting as advisors and mediators for the Watara. Until today, the Imam of the Watara mosque in Kombougou is a Saganogo, and the relations between the Saganogo in Darsalamy and Bobo-Dioulasso are very close.

Dafra: A Sacred Place

Visitors to Bobo-Dioulasso are told to be aware of approaching the banks of the streams Houet and Sanyon which are inhabited by sacred silurids (catfish, j. *manɔgɔ*). These catfish are considered as tutelary spirits of Bobo-Dioulasso and figure in the city's coat of arms. Should anybody intentionally or by accident kill one of the fishes, he or she will be flogged and must pay a fine to the elders of the respective quarter through which the Houet flows.[34] They will

---

33 The Watara are subdivided into lineages or houses such as the Janguinajon, Sissira, Numabolo, Kinibolo, and Bambajon (Quimby 1972: 15; cf. Şaul 1998: 563). According to Traoré (1996: 294), these groupings corresponded in fact with military divisions or *garnisons*, comparable to the Zara houses of Forobakonso, Sangouélélouma, and Dagasso.

34 This and the fact that there are some masks which are thought to flog innocent passers-by are one of the reasons why many inhabitants of Bobo-Dioulasso who are not Bobo or Bobo-Jula never venture into the old quarters. Only tourists do that.

make a sacrifice in order to appease the powers embodied in those fishes, and the dead fish is going to be buried like a person.[35] The source of the Houet is at Dafra, a gorge some eight km southeast of Bobo-Dioulasso. Dafra is a sacrificial site that is visited by people from all over Burkina Faso and the neighboring countries. It has the reputation of being a powerful place where wishes made and confirmed by vows will be fulfilled.[36]

A pilgrim to Dafra is led on a footpath down a slope into the gorge. At bottom level, the source of the Houet forms a kind of basin. The pilgrims, each of whom has brought a chicken, are led to a shrine, a large boulder on one side of the banks of the basin covered with feathers, blood, and millet beer. The chicken is killed and some blood and feathers sprinkled on the rock. If the pilgrims are Muslims, however, they will not go to the shrine but kill their chicken directly on the rocky ground beside the basin. Before killing the chicken, the visitors hold them for a moment and silently utter their respective wishes to them. After the chickens have been killed, they are plucked and grilled on the spot at several fireplaces. Then the visitors proceed to the edge of the basin, throw pieces of *dɛgɛ* (fermented balls of millet paste) and the intestines of the chicken into the water, and call the fishes: "Dafra na tɔ!"—"Dafra, come and take!". Dafra is the name of the *genius loci* and encompasses the place and the fishes. Soon there will be a number of fishes (some of which easily measure about one meter) who snap at the food.

Having finished feeding the fishes in the basin, the pilgrims follow a small footpath to the other side of some big rocks. There is another basin where they can feed the fishes, and those who wish may strip and take a bath (a 'guard' will be posted on the footpath above in order to prevent other people from coming around the bend that hides those who bathe from view). The water of Dafra is considered to be purifying and healing in a spiritual sense and can be taken home in plastic bottles.

When all of this is done, the pilgrims either eat the chicken directly, sharing out pieces to other visitors who came after them, or take them home. On Fridays, when most pilgrims arrive, the scene resembles a kind of picnic site with groups or families gathered around a meal, were it not for the cadavers of a dozen or more goats and rams cut into large pieces, lying on their skins on the ground next to the basin. The goats and rams are offerings of thanks

---

35 Normally the fish will be buried on the spot where it is found. The quarters or former villages which share the ritual responsibility for the Houet and the fishes are Bindougousso, Dioulassoba, Kuinima, and Tounouma. In 2007, more than 60 fishes died of poisoning after an industrial accident on the level of Kuinima. They were buried next to a shrine along the Houet (interviews with the village heads of Bindougousso, Dioulassoba, Kuinima, and Tounouma in August 2007).

36 One football team in Bobo-Dioulasso is named 'Les Silures' after the sacred fish. Before home matches, its members collectively visit Dafra and make offerings (Royer 2002: 475).

made to Dafra according to a vow made once the respective wish has been fulfilled. The entire ground is covered with feathers, and skins that were left behind hang in the branches of two or three trees on the side.

There is no way of establishing how long Dafra has been a sacrificial site or *lieu de pèlerinage* (Sanou 1996: 128)[37] for the local populations. Dafra has probably always been an important place in the spiritual landscape of those who inhabited the region, who, like other populations elsewhere, made a 'pact' with the spiritual beings of the localities where they settled.[38] Today, visitors come from all over Burkina Faso and the neighboring countries, even from as far as Europe and the US. There are Muslims, Christians, and adherents of local religions. Their social backgrounds vary widely: on several visits my interpreter Alimatou Konaté and I met people as diverse as a doctor, a sociologist, traders, farmers, students, etc. Some people clearly did not like having witnesses and refused to talk to us, but others were quite open. Most visitors said that people come to Dafra because of some personal problem such as illness, infertility, lack of money, failure in school or business, nightmares, etc. We did not ask for personal information other than that which was provided voluntarily, but obviously there were some people who had tried other means of solving a serious problem before coming to Dafra as a last resort. Otherwise it would not be conceivable, for instance, to leave a town in southern Côte d'Ivoire and undertake a journey of several days, including the crossing of the military buffer zone that has separated the North and the South since the beginning of the civil war in 2002, just to get directly to Dafra and then back again.

Dafra lies on the land of Kuinima which was a Bobo village in precolonial times and is a quarter of Bobo-Dioulasso today. According to the present-day *chef de village* de Kuinima, the inhabitants of Kuinima were firstcomers in the region and thus have a special relationship with the site of Dafra and with the silures, and likewise other ancient Bobo villages that border the rivers Houet and Sanyon.[39] Therefore members of these Bobo communities act as 'sacrifice attendants' for the visitors. Today, the pilgrimage to Dafra clearly has an economic dimension. For the people who act as sacrifice

---

37 Sanou (1996: 128) cites two main reasons for the Bobo for making a pilgrimage to Dafra: in order to conduct a sacrifice after having breached certain interdictions concerning Dafra or the river Houet, and in order to ask for a child in case of infertility.
38 In Timothy Insoll's book on archaeology, ritual, and religion (Insoll 2004), the description of a visit to Dafra serves as a prologue.
39 Interview with Sanou Famara, *chef de village*, and Sanou Mamadou, Kuinima, Bobo-Dioulasso, 21.3.2007; Sanou (1996: 96). This version is contested by the *chef de terre* of the Tiéfo village of Kwakwalé who claims that Dafra belongs to the land of Kwakwalé (interview with Mori Ouattara, 10.3.2008).

attendants or tourist guides, going to Dafra has become a way of making money, which in turn attracts other less desirable visitors such as thieves.

Certain interdictions have to be observed when visiting Dafra. One should not wear clothing in red; on the way to and from the site, one should not speak to other persons; one should not wear shoes when approaching the edge of the basin and the shrine; no blood should get into the water. Most people come accompanied by guides, either some of the attendants who wait for 'clients' in a compound along the dirt road leading to the site, or relatives, or friends who have been there before. On the spot, every pilgrim is instructed and accompanied by one of the attendants while making the offerings. The attendants then pluck and roast the chicken or slaughter the other animals, and receive meat, millet beer, or cash by way of payment.[40]

In former times, visits to Dafra were only permitted on Mondays and Fridays, but nowadays people come on every day of the week, many at weekends. The visits continue from early morning to early afternoon; around 4 p.m. the stream of visitors ceases and vultures start descending to pick up the left-overs. Due to the constant coming and going, we were not able to count people systematically, but just to give an impression: on February 9, 2007, a Friday, we conducted brief interviews with 78 people, some of whom arrived in small groups of three to six people (among them a group of tourists), some alone or with a guide. These 78 people were probably half of the total number of people who visited that day. Most of the visitors we spoke to came from Bobo-Dioulasso or some towns and villages in the region such as Pala, Bare, Numudara, or Banfora, but there were also people who came from Abengourou and Korhogo in Côte d'Ivoire. Other Ivorian cities mentioned on other days were Abidjan and Gagnoa. Among the visitors were Muslims, Christians, and 'animists'; the ethnic affiliations mentioned were Bobo, Bobo-Jula, Lobi, Mossi, Tiéfo, Samo, Senufo, and Turka.

When asked what they knew about Dafra, most people said that Dafra is a place where you can go with any kind of problem. People come to make offerings (*saraka*) there. They had heard about Dafra either because they were from Bobo-Dioulasso, or because some relative or friend had already been there and a wish had been fulfilled. Some said that Dafra is a pagan place (*sɔnni kɛ yɔrɔ lo*). Others, on the contrary, stressed that Dafra is not a pagan shrine (*jo yɔrɔ* or *josɔnyɔrɔ*), but a place for the worship of God (*Ala dari yɔrɔ*). In the same vein, some said that Dafra is not a god, but a gift of God, and that their ancestors already had the habit of going there. These answers

---

40 It is forbidden to charge fees for these activities, but some of the attendants do so. Apart from theft, there have also been cases of attacks on tourists (John Messer: Travel: holiday disasters, The Independent, London, May 23, 1999, http://findarticles.com/p/articles/mi_qn4158/is_19990523/ai_n14237317, download 1.6.2007).

mirror the differences between Muslims and Christians who tended to declare Dafra as a part of local 'tradition' or something that did not have anything to do with religion at all, and those who were either 'non-practicing' Muslims and Christians, or outright proud to be 'animists' or 'fetishists' in popular Burkinabè French parlance.

Whatever the case, the 'discovery' of Dafra is attributed to a Muslim saint (*wali*) or scholar (*karamɔgɔ*). This Muslim is credited to be the ancestor of the Kassamba-Diaby, one of the Muslim families in Bobo-Dioulasso. According to a legend that is not only told by the Kassamba-Diaby but also by non-Muslims,[41] their ancestor came to the area on his way from Samatiguila in present-day Côte d'Ivoire. According to different versions, the Kassamba-Diaby ancestor either found the source by praying and then looking around, or by following an animal, or he prayed for water and lightening struck the earth, opening up the source.[42] Therefore, to the present day, the Kassamba-Diaby have a special relation to the site, although they are not its 'owners'.

The Kassamba-Diaby are a group of Mande origin who came to the region of Bobo-Dioulasso in the 18th century.[43] They became assimilated to the Bobo-Jula by intermarriage and by adopting their hosts' language. In the late 19th century, however, there were misgivings between the Kassamba-Diaby and the Bobo-Jula because the latter did not give up their pagan practices. Therefore, a part of the Kassamba-Diaby followed the branch of the Saganogo family who left for Darsalamy (Traoré 1996: 798). However, close relationships have existed between the Kassamba-Diaby and the Bobo-Jula up to the present day, and they still act as *maîtres de pardon* for each other.[44]

Concerning Dafra, there is no unanimous opinion among family members. Some have never gone and would never go to Dafra; others accompany visitors quite regularly and make offerings. The present-day Imam Muhammad Kassamba-Diaby stopped visiting Dafra many years ago. Nevertheless, he talks openly about it. He explained, for instance, that if a person has to make an offering of thanks but cannot do so because he or she is abroad, it is possi-

---

41 Interviews and conversations with Bobo elders, sacrifice attendants, and visitors at Dafra on several visits in February 2007; Interview with Sanou Famara, *chef de village* de Kuinima, Bobo-Dioulasso, and Sanou Mamadou, 21.3.2007.
42 Traoré (1996: 332); Interview with Imam Muhammad Kassamba-Diaby, 4.11.2006; Interview with Souleymane 'Doudou', 3.3.2007. A similar story is told about the springs at Sindou (interview with Bafaga Diané, Kotédougou, 17.2.2007).
43 According to Traoré (1984: 22, see also Roth 1996: 45-46), they arrived before the Saganogo, but the current Kassamba-Diaby Imam says the Saganogo and other Muslims were already there when their ancestor arrived.
44 According to the historian Bruno Sanou (personal communication, 22.8.2007), discussions about the origin of Dafra only emerged during the past 30 years in the context of political disputes about historical origins of collective identities in Bobo-Dioulasso.

ble to send money to a member of the Kassamba-Diaby family and they will take care of it. He also said that not all wishes will be fulfilled. This does not mean, however, that God has not heard the wish. Instead it means that God knows about the counter-productive consequences a wish may have for a person. For example, a person makes a wish to be promoted at work; but if he or she will be promoted at the expense of a colleague, this colleague will be angry and try to do harm to the person. Other Muslims in Bobo-Dioulasso, such as, for instance, Gaoussou Sanou, a son of the late Imam Salia Sanou, would ridicule people who go to Dafra on the grounds that everything is made by God anyway: there is no use of killing chicken and feeding them to fishes if you can speak to God directly through prayer.

The sacrificial practices at Dafra appear archaic but, although blood sacrifices are made at various shrines throughout the region, the killing of chickens in Dafra appears to be a recent introduction. Formerly the non-Muslims only made their vows and then washed with Dafra water, and the Muslims prayed two *rakat* at the site.[45] Twenty five years ago Mahir Şaul was told by Bobo informants that a blood sacrifice in Dafra was an abomination. The proper sacrifice was fried cakes or balls made of millet (*ɲɔmi, dɛgɛ*).

The associations here are double and both interesting. First the centrality of millet, which is a kind of sacred crop among the Bobo and other savanna people (the pagan element if you wish). Second, it is vegetable food, which enters into the notion of *salaka/saraka* [from ar. *sadaka*]. Whenever village people say *salaka* they mean a non-blood offering.[46] It is an interesting case of continuity/reinterpretation. It goes with the prohibition of red, which is the color of very bloody shrines such as Komo/Kono[47] (Mahir Şaul, e-mail, 10.6.2007).

Obviously, not all Bobo people shared the notion that non-blood offerings are the only acceptable way to communicate with Dafra, but it is impossible to find out when, why, and by whom blood sacrifices were introduced in Dafra. However, it is conceivable that the ritual practices at Dafra changed several times ever since it first served as a sacrificial site. Since Dafra does not 'belong' to any one group, the Kassamba-Diaby Muslims could not prohibit blood sacrifices or the consumption of sorghum beer right next to the water. Likewise, it is difficult to set up rules or sanctions against those who violate the interdictions, because nobody can effectively control the site. The village heads who are responsible for sacrificial matters along the Houet say that Da-

---

45 Interview with Sanou Famara, *chef de village* de Kuinima, Bobo-Dioulasso, and Sanou Mamadou, 21.3.2007; interview with Fousséni Kassamba-Diaby, 1.9.2007.
46 Cf. Le Moal (1999: 80).
47 'Power associations' or 'initiation societies', sometimes transformed into witch-hunting cults in the Mande-speaking areas of West Africa.

fra will punish wrongdoers in its own time, which means that the person will drown, be killed by a wild animal (i.e. a bush spirit), or otherwise. It is probably the fear of this kind of punishment that keeps most visitors from breaking the rules of conduct at Dafra.

Even in the context of western Burkina Faso where earth shrines, ancestor shrines, and individual shrines are important for personal and collective well-being (regardless of the attachment to the universal religions), Dafra is an exceptional place. It does not 'belong' to any specific group or individual, although the Kassamba-Diaby and some Bobo and Tiéfo communities claim a special relation with it. Although frequently described as a pagan or 'traditional' place, Muslims do go there (according to some, even Wahhabites). Some Muslims who go there maintain a difference to the non-Muslims by not killing chickens at the shrine, and by not offering or drinking sorghum beer. Muslims who consider themselves as more orthodox and who would never go to Dafra argue that sacrificing chickens is a pagan practice and that if a Muslim does so, he is in fact a pagan.

As the example of the Kassamba-Diaby Imam has shown, an individual may find himself on both sides of this divide, and deal with the dilemma pragmatically by not going to Dafra himself, but not preventing other family members from going there. It is possible that other Muslim groups and families in Bobo-Dioulasso secretly doubt the orthodoxy of the Kassamba-Diaby Imam, but they do not do so openly. When the Kassamba-Diaby held a *tafsir* on 5 November 2006, during Ramadan, they routinely invited the 'grand Imam' and other Imams and Muslim notables. Whatever their personal views, the grand Imam and other Imams honored the *tafsir* with their presence, just as they would invite the Kassamba-Diaby in turn.

Conclusion

Darsalamy and Dafra are important localities in the spiritual landscape around Bobo-Dioulasso. Interestingly, places like these are terminologically differentiated both in French and in Jula. Whereas a Muslim place such as Darsalamy is called 'saintly' ('lieu saint' or 'lieu de prière'; *yɔrɔ sanyiani, Ala dari yɔrɔ*), places like Dafra are called 'sacred' ('lieu sacré': *joyɔrɔ* place of shrine, or *josɔnyɔrɔ* place of offering at a shrine).

The two places have some common features. Both are important places in present-day accounts of the history of Bobo-Dioulasso. For both places, Islam is a point of reference, though in different ways. Both are known beyond the region and are visited by people who look for help and spiritual support. In both places, the religious practice has a commercial dimension.

There are also some obvious differences between the two places. The creation of Darsalamy seems to have been modeled on the *hijra*.[48] The village was founded by Muslims for Muslims who wanted to set themselves apart from non-Muslim or only nominally Muslim people and practices such as masks, dances, shrines, and the consumption of alcohol. Dafra, on the other hand, is an inclusive place that does not 'belong' to any specific individual or group and is visited by all kinds of people, regardless of their professed faith.

Islam serves an important element in discourses about the constitution of collective identities. As elsewhere in West Africa, the reference to Muslim ancestors is thought to convey a somewhat superior status on a population. Historically, there were shifts between more and less Islam in the sub-region. This is mirrored in the present-day relations—and conflicts—between different groups of inhabitants of Bobo-Dioulasso. The Kassamba-Diaby—whose ancestor, a Muslim saint, is said to have 'discovered' Dafra—are labeled as 'guests' (i.e. socially juniors) of the Bobo-Jula/Zara in Bobo-Dioulasso who consider themselves as founders of Bobo-Dioulasso (a claim which is contested by the Bobo). The Zara themselves refer to a Muslim ancestor.

Today, both Islam and the sacred fish figure in the city's coat of arms: it shows four silurids forming a stylized S, the upper end surrounding a baobab, the lower end surrounding the old mosque. Thus, the coat of arms symbolizes the different religious traditions, and the co-existence of Muslims and non-Muslims in Bobo-Dioulasso.

The examples of Dafra and Darsalamy shows that there is no neat distinction between Islam and non-Islam in this part of West Africa. Although Dafra is clearly not an 'Islamic saintly place', Muslims do visit there and make offerings, and the story of its 'discovery' by a Muslim is acknowledged by Muslims and non-Muslims alike. On the other hand, even the *marabouts* of Darsalamy were not able to eradicate the custom of *kurubi* (dance by girls and young women during the 14th and 27th night of Ramadan)[49]. In fact, *kurubi* presently seems to be more important in Darsalamy than in Bobo-Dioulasso.

It would be too easy to dismiss the attitude of Muslims who go to Dafra as 'not really Islam' or to discredit them as pagans—as many people in Bobo-Dioulasso actually do. Debates about what constitutes 'true' or 'false' Islam are probably as old as the religion itself, but the contents of the actual disagreements vary according to the local and historical circumstances. It makes sense that disagreements in this case revolve around a sacrificial site, because sacrificial sites are an important feature of the spiritual topography of western Burkina Faso, much more than the tombs of Muslims saints, as discussed in

---

48 For a discussion of *hijra* as a form of liminal action with reference to a similar case of the spatial separation of 'true' and 'false' Muslims by the West African *jihad* leader Usman Dan Fodio in the 19th century, see Fisher (1986).
49 For modern-day debates about *kurubi*, see Quimby (1979).

other contributions to this volume. Other debated issues that seem to be typical for the region of Bobo-Dioulasso are the ongoing practices of masking traditions or the dances of *kurubi* and *jɔmɛnɛ*, all of which are condemned in the speeches of Muslim preachers but at the same time heralded as 'tradition', 'custom', and 'cultural heritage' during festivals such as the biannual *Semaine Nationale de Culture* or the *Festival de la Rue*. More generally, the coexistence of the diverging attitudes concerning religious practice itself points to the fact that there is no central religious authority on either side which could define general and binding norms. The ambiguity of certain practices—on the one hand deemed by many to be against religion and at the same time held to be important parts of cultural heritage and collective identity—appears to be a general pattern in regard to modernization and religious reform in much of the Muslim world.

References

Bauer, Kerstin (2005) *Kleidung und Kleidungspraktiken im Norden der Côte d'Ivoire*, Berlin: LIT.

Binger, Louis (1892) *Du Niger au Golfe de Guinée par le pays Kong et le Mossi* (2 vols.), Paris. [Reprint, Société des Africanistes, 1980].

Cissé, Issa (1998) "Les médersas au Burkina. L'aide arabe et l'enseignement arabo-islamique". In: Ousmane Kane/Jean-Louis Triaud (eds.) *Islam et islamismes au sud du Sahara*, Paris: Karthala, pp. 101-115.

Clark, Peter B. (1982) *West Africa and Islam. A Study of Religious Development from the 8th to the 20th Century*, London: Edward Arnold.

Dassetto, Felice/Laurent, Pierre-Joseph (2006) "Ramatoulaye. Brotherhood in Transition". *Isim Review* 18, pp. 26-27.

Deniel, Raymond (1970) *Croyances religieuses et vie quotidienne: Islam et christianisme à Ouagadougou*, Paris: C.N.R.S.

Fisher, Humphrey J. (1986) "Liminality, Hijra and the City". In: Nehemia Levtzion (ed.) *Rural and urban Islam in West Africa*, Boulder/London: Lynne Rienner, pp. 147-171.

Fourchard, Laurent (2002) *De la ville coloniale à la cour africaine : Espaces, pouvoirs et sociétés à Ouagadougou et Bobo-Dioulasso (Haute-Volta), fin 19ème siècle-1960*, Paris: L'Harmattan.

Green, Kathryn (1986) "Dyula and Sonongui Roles in the Islamization of the Region of Kong". *African and Asian Studies* (Haifa) 20, pp. 97-117.

Griffeth, Robert R. (1971) "The Dyula Impact on the Peoples of the West Volta Region". In: Carleton T. Hodge (ed.) *Papers on the Manding*, Bloomington/The Hague: Indiana University/Mouton & Co., pp. 167-181.

Insoll, Timothy (2004) *Archaeology, Ritual, Religion*. London & New York: Routledge.

Kodjo, Georges Niamkey (2006) *Le royaume de Kong (Côte d'Ivoire). Des origines à la fin du XIXème siècle*. Paris: L'Harmattan.

Koné-Dao, Maïmouna (2005) "Implantation et influence du wahhâbisme au Burkina Faso de 1963 à 2002". In: Muriel Gomez-Perez (ed.) *L'islam politique au sud du Sahara: Identités, discours et enjeux*, Paris: Karthala, pp. 449-459.

Kouanda, Assimi (1989) "La religion musulmane: facteur d'intégration ou d'identification ethnique". In: Jean-Pierre Chrétien/Gérard Prunier (eds.) *Les ethnies ont une histoire*, Paris: Karthala, pp. 125-134.

Kouanda, Assimi (1995) "La progression de l'islam au Burkina pendant la période coloniale". In: Gabriel Massa/Y. Georges Madiéga (eds.) *La Haute Volta coloniale. Témoignages, recherches, regards*, Paris: Karthala, pp. 233-248.

Kouanda, Assimi (1998) "Les conflits au sein de la Communauté musulmane du Burkina: 1962-1986". In: Ousmane Kane/Jean-Louis Triaud (eds.) *Islam et islamismes au sud du Sahara*, Paris: Karthala, pp. 83-100.

Kouanda, Assimi (2000) "La Hamawiyya et les changements toponymiques au Burkina". In: Jean-Louis Triaud/David Robinson (eds.) *La Tijâniyya. Une confrérie musulmane à la conquête de l'Afrique*, Paris: Karthala, pp. 249-267.

Langewiesche, Katrin (2003) *Mobilité religieuse. Changements religieux au Burkina Faso*, Münster: Lit Verlag.

Langewiesche, Katrin (2005) "Religiöse Mobilität. Konversionen und religiöser Wandel in Burkina Faso". *Paideuma* 51, pp. 67-88.

Launay, Robert (1982) *Traders without Trade: Responses to Change in two Dyula Communities*, Cambridge/New York: Cambridge University Press.

Launay, Robert (2006) "An Invisible Religion? Anthropology's Avoidance of Islam in Africa". In: Mwenda Ntarangwi/David Mills/Mustafa Babiker (eds.) *African Anthropologies. History, Critique and Practice*, Dakar/London/New York: CODESRIA/Zed Books, pp. 188-203.

Le Moal, Guy (1960) "Note sur les populations ‚Bobo'". *Etudes Voltaïques* 1, 5-17.

Le Moal, Guy (1999) *Les Bobo: nature et fonction des masques*, Tervuren, België: Koninklijk Museum voor Midden-Afrika.

Lentz, Carola (1995) "'Tribalismus' und Ethnizität in Afrika. Ein Forschungsüberblick". *Leviathan* 23, pp. 115-145.

Levtzion, Nehemia (1968) *Muslims and Chiefs in West Africa. A Study of Islam in the Middle Volta Basin in the Pre-Colonial Period*, Oxford: Clarendon.

Otayek, René (1988) "Muslim Charisma in Burkina Faso". In: Donal B. Cruise O'Brien (ed.) *Charisma and Brotherhood in African Islam*, Oxford: Clarendon, pp. 91-112.

Otayek, René (1993) "L'affirmation élitaire des arabisants au Burkina Faso. Enjeux et contradictions". In: René Otayek (ed.) *Le radicalisme islamique au sud du Sahara*, Paris: Karthala, pp. 229-252.

Pelzer, Christoph/Müller, Jonas/Albert, Klaus-Dieter (2004) "Die Nomadisierung des Sahel. Siedlungsgeschichte, Klima und Vegetation in der Sahelzone von Burkina Faso". In: Klaus-Dieter Albert/Doris Löhr/Katharina Neumann (eds.) *Mensch und Natur in Westafrika*, Weinheim: Wiley-VCH, pp. 256-288.

Person, Yves (1968) *Samori. Une révolution dyula* (Vol. I), Dakar: Ifan.

Person, Yves (1975) *Samori. Une révolution dyula* (Vol. III), Dakar: Ifan.

Quimby, Lucy Gardner (1972) *Transformations of belief: Islam among the Dyula of Kongbougou from 1880 to 1970* (unpublished dissertation), University of Wisconsin.

Quimby, Lucy (1979) "Islam, Sex Roles, and Modernization in Bobo-Dioulasso". In: Bennetta Jules-Rosette (ed.): *The New Religions of Africa*. Norwood: Ablex Publishing Corporation, pp. 203-218.

Rey, Pierre-Philippe (1998) "Les gens de l'or et leur idéologie. L'itinéraire d'Ibn Battuta en Afrique occidentale au XIVe siècle". In: Bernard Schlemmer (ed.) *Terrains et engagements de Claude Meillassoux*, Paris: Karthala, pp. 121-155.

Robinson, David (1985) *The Holy War of Umar Tal. The Western Sudan in the Mid-Nineteenth Century*, Oxford: Clarendon Press.

Roth, Claudia (1996) *La séparation des sexes chez les Zara au Burkina-Faso*, Paris: L'Harmattan.

Royer, Patrick (2002) "The Spirit of Competition: *Wak* in Burkina Faso". *Africa* 72/3, pp. 464-483.

Sanou, Alain (1993) *Les chanson du danse de Zɔmɛlɛ* (Cahiers du Centre de Recherche en Lettres Sciences Humaines et Sociales, 9), Université de Ouagadougou: F.L.A.S.H.S.

Sanou, Doti Bruno/Sanou, Sma (1994) *Odonymes et noms de places de Bobo-Dioulasso: La mémoire collective à Sia, source d'inspiration, à travers les rues et places, 1927-1993*, Bobo-Dioulasso: Centre africain de recherche pour une pratique culturelle du développement.

Sanou, Doti Bruno (1996) *Commune de Bobo-Dioulasso. Les racines du futur*, Bobo-Dioulasso: Édition CAD.

Sanou, Doti Bruno (2005) *Promotion culturelle à Bobo-Dioulasso. Proposition d'une méthode dans un contexte de décentralisation*, Ouagadougou: Éditions Découvertes du Burkina.

Şaul, Mahir (1997) "Islam et appropriation mimétique comme ressource historique de la religion bobo". *Journal des Africanistes* 67/2, pp. 7-24.

Şaul, Mahir (1998) "The War Houses of the Watara in West Africa". *The International Journal of African Historical Studies* 31/3, pp. 537-570.

Şaul, Mahir (2003) "Les maisons de guerre des Watara dans l'ouest burkinabè précolonial". In: Yénouyaga Georges Madiéga/Oumarou Nao (eds.) *Burkina Faso. Cent ans d'histoire 1895-1995*, Paris: Karthala, pp. 381-417.

Şaul, Mahir (2006) "Islam and West African Anthropology". Africa Today 53/1, pp. 3-33.

Şaul, Mahir/Royer, Patrick (2001) *West African Challenge to Empire. Culture and History in the Volta-Bani Anticolonial War*, Athens/Oxford: Ohio University Press/James Currey.

Skinner, Elliott P. (1966) "Islam in Mossi society". In: Ioan Lewis (ed.) *Islam in Tropical Africa*, London: Oxford University Press, pp. 350-373.

Soares, Benjamin F. (2005) Islam and the Prayer Economy: History and Authority in a Malian Town. Edinburgh: Edinburgh University Press.

Traoré, Assane (1993) *Sakidi Sanou: la légende et l'histoire* (unpublished thesis), Université de Ouagadougou.

Traoré, Bakary (1984) *Le processus d'islamisation à Bobo-Dioulasso jusqu'à la fin du XIXe siècle* (unpublished thesis), Université de Ouagadougou.

Traoré, Bakary (1996) *Histoire sociale d'un groupe marchande: Les Jula du Burkina Faso* (unpublished dissertation), Paris, Université de Paris 1.

Traoré, Bakary (2005) "Islam et politique à Bobo-Dioulasso de 1940 à 2002". In: Muriel Gomez-Perez (ed.) *L'islam politique au sud du Sahara: Identités, discours et enjeux*, Paris: Karthala, pp. 417-447.

Wilks, Ivor (1968) "The transmission of Islamic learning in the Western Sudan". In: Jack Goody (ed.) *Literacy in Traditional Societies*, Cambridge: Cambridge University Press, pp. 162-197.

Wilks Ivor (1989), *Wa and the Wala. Islam and Polity in North-Western Ghana*, Cambridge: Cambridge University Press.

Wilks, Ivor (2000) "The Juula and the Expansion of Islam into the Forest". In: Nehemia Levtzion/Randall L.Pouwels (eds.) *The History of Islam in Africa*, Athens: Ohio University Press, pp. 93-115.

Chapter 7

The Making of a 'Harari' City in Ethiopia: Constructing and Contesting Saintly Places in Harar

Patrick Desplat

Introduction: Debating Muslims, Contested Practises

The East Ethiopian town of Harar is considered the most important centre of Islam in the Horn of Africa. Its symbolic capital is reflected in its local representation as *madinat al-awliya'*, the city of saints, which emphasizes the spiritual value of the hundreds of saintly places within its old walls and the many shrines in the countryside beyond them. Some inhabitants go as far as referring to their city as the fourth holiest place in Islam—i.e. after Mecca, Medina, and Jerusalem. However this claim is rejected by the majority and is currently used mainly in the tourism sector to attract more visitors. Nonetheless, the associated saints, their legends, and practices of veneration continue to play a significant role in the religious life of the town of Harar and, similar to its ascription as the fourth holiest place in Islam, the saintly tradition is the focus of much debate concerning it legitimacy. This attitude is reflected in the following exchange between two employees of a local administration office:

Fathi: "What are people doing there, at the shrines? You know that it is forbidden to pray to someone other than God."
Imadj: "Of course. But people are not praying to the saint. That would be *shirk* (polytheism). They pray to God and they do it in communal way, since praying together increases the effectiveness of the prayer."
F: "So? But why are people doing it at the shrines? What is their importance? I may pray at home, it has the same effectiveness. I don't have to go there since God hears me everywhere!"
I: "No, no. Look, the saints are very important individuals, the friends of God. They have been great figures of Islam and they stand out due to their deeds and their character. It's better to pray at their places. It's also better to pray in a mosque than at home. The same thing is true with shrines."

F: "O.k., but let me ask you one question: When have you been there for your last time?"
I: "Hhm ... That was long time ago. When I was a child I went there with my father or mother. I don't remember exactly. But that doesn't matter. The saints are important and righteous."
F. "You see. I even didn't meet any Harari, who's going to the shrines for *ziyara*. Only women may do it and a lot of Oromo people. Well, I just don't believe in it. And when I make this statement openly, they will call me a '*Wahhabi*' and I will have a lot of problems!"

This argument between the administrative employees is an illuminating example of the different perceptions of the saintly tradition. Both participants were Hararis and both were from the local middle class, who claim to be the original settlers of the town and differentiate themselves from other ethnic groups, such as the Oromo, Somalis, Argoba, and Amhara. Despite being a minority—they represent merely twelve percent of the town's population—the Hararis enjoy a privileged status among their ethnic neighbours based on their political power. As a result of the reorganization of administrative structures by the state from 1991, Harar became the smallest administrative unit in Ethiopia, the *Harari National Regional State* (HNRS). This development guarantees special legal rights for the Hararis and underlines the importance of their current political role. Today, most of the Hararis live in diaspora communities in other Ethiopian cities or overseas. Fathi is an exception as he returned to Harar a few months earlier to take up a job opportunity, while Imadj was born and raised in Harar.

Their discussion illustrates that the contestations of local saint veneration includes at least three categories of actors. First, there are people who position themselves against the saint tradition. These individuals clearly constitute a minority within the Harari society and are fearful of expressing their point of view openly as they will be accused of 'Wahhabism' which is equated with extremism (*akrari*) in local parlance. The accusation of being a 'Wahhabi', mostly made in the context of gossip, can have severe social consequences. In reality, only a few Oromo, mainly graduates of Saudi universities, and their followers publicly accuse saint veneration as 'un-Islamic'.

Second, the supporters of the saintly tradition, who may visit shrines for veneration, are identified by Fathi as 'women' and 'Oromo'. Fathi used these terms as collective references for people from the margins of society, which includes the 'crazy Sufis', peasants, and illiterates and reflects the image the local middle class has of the 'ordinary people'. This also includes the belief that they are ignorant of 'correct' religious practice. Those who believe in saint veneration, on the other hand, resist this allegation and see themselves as agents of an 'orthodox', but mystical inspired Islam. They justify their argument by referring to a mystical world view which underlines the hidden inner dimension which would not be captured by either middle-class secular education or the abstract knowledge of religious scholars.

This debate between followers and their opponents is not new, but a comprehensive phenomenon of Islamic societies and must be understood in the context of the continuous purification of religious practice through the influence of modernity and ideas of Islamic reform. However this arena of debate is supplemented in Harar by a third group, a characteristic of which is its ambiguous attitude towards the saint tradition. Like Imadj, the members of this group praise the saints, but will never visit the local shrines or participate otherwise in their activities. At the same time they lament the decline of the saintly tradition and may criticize the related rituals without, however, categorizing them as un-Islamic while defending them vehemently against those who openly question the practices at the shrines. This group includes a variety of people from the well-educated middle class, shop-keepers, traditional religious scholars, and even reformers from the *Tablighi Djamat* or the *Habashiyya*.[1] This heterogeneous group is characterized by its ambivalent stance: people from this group visit the local shrines seldom or never and may even criticize some of the related practices. However, like Imadj, these people never fundamentally question the saints and even defend them in disputes.

The question that arises here is why these influential and, in part, prominent people in Harar stand up for saintly places although they never visit them for religious practice. This question is directly related to local imaginations of the self and locality. As the city of saints, Harar is an important resource not only in the context of religious contestations but also in relation to identity politics. This chapter will explore the problems of the construction and negotiation of saintly locality. The aim is to show that local saintly places are not marginal, but an important factor of religious and cultural order. The spatial dimensions of sanctity play a part in the disputes surrounding their legitimation. This paper will show that the conflation of culture, history, and locality with religion are an important project for the maintenance a Harari identity, in which the city of Harar is constructed as Islamic but rather resembled a predominantly 'Harari' city. The question concerning the contemporary role of saint tradition must be seen in a wider context, in which Harari Muslims are trying to positioning themselves as modern Muslims in a wider sense of the *umma*, while defining themselves in a local and regional context through their distinctiveness.

---

1 Both movements have different theological and practical approaches but share the objective of a renewal of the Islamic faith. The *Habashiyya* is locally known as *Sheikh Abdullahi Djama* and was initiated in Lebanon by a Harari scholar in the 1980s. Similarly the *Tablighi Djamat* is quite popular in Harar as the *Dawa Djama* and developed in India in the early 20th century.

Symbolic and Historical Configurations of Local Sanctity, Saints, and their Places

Harar is known by its inhabitants as *Bändär Abadir*, the city of the saint Abadir or, even more distinctively, as *madinat al-awliya'*, the 'city of saints'. This term reflects the density of saintly places in and around Harar. Emile Foucher (Foucher 1988, 1994), a catholic priest from the Capuchin mission in Harar, identified 235 saints, while several years later the anthropologist Camilla Gibb counted about 272, i.e. 232 male and 40 female (Gibb 1996: 291-309). More recently, the University of Rome published a map of the old town in cooperation with the Harari People National Regional State which contains the location of 100 saintly places (CIRPS/State 2003). However, the exact number of saintly places and their associated saints in Harar and its surrounding is not known as many sites are considered locally as *khuddun*, which means 'to be covered', a synonym for the Arabic *batin*, i.e. esoteric, hidden.

This bundling of locally perceived religious importance into a meta-term 'city of saints' has its significance even today. Although some religious scholars may not accept the term because of its relationship to a mystical and, in their view, 'popular' Islam, many people from the middle class appreciate it. As they see it, the expression 'city of saints' not only underlines the importance of the town, but also explains the obvious density of saintly places in Harar. Other Hararis may justify the expression with reference to mystical knowledge. According to a popular legend, the denomination of Harar as the city of saints goes back to the prophetic ascension (*mi'radj*):

> During the nocturnal journey the prophet Muhammad saw from above a shining spot on earth. He was drawing the attention of his escort, the angel Djibril and asked him about the place and its name. The angel answered him that this is the city of saints and they continued their journey.[2]

In addition to this story there is a saying that embeds two of the most venerated saints of Harar, Abadir and 'Abdulqādīr Djilānī, the famous founder of the Qadiriyya, into the wider context of the ascension of the prophet: *Bād zaleyu Abādir. Bāri zaleyu 'Abdulqādīr* (The land belongs to Abādir. The gate belongs to 'Abdulqādīr).[3] According to local interpretations the prophet was expected by the later Caliph Abu Bakr as-Siddiq. Abu Bakr was already in-

---

[2] This legend was already published in a similar form by Foucher, i.e. Foucher, Emile (1994) "The Cult of Muslims Saints in Harar. Religious Dimensions". In: Bahru Zewde/Richard Pankhurst/Taddese Beyene (eds.) *Proceedings of the 11th International Conference of Ethiopian Studies, Addis Ababa (1-6.4.1997)*, Addis Abeba: Institute of Ethiopan Studies, Addis Abeba University, pp. 71-83.

[3] A local adaptation of a *hadith* which is especially recognized by the Shia: "I [Prophet Muḥammad] am the town of knowledge and Ali is the gate."

formed about the sighting of the *madinat al-awliya'* by Muhammad through their close relationship and the possibilities of dream communication. As a result he tried to claim the city for himself. However, the prophet said that he would not give it to him but to his great-grandchild. After all, the local saint Abadir is genealogically related to Abu Bakr, and the Hararis see themselves as the descendants of the saint, which means that their claim to the town of Harar was finally legitimated through the prophet himself. Djilani was mentioned because he met the prophet on one of his spiritual journeys and he was assigned to rule the wider region, emphasizing his spiritual role in the Horn of Africa.

These overlapping stories of spiritual belonging and leadership in a specific territory are set into a repertoire of legends that construct a connection between the local spiritual order of Harar and a semantic Islamic imperative, the *mi'radj* in this case. All these legends of spiritual claim and protection are connected to a cognitive map which extracts meanings that individuals and groups assign to places. They are more or less embedded in historically contingent and shared cultural understandings of the terrain and sustained by diverse imageries, through which people see and remember the city of Harar as a regional centre, which obtained its legitimation as saintly from the prophet itself, distributed genealogically through the first caliph to Abadir, the final owner of Harar.

Saintly landscape and local cosmology—
the manifestations and meaning of saintly places

As in the case of other traditions of saint veneration throughout the Muslim world, the saints in Harar are believed to have the capacity to heal diseases, find of stolen goods, bring good fortune, generate fertility, and redirect lazy pupils from Qur'anic schools back to the path of learning. In a particular case the ascribed meaning of sanctity does not necessarily reflect an Islamic or Sufi doctrine, but rather concrete needs and cosmologies of the local community. This kind of contextualization causes the high level of identification of the people with the saints, who lived, acted, and ultimately died at the shrines as neighbours, ancestors, teachers, healers, friends, and even foes. In Harar sanctity is partly ideological and not related to purity and taboo but mainly to protection and the common good, both spiritually and worldly.

The historical sanctity of the 'golden age' is bound to protection and the common good. This is reflected today in the local cosmology of temporal and spatial protection. Like the town of Harar itself, virtually all visible shrines are constructed on top of hills. Taken in combination they constitute characteristic landmarks forming a saintly topography. The material appearance of these places is highly diverse. They exist in the shape of niches, trees, simple graves, rocks, and the typical cupola. Some shrines have rooms, which are used for the veneration of saints (*gelma*). Many of the shrines have a mosque with a small cemetery attached to it. Saintly places in the countryside in particular are erected close to enormous overhanging sycamore trees.

The temporal aspect of protection is provided through local interpretation, according to which Harar is safeguarded by 355 saints. This figure correlates with the days of the Islamic lunar year. Thus every day of the year is protected by one saint. Oral histories tell that each weekday is represented by a specific saint, however in most cases their names are not known. All of the saints belong to a spiritual 'parliament'. According to legend, all of the saints of Harar meet every week on the top of nearby Mountain Hakim to debate about the well-being of the city. These weekly meetings are supplemented by monthly and yearly gatherings. This belief in protection conducted by a saintly 'parliament' corresponds to a common notion in Sufism of a 'hidden government' (*hukuma batiniyya*), who debates and judges the affairs of the mortals and the worldly authorities, the 'visible government' (*hukuma zahiriyya*) (Reeves 1990).

In addition to this temporal perspective the Hararis perceive saintly places as spatial landmarks of protection. The city wall of Harar has five gates which lead to the region's main trade routes. Many saints have their last sanctuary on these routes. The saints with the first shrines beyond the gates are seen as important patrons of protection. This is undoubtedly related to their location as the gates were known as obvious points of attack. Shrines in the countryside are also known for their protection, but also combine other functions. On the one hand the shrines are believed to be places of education, Islamization and healing during times of peace. On the other hand these graves are seen as intersections of a wider network of communication which helped to transmit information concerning attacks, epidemics, etc. as quickly as possible during times of crisis.

The 'golden age' of saints as reflection of historical crisis and marginality

The symbolic configuration of local sanctity is historically situated and demands a perspective that brings together hagiographical sources and historical events. The reference to a 'golden age' of saints is more than a mere glorification of the past. The 'golden age' was, in fact, anything but golden. It was a time of crises, in which Harar lost its political, military, and economic power. As the capital of the Sultanat of Adal, the city became the most important centre in the region during the 16th century. It was the breeding ground for a new religious elite who waged a 14-year *djihad* (1529-1543) against the Christian empire in the Ethiopian highlands. Their most popular leader, Imam

Ahmed b. Ibrahim, conquered extensive parts of Ethiopia during the war but was finally vanquished with the help of Portuguese troops. From this point on the situation in Harar changed dramatically, particularly due to the intervention of a third party; for unknown reasons, the pastoralist non-Muslim Oromo started to migrate to the western and eastern parts of today's Ethiopia, driving a wedge between Christians and Muslims and party benefiting from the war-devastated land and the resulting power vacuum in these regions. In the eastern regions, which had been dominated by Muslims, the Oromo migration only left small enclaves of the former Islamic dominions. For the first time the inhabitants of Harar saw themselves as a Muslim minority against a foreign majority of Oromo who constantly attacked the town. Islam remained the only resource for superiority and civilization. This symbolic distinction between town and country, physically manifested in the wall, is reflected in local terminology which classifies the town as 'civilization' (*ge*) while the outskirts in the countryside are associated with 'barbarism' (*därga*).[4] Thus, Harar became a historical Islamic bulwark which influenced the perception of the city as an Islamic center more than its role in education and scholarship. Surviving the tremendous tragedy contributed to the glory of the city, which is acknowledged throughout the wider region of Ethiopia.

The most popular saints and the ascription of their sanctity must be understood in this context of ideologization. They are historical figures who are venerated on the basis of their deeds as leaders and protected the community, while miracles transmitted in oral or written form provide supplementary material not the primary legitimation of their saintly status. The most important saint of Harar is Abadir. He is considered as the main patron of the city and nicknamed *imam al-quṭb* or *shaykh ash-shuyukh*. He is not seen as the founder of the city or the first person who Islamized the region, but is instead associated with the reorganization of Harar and the establishment of the local saint tradition. According to the legendary local hagiography, *Fath madinat Harar*, he arrived in the already Islamized region of Harar from the Hidjaz with 405 saints the 12th century (Wagner 1978). Abadir, who was elected by the saints as their leader, ordered the reorganization of the town, which was formerly divided into seven villages. He asked each of the surrounding tribes, i.e. the Somalis, Argobas and different Oromo clans,[5] to bring their agricul-

---

4 There is an entire repertoire of words relating to this division: the Harari named their town *ge* and call themselves *ge usu*, the people of the town. These *ge usu* speak a Semitic language called *ge sinan*, the language of the town, they claim a specific *ge ada*, a town culture, live in *ge gar*, the traditional town house, and send their children to *quran ge,* the urban Qur'anic school.
5 This is an obvious invention of a tradition. While Wagner made clear that the time of the arrival of Abadir is historically more or less correct, the Oromo came not before the 16th century into the region of Harar at least not as permanent settlers.

tural products to the town and trade them. Moreover, these tribes had to elect one of the saints to be their leader. Subsequent to this initial action, he fought the surrounding unbelievers and after the final victory transferred the conquered land to his saintly companions, while staking a claim to the town of Harar for himself. Each saint was assigned to a specific site where he should act as scholar, local doctor, military commander, teacher, and/or miracle worker. After their deaths they were buried at their sites of action, which then became centres of attraction for local veneration and pilgrimage. Those places became saintly as spatial materializations of the saints and their transcendental power. Through Abadir, Harar became a both secular and spiritual administrative unit, with the city at its centre. Topographically, sanctity in Harar is organized as an urban-rural continuum and is not centred on a single grave. The saint tradition in Harar comprises a diffuse network of saintly places, which together form a saintly landscape restricted to a radius of about 40 miles. Moreover, this limited space of spiritual authority coincides with the territory of the independent emirate of Harar which was established during the 17th century. This may explain why, unlike Sheikh Hussein in southern Bale, Harar does not attract pilgrimages from all over Ethiopia, but appeals more to the immediate inhabitants of the region.

The second most popular saint is Amir Nur b. Mudjahid (1551-1567). Like Abadir he was a historical figure who is mainly praised for his deeds as military leader. Amir Nur tried to remobilize the *djihad* and succeeded in killing the ruling Christian emperor. On the way back to Harar he became involved in a military conflict with the approaching Oromo, but lost the fight and fled back to Harar. There he ordered the construction of a wall around the town, which provided effective protection against the continuous attacks of the Oromo and retains its high symbolic value to the present day. Abadir's approach was more inclusive; he organized the surrounding tribes to serve Harar, but excluded the Christians, with whom he fought in several battles. In contrast, Amir Nur's agenda may be interpreted as rather exclusive, involving the construction of a wall to exclude other foes, now the Oromo. However, this view neglects an important and mostly overlooked aspect; oral histories point out that it was Amir Nur who gathered the surrounding Muslims and resettled them in Harar to protect them against the Oromo. Due to their heterogenous backgrounds, fights broke out between the initial and later settlers. Amir Nur arbitrated in the dispute and ordered the destruction of all genealogies so that all inhabitants of the town could be considered equal as Hararis, a term which had not been used hitherto. This means that Amir Nur was not only responsible for the wall, but also for the genesis of a Harari identity. Seen from this perspective, sanctity in Harar is related to the exclusion of the foreign and the inclusion of the self—showing strength to the outside and at the same time endowing identity. However, during the reign of Amir Nur, the spatial structure of sanctity in Harar was transformed into a more restricted area of what is today called the old town, the core of the city surrounded by its wall.

The third saint is Sheikh Hashim. He lived in the 18th century and represents a different type of saint. He is also seen as an innovator and is associated with the popularization of the Qadiriyya. However, the sanctity he represents is less concerned with protection and the common good than with asceticism and miracles. The conflict between Sheikh Hashim and the community is continuously underlined in the oral histories, cumulating into a story in which the saint fought with the ruling emir regarding the correct recitation of *dhikr*. Disappointed by the both ruler and the people, he ultimately left the town, announcing that all saints after him should be hidden (*khuddun*) and that spirit possession should instead enter Harar. This tradition is deeply symbolic and addresses the decline of the 'true' saintly Islam, while Sheikh Hashim is considered as the 'seal of the saints' (*khatam al-awliya'*). This is basically related to a different historical context: the inhabitants of Harar in the 18th century were less exposed to wars and crises, but experienced instead increasing security and prosperity due to alliances with the Oromo. Finally, the consolidation of Harar correlates with the end of the 'golden age' of saints; spatial sanctity itself expanded during Sheikh Hashim beyond the city wall.

Decline and Revival of Pilgrimages and Festivity

Saintly places must be 'charged' to maintain their status. A *ziyara*, the visit to a shrine, is probably the predominant practice involved in keeping such places alive. The organization of a *ziyara* may be based on a range of motivations. However, these can be differentiated into two categories. First, the individual *ziyara* whereby the faithful visit the grave of a saint for intercession and, second, the communal ziyara, which is usually connected to a specific time. During the individual *ziyara* the person approaches the representative of the shrine (*murid*) to beg for something, to seek for a solution, or to thank the saint for a fulfilled wish. The pilgrim usually hands over a gift for the saint, utters the problem to the *murid* who will first bless the donations and then recite specific prayers to gain the help of the saint. Incense is burned during this process. The *murid* ends the ritual with a blessing, spitting water in the face of the pilgrim. If the vow is fulfilled, the pilgrim must return to the shrine, not only to make further donations but also to participate in the regular communal *ziyara*. This kind of *ziyara* is always an overnight session and is organized on a weekly basis on Thursday night or on one of the eight 'big days' in a lunar year. These big days (*gidir jam*) are not related to the birth or death of a saint but are associated with generic occurrences in Islam such as the *mi'radj* or *badr*. On rare occasions, a communal *ziyara* may be organised due to catastrophes such as famines or family disputes. Despite the varying temporal settings, the practice is very similar: the scene is dominated by drum playing, dance, and the recitation of religious text in Arabic, e.g. the *mawlud*, supplemented by *zikri*, local songs to praise God, the prophets, and saints in vernacular languages. Large quantities of *Qat* and coffee are consumed and incense is burned continuously. The recitation is led by the murid and his *djamā'a*, an equivalent to a Sufi order but less organized, while others follow with the chorus of the songs, dance in a group forming a circle, or clap their hands to the beat of the drums. Depending on the shrine and the occasion, the *ziyara* may attract anything between ten and 200 participants.

While most saints and saintly places in Harar are not discussed, the middle class and religious scholars in particular criticize the religious practise and the participants. Theologically they agree about the righteousness of personalized sanctity in general and the historical role of the saints for Harar in particular, however they accuse the participants of being 'wrong Sufis', 'illiterate', and 'uneducated'. This argument is common among the middle class in different Islamic societies. However, the interesting fact is that, although they keep away from shrine activities, at the same time they defend them when sanctity comes under the attack, for example by the Wahhabis, whom they accuse of being extremists and, in some cases, even unbelievers. The consensus between the Sufis and the middle class concerning the significance of sanctity is based on different normative views of religion. While the Sufis have a mystical inspired world view and differentiate between the 'hidden' and the 'visible', a structure, which is dissociated from human intervention, the middle class argues that sanctity represents a paradigm from the past which is not practicable in the modern context. Their view on saint veneration is an ambivalent one, best reflected in an article published by Ahmed Zekaria, a Harari scholar. On the one hand he assesses the *ziyara* as 'syncretistic' and dismisses any form of intermediation through the saints as being strong blasphemy. On the other hand, however, he legitimates the practice in an historical framework and for today only if the believer has the 'right' intention before and during his pilgrimage (Zekaria 2003: 26). This attitude is a strategy of distinction which is addressed to both Sufis and the Wahhabis. I will not follow this line, but will recapitulate an incident in 2003 in which members of middle class attended a festival called *shawwal id* to deconstruct the thesis that members of the middle class will never visit any kind of *ziyara*.

As opposed to a 'generic' *ziyara*, the *shawwal id* is a public feast and also known as *Harari Id* as, traditionally, other ethnic groups did not participate in it. The *shawwal id* takes place at two shrines near the two northern gates following seven days of fasting in addition to the month of Ramadan. In 2003 these places where colourfully decorated with pennants and banners in Amharic or Arabic script. Flags of Ethiopia and Harar were on show everywhere, underlining the role of the municipality as the main sponsor of the decorations. Schools and some shops were closed during the period of festivity. As in the case of other forms of *ziyara*, people recited local songs devoted to God, Muhammad, and the saints (*zikri*). The singing was accompanied by drums. The participants danced or clapped their hands, while others hung around, chewed *qat*, or strolled from one place to the next and back. Unlike in the case of a generic *ziyara*, men and women mixed freely, a religious text was not recited and there was no *murid* present. The scene in the evening was dominated by young people, both male and female. Many youngsters from the diaspora, easily identifiable by their style of clothing, recorded the dancing crowd on their video cameras and sold their recordings on CDs several days later. The young people were also present during the day when a lot of older women and children participated in the festival. The number of participants is likely to have reached several hundreds, mostly Hararis, but also people from other ethnic groups.

The success of the festival was highlighted by the comments of many Hararis who were surprised by the revival of the *shawwal id* as, previously, people had to be forced to attend the *shawwal id*. Similarly, some Hararis argued that the regional state, represented by the president and an employee of the municipality, once tried to ban the feast while others denied this and referred to religious scholars who were against it because of the lax attitude towards alcohol and the mixing of the sexes. The festival of 2003 presented an entirely different picture. This change of attitude brings us to the central questions as to what attracts people to saintly places and what draws them away from them.

Shawwal id stands in clear contrast to the generic *ziyara*. It is a remarkable case of the reinterpretation and a change of purpose, in particular in relation to the protection of the city. In the past it had two main functions. It reflected, first, the need for protection and, second, the presentation of strength. In the past, the practice of wandering between the two shrines at the night was intended to convey to potential enemies that the Hararis were not weak after the fasting period but alert to potential threats. The establishment and use of two shrines as places of festivity has nothing to do with the saints themselves. The *shawwal id* is considered to be historically linked to the coming of Abadir, who taught the Hararis the 'right' way to fast. There are several other oral histories concerning the festivity, but none ever mentioned the two saints' shrines where the *shawwal id* takes place. This is unusual, but taking into account that those two shrines are the nearest to the northern gates of the wall, historically the weak point of attack by Oromo and other groups, they may serve as spiritual guardians due to their location.

Nowadays, the symbolic frame of the parade between the two shrines is missing: people can take the most comfortable path and most participants do not know about the protective function of the festival. While, previously, participation in the *shawwal id* was rather insignificant, today, the involvement of the young people has made a strong contribution to its revival. This may be related to another traditional function of the feast whereby it is intended to provide an occasion for the adolescent male to choose his future fiancée. The feast was the only occasion within a religious context when men and women were allowed to meet in the public. This partly explains the nicknaming of *shawwal id* as *Harari id*, since the Harari marry endogamously and may dislike the participation of other groups for that reason. Even if the original function sounds inappropriate in today's context in which the young people mix relatively freely, the *shuwwal id* is mainly being revived through them and members of the middle class who meet at the shrines, flirt, and hang around in groups and do not necessarily participate in the recitations of *zikri* or dancing. Visiting youngsters from other towns have a significant influence on the local event and use it as a platform for new cultural identity, a typical element of diaspora communities.

However, the popularization of the festivity is also due to the fact, that it offers a broad scope for interpretation. The greatest potential for attracting the otherwise prejudiced middle class lies here as the *shawwal id* has been always popular festival which departed from social rules and constraints. This meaning is documented in different traditions, in which tension arose between the people who wanted to celebrate a festivity and a ruler who tried to forbid it, but failed due to spiritual powers. The inversion of hierarchical structure is not only obvious in several legends, but also evident in the conception of the *shawwal id* itself. In contrast to the 'generic' *ziyara*, the *shawwal id* is not about obtaining the blessing of the saint or making vows. There is no hierarchical order between the *murid*, *djama'a*, and the participants. Another point of distinction is that families or some of their individual members are usually connected to a specific shrine due to the fulfilment of their vows and therefore bound to attend the *ziyara* there. The *shawwal id* is the only festivity related to saintly places in Harar, which all Hararis should attend, irrespective of their relationship with a particular saint. Strictly speaking, the feast is not too embedded in the framework of mystical knowledge. The symbolization of protection through the wandering around and the selection of a fiancé are more acceptable by the middle class than any Sufi explanation.[6] Another trend is the increasing commercialization of the festivity and the involvement of the state through donations. Moreover the *shawwal id* is celebrated in Addis Abeba and Dire Dawa and thus reconstructs locality in another context.

---

6   It must be admitted that some Sufis have an explanation for the *shawwal id*. They relate it to a 'mystical fiscal year'. This is interesting because the 7th of *shuwal* is sometimes known as New Year of the pre-Islamic age. However, this explanation is relatively unknown and therefore of little relevance for most of the Sufis and the middle class.

The most important aspect of the *shawwal id* at present may be the presentation of Hararis as a homogeneous cultural group. This is reflected in the in different cultural-political programs of events. In the year 2005 the festival was further enlarged with the help of the diaspora organization *Harari Unity Youth Association* and additional events were staged, ranging from an anti-HIV campaign to musical and cultural shows at which popular local musicians performed Harari songs and women presented traditional Harari clothing. In 2006 the course of events was similar, but on this occasion the *shawwal id* also revealed a political connotation. The festivity was used to welcome the representatives of different groups, namely Somalis, Afar, and in particular Silte, a Gurage-group. The Silte party comprised 300 people who were welcomed by a brass band and fireworks. During the dinner the representatives gave a speech, in which the need for a reunion of Hararis and Silte was addressed:

we have seen the reunification of South and North Yemen, East and West Germany and insh-Allah one day we want to see all Hararis 're-united' with their motherland.[7]

That other groups define themselves as 'Hararis' is a new phenomenon, but could be interpreted as reference to the 'golden age' as it is said that the Silte and the Hararis belonged to one group before the Oromo overran the region in the 16th century. Thus, the event forms part of a policy of remembrance, in which the heyday of the Islamic Sultanate under Imam Ahmed is celebrated—a fact furthermore underlined by the exclusion of the Oromo, the immediate neighbours of the Hararis.

The *shawwal id* offers different interpretations not necessary bound to the rules and regulations of the more 'generic' *ziyara*. The motivations for going to or staying away from shrines are diverse: i.e. to search for the spiritual inspiration, to meet friends and have fun with them, to compete with others in the recitation of religious texts, to dance and chew *qat* the whole night long. Some may go to shrines to gain the blessing of the saint, to find a solution for a problem, or to ask for the fulfilment of a wish. This rather individual *ziyara* is locally associated with the belief in intercession (*tawassul*) and is contested locally but also widely practiced and tolerated. First, this ambivalence is inherent to the saint tradition itself, which is not an explicit theology but an implicit belief and therefore open to different, often competing interpretations. Second, it is generally tolerated by those who do not believe in it because only few people visit shrines for intercession, or do so discreetly. It is considered a matter of personal religiosity whereby what matters is the intention be-

---

7 http://hararconnection.blogspot.com/2007/01/historical-shawal-eid-in-harar-2006.html [10.10.2007].

hind the visit matters and this will ultimately be judged by God himself. However, the revival of *shawwal id* and its meaning for the modern context must be seen in the context of two recent developments: the revival of religion and a revival of cultural identity.

Islamic Reform and the Revival of Cultural Identity in Harar

Islam had been constantly marginalized following the incorporation of large Muslim-populated regions into the Ethiopian state at the end of the 19th century. This was, in fact, the fate of all religions except Orthodox Christianity. This corresponds to the imagination of Ethiopia as a 'Christian island surrounded by infidels' and the projection of the country as predominantly Christian, despite the fact that approximately 45 percent of the population is Muslim. This attitude changed slightly with the change of government in the 1970s. Initially the socialist regime (1974-1991) treated all religions equally, but set up restrictions on religious networking, mainly the importing of religious literature, pilgrimages to Mecca, and visits by foreign scholars.

It was not until the current government came into power in 1991 that the state developed a more liberal attitude towards the religious sphere: religious freedom became an item on the political agenda and was written into the constitution and the previous restrictions were abrogated. These changes prompted a revival of Islam reflected in a new Islamic identity, the construction of new mosques and Islamic schools, the emergence of numerous magazines and newspapers with an Islamic focus, the participation of Muslims in public discussions, conferences, an increase in pilgrimages to Mecca, and the establishment of Islamic organizations (Ahmed 1998).

The non-interventionist stance by the state changed with the allegation of 'fundamentalism'. There had been fights against some groups at the Somali border and in June 1995 a significant incident occurred in capital Addis Abeba, in which Hosni Mubarak, the Egyptian president, survived an assassination attempt. As a result, the state began to intervene in the religious sphere again by banning several Islamic NGOs. The term 'fundamentalism' became synonymous with an Arab-inspired, foreign Islam that divides Ethiopian Muslims. This has a clearly political background as 'fundamentalists' are always depicted as 'foreign' by the state, i.e. associated with the neighbouring states of Sudan, Eritrea, and Somalia, with whom Ethiopia has a hostile relationship. Based on this attitude, local groups also came into the potential focus of the Ethiopian state.

In Harar the revival of religion and the tension between the alternating state restrictions and liberal attitude is clearly reflected in the presence of Egyptian teachers in Harar in the early 1990s. Interest in religion increased at the time and was reflected in the establishment of new educational institutions which combined secular and religious curricula or focused strongly on Arabic. The *Tablighi djamaat* succeeded in attracting a lot of followers, new religious literature circulated, and the access to cheap television and satellite equipment due to contraband trading offered access to Arabic channels broadcasting on religious topics. The arrival of the Egyptians and their engagement in religious education prompted a positive response by many Hararis. However, despite being tolerated for some time, they were suddenly expelled from the country by the Ethiopian State on the grounds of their lack of work permits. Hardly uncoincidentally, this happened soon after they exposed themselves as members of the Muslim Brotherhood and started to use the mosque's loudspeakers for preaching. The broadcasting and the content of the sermons were reason for both state and the Hararis to act against the Egyptians on the ground of their 'extremism'. While the Hararis embraced a renewal of Islam, they were not interested in appropriating ideas they consider as deviating from the established interpretation of religion—particularly when it is done openly in public. The Ethiopian state, on the other hand, was motivated by its concern about potential threats to national security which became an increasing issue after the failed assassination of the Egyptian president.

This rather brief incident was accompanied by a similar development on a wider scale. During the 1980s some Oromo received scholarships for religious studies from the Saudi government (Gnamo 2002). On completion of their studies they returned to their home country and preached that some long-established religious practices were un-Islamic. However their activities were only partly successful, mainly in the in rural areas and on the outskirts of the towns. In Harar, the reformist Oromo condemned saint veneration as a 'Harari cultural invention' which is alien to 'original' Islam.

But what kind of influence did the reformists have on the Hararis? The term 'Wahhabi' is locally indexed and embedded in an historical incident that occurred in the 1940s when a small group of pilgrimages came under the influence of Wahhabi ideology and after their return became involved in a local school. This group was challenged by local scholars and, again with the involvement of the state, their leader was arrested and the school closed down. The concept of 'Wahhabi' was initially used as a synonym of 'otherness' and the misinterpretation of Islam. Of course, this does not mean that new ideas were and are not appropriated by some Hararis. However, the people who embrace such views tend to express them in the context of small groups of friends and keep a low profile in public.

This conflict between the followers of different religious interpretations had a rather strong effect on saint veneration: people who venerated local saints were suddenly harassed and forced to justify their practice and members of the middle class, in particular people who never visit the shrines, started to defend local sanctity. The two groups attack the Wahhabis, on theological grounds and accuse them of distorting the doctrine of the unity of god (*tawhid*). However, views based on a polemic text, in which Wahhabism is exposed as being an invention by the British colonial power with the deliberate intention of dividing Muslims in order to control them have become even more popular in this debate. These kinds of conspiracy theories have a great impact on the debate as they are inherently disprovable. However, the middle class is probably not so much concerned about Wahhabism itself as the question of theological righteousness. They are more agitated by the fact that some Oromo are attacking the historical core of Harari identity, namely the saints and their deeds. Members of middle class see this as a direct attack on the legitimacy of the Hararis themselves and their role in the political and religious administration of Harar. This brings us to the recent process of culturalization and identity politics.

The culturalization of Harari society—locality as a cultural resource

The question of locality remained relatively untouched in the context of religious contestations in the past but has now re-entered the arena in the context of identity, since the conflict between people for and against saint veneration is intertwined with another set of conflicts between the Hararis and Oromo. Another facet of locality has entered the arena here focused on question as to who ultimately owns Harar.

The Ethiopian state again assumed an important role in this debate. With the change in government in 1991, the Ethiopian state not only liberalized the religious sphere, but also implemented a federal policy. While in the past the state was controlled by the Christian Amhara, the new state tried to concede more rights and autonomy to different ethnic groups. To that end, new regional states, each with their own parliament, budget, and tax authority, replaced the previous administrative zones. The most distinctive feature of the restructuring process was its ethnic and linguistic dimension. The smallest regional state, i.e. *Harari People's National Regional State* (HPNRS) was established in 1995. At the expense of other ethnic groups in the region, most notably the Amhara and Oromo, the Harari minority obtained political privileges which permitted them for the first time since the incorporation of Harar into the Ethiopian state not only to lay claim to the city of Harar but also to administer it. This governmental empowerment of Hararis triggered a revitalization of ethnic-linguistic identity and also gave rise to conflicts with the local Amhara and Oromo who see themselves as politically unrepresented.[8]

---

8   It must be added that the above-mentioned groups and the Somalis, have their 'own' regional state. However, due to the symbolic role of Harar, its characteristic as a historical crossroads, at which many groups interacted, the town is also claimed by others. The militant *Oromo Liberation Front* (OLF) is striving for an

This search for a Harari identity was supplemented by the search for 'authentic' Harari culture understood as a rather static system of binding rules. The ideological power of 'culture' is based on the essentializing politics of identity, through which the meaning of being Harari is currently discussed. The establishment of museums, publications in the Harari language, and also the successful application for inclusion in the UNESCO list of world cultural heritage sites are exemplary of this process. The city of Harar has become a political and economic resource. To underline the continuity of its significance, in a recent publication the former president of HPNRS explained the central theme in the preface: "This book will help the cause of protecting the heritage in no uncertain manner. [It] will surely help to prevent losing our heritage" (Revault/Santelli 2004: 5).

While the religious meaning of the city for the region was constantly underlined in this book, the main focus was on historical and cultural manifestations. It is worth noting that the publication classifies shrines in Harar as 'culture'. This structure reflects the common middle class discourse that today categorizes shrines as cultural and historical manifestations. Parts of the new regional government are particularly concerned about the areas of language, culture, and the administration of historical places, in particular "mosques, shrines and graves of saintly figures" (Abubeker 2001: 27).[9]

Local sanctity is a symbol, in which the complex imagination of the own group is mobilized. This is only possible because they are historically 'proven'. The saint tradition is one of the many aspects Harari society, in which a territorial and spatial concept of representation and symbolization is mediated. Saintly places along with the wall and mosques are used as places of memory. A sense of belonging and, moreover, belonging to a certain place and involvement in its administration is part of this culturalization. The conflation of culture and history with religion are inherent to the Harari project of identity. From the perspective of the regional state and the middle class, saintly places are historical-cultural landmarks and only secondarily religious sites.

---

independent Oromo state including Harar. According to some Somalis, Harar should play an important role in the context of an idea of 'Great Somalia', including the war-torn Somalia, as well as Djibouti and parts of northern Kenya and eastern Ethiopia. The Amhara, on the other hand, would like to place the Harari regional state under the central government of Addis Abeba, as was done with the town of Dire Dawa, due to its multi-ethnic status.

9 In practice, however, the regional state provides sporadic help to economically weak shrines. It usually focuses on the repair of shrines and related buildings, e.g. the festivity rooms. The municipality will sometimes donate a camel or goat for a *ziyara*, but mainly to shrines with a female clientele which are economically weaker than other saintly sites.

Religious meaning and cultural use of saintly places

In this context it is understandable why people feel so attracted to festivities like *shawwal id*, while they may neglect other forms of pilgrimage. It is worth noting that the term 'culture' is interpreted in different ways: while some Oromo, who are associated with the Wahhabi movement may attack the saint veneration as 'cultural', the Hararis, i.e. both middle class and Sufis, justify their practices as religiously legitimate. They argue from the same logic but with different normative claims. However, outside this debate saintly places become indeed a cultural resource of the regional state and the well-educated middle class. For them, 'cultural' becomes an attribute of positive self-representation that does not contradict the 'religious'. Both levels of culture and religion are intermingled and used as arguments in particular situations. There may be situations in which many Hararis will strictly divide between religious and cultural practice. However, if the 'other' is claiming the same thing, the argument will be strongly rejected. This middle-class ascription of shrines as primarily cultural (rather than religious) sites explains why Hararis today may defend these places and even the associated practices. It is not even about not going to the saints' graves, but about a different way of going and the attachment of an altered significance to the shrines.

Against the background of the initial question it is evident that the tradition of saints is of significant relevance, but the nature of the relevance has changed. This development cannot be reduced to processes of rationalization, secularization, or 'Wahhabization' of their own religion, which means the confrontation and contestation with modernistic ideas. In fact the reinterpretation and refunctionalization of saintly places has become obvious: i.e. from the classical model of intercession between God and Muslims to the production of mainly local and collective identity. The modification is the result of the interaction of different groups of actors and the continuous negotiation of the 'true' Islam. Processes of increasing transnational integration simultaneously strengthened processes of definition and redefinition concerning the self and the other. The apologetic discourses in the context of recent contestations display a feeling of loss. Saintly places are promoted as moments of cultural and historical remembrance without losing their inherent ambivalence. For this reason the relation between the locality of urban Harar, a saintly topography, and collective identity have produced a new meaning. The construction of saintly locality, manifested in individual shrines or in the town itself, comprises processes of uprising against the recurrent waves of purification that involve the attempt of a hegemonic reduction of the natural heterogeneity in Islam.

References

Abubeker, Abdulhamid (2001) *The Process of Decentralization in Ethiopia. A Case Study of the Harari Peoples' National Regional State* (B.A. thesis), Addis Abeba: Addis Abeba University.

Ahmed, Hussein (1998) "Recent Islamic Periodicals in Ethiopia (1996-1998)". *Northeast African Studies* 5, pp. 7-21.

CIRPS/State HPNR (2003) *Cultural Heritage of Harar. Mosques, Islamic Holy Graves, and Traditional Harari Houses. A Comprehensive Map*, Brüssel: European Commission.

Foucher, Emile (1988) "Names of Mussulmanes Venerated in Harar and its Surroundings". *Zeitschrift der Deutschen Morgenländischen Gesellschaft* 138, pp. 263-282.

Foucher, Emile (1994) "The Cult of Muslims Saints in Harar. Religious Dimensions". In: Bahru Zewde/Richard Pankhurst/Taddese Beyene (eds.) *Proceedings of the 11th International Conference of Ethiopian Studies, Addis Ababa (1-6.4.1997)*, Addis Ababa: Institute of Ethiopan Studies, Addis Abeba University, pp. 71-83.

Gibb, Camilla (1996) *In the City of Saints. Religion, Politics and Gender in Harar, Ethiopia* (Ph.D. thesis), Oxford: University of Oxford, Michaelmas.

Gnamo, Abbas Haji (2002) "Islam, the Orthodox Church and Oromo Nationalism (Ethiopia)". *Cahiers d'Etudes Africaines* 165, pp. 99-120.

Reeves, Edward (1990) *The Hidden Government. Ritual, Clientelism and Legitimation in Northern Egypt*, Salt Lake City: University of Utah Press.

Revault, Philippe/Santelli, Serge (2004) *Harar. A Muslim City of Ethiopia*, Paris: Maisonneuve&Larose.

Wagner, Ewald (1978) *Legende und Geschichte. Der Fath Madinat Harar von Yahya Nasrallah*, Wiesbaden: Franz Steiner.

Zekaria, Ahmad (2003) "Some Remarks on the Shrines of Harar". In: Bertrand Hirsch/Manfred Kropp (eds.) *Saints, Biographies and History in Africa*, Frankfurt am Main: Peter Lang, pp. 19-29.

Chapter 8

Merchants and *Mujahidin*: Beliefs about Muslim Saints and the History of Towns in Egypt

Souzan El Saied Yousef Mosa

Introduction: History and Folklore

In Egyptian anthropology, folklore is considered to be a creation expressing the spirit and symbols of popular cultural attitudes in everyday life. It is considered to determine the immediate relationships between man and environment, between people interacting with each other, and between people in their material, social and intellectual worlds as represented by symbols in language, art and religion.

There are cultural generalities that are shared by local people and, more specifically, there are different attitudes which are related to gender, age, class, occupation and geographical location. Although people inherit the values and beliefs that feature in the symbols, tales and rituals, they also change these values and beliefs and use them in different ways.

Popular beliefs and practices draw on the past and interpret it with respect to present daily life and future expectations. It is increasingly acknowledged today that popular beliefs represent a mixture of folklore, religions and other forms of knowledge. However, they also transport the belief in supernatural powers that can be avoided or controlled through rituals that repel evil creatures and invite benevolent ones. Based on the German tradition of *Volkskunde*, Muhammad al-Gawhary has introduced folklore studies as a specific approach in Egyptian anthropology. Today, however, American approaches to folklore studies, such those developed by Alan Dundes (1992) and Michael C. Howard (1995), exert significant influence in Egypt.

With respect to history and its impact on folkloric expressions as they relate to the cultural nature and collective personality of people, the influence of German *Volkskunde* and, specifically, the Munich School, which was concerned with the history of beliefs, and modern continuities in language and art (Brandish 1992: 60-65), remains influential. This approach goes back to the *Volkskunde* studies of the German philosopher Johann Gottfried Herder (1744-1803). Herder attached major significance to the inherent relationship between the formation of personality and popular traditions. He argued that folk tales contained representations of community principles and local history, law and morality. For him it is a kind of poetry that emerges spontaneously from the conditions of life at the moment of redemption, and people express it in a simple spirit, each individual considering it a real expression of himself or herself (cf. Oring 1994).

It is important to note that the specific dimension of locality is important within these traditions of folklore studies, which largely deal with modern identity formations. In this framework, it becomes possible to map mentalities on the basis of an historical-geographical view (cf. Dundes 1980: 18-20). As opposed to this, it has been debated whether it is still possible to sustain a pure identity/history relation. The notion of the past changes and folklore is seen to represent only a certain period that the community sees as particularly important for it (e.g. Ben Amos 1971).

Based on these discussions of Egyptian folklore studies, in this study, I will lean on this concept of change. I will concentrate on the tales about a *wali* (saint) and shift the ritual aspects of celebrating the *awliya'* into the background of my analysis. Visiting the shrine, offering votives, and celebrating the *mulid*, the annual saints-day festival, are key elements of the veneration of a saint. However, there is difference in the way rituals are performed and symbols used. These differences are mainly dictated by the specific character of each *wali*. My argument here is that each town has created different *wali* characters and related to them a special historical imagination. Some of these *awliya'* are associated with ruins of ancient cities, such as Abdallah Ibn Salam near the well known Tell el-Rub', which is the ancient town of Mendes, the capital of the sixteenth nome in old Lower Egypt. Tell al-Muqdam (Busiris), which was the capital of the 19th nome in old Lower Egypt and is located near to Mit Ghamr, hosts the shrine of Al Muqdam Ibn al-Aswad (Selim Vol. VI: 407-408). Some villages are related to the Coptic history, for example Bussat al-Nasara and Tonnamel where tales about Maria the Copt and Caliph al-Ma'mun are found.

It is believed that *awliya'* (saints) are people who performed *karamat* (miracles and extraordinary deeds). These *karamat* may have taken place during their lifetime or after their death. Examples of these *karamat* as described in hagiographies and vernacular traditions include travelling away and returning on the same day, walking on the surface of water, and curing serious illnesses without medical intervention. Since saints are believed to have a special relationship with God, people ask them to act as intermediaries between themselves and God so as to bring blessing to people. While present in localized Muslim cults around the world, this phenomenon also has deep roots in ancient Egyptian culture (Hassan 2000: 219-220). Old beliefs and practices continued and featured in the life of people in different periods, although they were often subject to restrictions imposed by and confrontations with orthodox religious and state institutions. An important question, therefore, concerns the reasons that lead to the continuation of the phenomenon of belief in *awliya'* and the role played by saints play in local communities and their historical imagination. An equally important question is how people adjust and redefine the cults of *awliya'* in the face of opposition from religious movements opposed to the veneration of saints. I will attempt to answer these questions below by explaining the relationship between the tales about *awliya'* and the history of al-Mansura, the capital of the ad-Daqahliya Governorate.

Al-Mansura and its Saints

Some of the *awliya'* of al-Mansura are related to the Crusades and Mamluk sultans. Others can be traced to the period of the British occupation and mixed courts which were intended for foreigners. Some of them were leaders of neighborhoods or cemetery guards. Their lineage may be traced to Ali ibn Abi Talib and Abu Bakr al-Siddiq. Some are martyrs of the Islamic conquests, others are leaders of Sufi *turuq* (orders), or natives of those villages who were famous for their piety or were exposed to injustice and oppression during their lives. Some were been *magazib*, divinely insane men and women, and finally some may be legendary characters representing the symbols of nature.

Daqahliya Governorate extends in a plain with a rural nature. It is divided into a number of districts along the Damietta branch of the Nile. Most of the districts are located on the east bank of the Nile, and a few of them are on the west bank. Al-Mansura became the capital of the Governorate at the beginning of the Ottoman rule. It was originally built by King al-'Adel Abu Bakr ibn Ayyub in 1218 A.D. during the 5th Crusade when Damietta was captured by the Crusaders. He stayed there until the Crusaders left Damietta. During the 7th Crusade in 1248 A.D., King al-Kamel Ayyub stayed in Al-Mansura. That decisive battle ended with the capture of King Louis IX of France in Ibn Luqman House (al-Maqrizi 1974: 194-210). Those incidents had their apparent effects on the popular mentality that wove a lot of tales on the *awliya'* related with that period.

Sufis played an important role in leading the popular resistance against the Crusades. According to the legend, Abu al-Hassan al-Shadhili, the founder of the Shadhiliyya *tariqa* in Egypt went with some Sufis to Al-Mansura to urge people to fight (Mahmud 1984: 19). Thus those Sufis were related in the popular thought with piety and supporting Islam, and shrines were built for them throughout the city.

In the Middle Ages, Sufis played an important role in spreading beliefs about *awliya'*. They spread tales about the *karamat* of those *awliya'*, and contributed in building shrines in other towns and villages. The State and the religious establishment, both closely associated with Islamic mysticism, where largely supportive of the veneration of *awliya'*. All classes of the people believed in sacredness of *awliya'*, because of their descent from the Prophet (peace be upon him) or a spiritual genealogy leading back to him. The rich were keen to build shrines for them at their own expenses to be buried beside major saints in the hope that the latter would intercede for them in the afterlife. Members of the ruling class were equally keen to build their tombs beside those of *awliya'* (The tombs of the royal family, for example, are located beside the shrine of Abu Shibbak in ar-Rifa'i Mosque in Cairo). Since the beginning, the shrines build around tombs were commonly attached to mosques. But some shrines were built inside markets, where a shrine was the center of the market, and a place where poor classes would gather for relief and cure, and to ensure blessing for their transactions.

With the multiplicity of Sufi *turuq*, the characters and symbols of *awliya'* became very diverse. With the growth of the city the number of *awliya'* increased and their characters varied. Belonging to all classes and categories (Ben-Ari/Billu 1987), some of them were members of Sufi *turuq* (Shadhiliyya, Rifa'iyya, and Burhamiyya) or ordinary people. The *wali* could be free or a slave, white or black, a man or a woman.

The members of all classes had a chance to turn into *awliya'* after their death, and thousands of folk tales have been told about their piety and *karamat*. Although those tales were a kind of literary creation invented by the popular imagination, they can be used to explore some aspects of the social history whose recording was neglected in formal history books. To some extent they give us a presentation of the real history of towns and their battles against invaders. More importantly, they also present a popular historiography of trades and craftsmen, the emergence and development of neighborhoods, and local families and the ways they tried to immortalize their names.

In late nineteenth century, Al-Mansura was a large city on the bank of the Nile. It had industries of silk, cotton, and wool. It had the main tribunal of the Governorate, a hospital, and foreign missionary schools. Beside its native Muslims, Copts and Jews, it was inhabited by a Greek community and some French and English (Mubarak 1990: vol. 15, p. 57). The city was divided into two main areas: the east and the west, further subdivided into smaller neighbourhoods. The inhabitants of the western neighborhoods were called *hawaryon* (those who live in alleys) and those who lived in the eastern neighborhoods were called *hadharyon* (the urban people). Each neighborhood had a leader who was obeyed at the times of hardship. Fights took place occasionally—once every three months at maximum. Preceded by boys throwing stones and brandishing a club the neighbourhood leader would lead the young mob of the neighborhood. Midway between the neighborhoods, he would be met by the leader of the other neighborhood followed by his people to the fight. Fighting would go on until the police came and dispersed the two parties. Sufi *turuq* tried to put an end to those fights and to change them into popular celebrations during which the inhabitants of a neighbourhood would come together with others in the celebration of their *wali*.

Sufi *turuq* had largely dominated popular thought until the end of the 19th century. At the beginning of the 20th century Sufi thought was seen by many to be marginal to the scientific approaches needed by the Egyptian society, while fundamentalist trends retreated. In the second half of the 20th century fundamentalist trends became active anew and overwhelmed the Egyptian society. These trends reached their climax in 1980s, when the clash between Sufi and Islamist groups was clear throughout of the Egyptian society. Shrines were demolished to build mosques in their places. The mosque of the Salafi organization al-Jam'iyya al-shar'iya in Port Said Street was first established beside the shrine of Sidi al-Masri who was a hero of the Crusade wars. In a recent enlargement of the mosque, the shrine was demolisched. Sometimes places were made for shrines at the back of mosques, and in some other case rebuilding the shrine was completely ignored. In some cases a shrine was destroyed to build a complex containing a clinic, a place for social services, and a place for memorizing the Qur'an and religious guidance through lectures for men and women.

Despite that campaign made by the Islamist groups against shrines, Sufi *turuq* had their own means to defend the shrines, and they have also built a number of new shrines in the second half of the 20th century. They have reinterpreted the biographies of saints to give them more legitimacy in face of the Islamists. Furthermore, they developed old shrines and attached to them associations providing social and health services, notably to orphans and widows.

Mediaeval Saints: From Mystics to Martyrs

Sidi Mashhur

The shrine of Sidi Mashhur is located in the Gidayla suburb east of the city. It is a new suburb that used to be dwelled by lower class families living from odd jobs beside working in the agriculture. Today it is known for its high percentage of educated people, as well as the activity of Islamist groups. In the past there were some shrines in this suburb, but the fundamentalist thought led to their demolition and the construction of mosques in their places. Those mosques carry names of the *awliya'* whose shrines used to be in those places. Nevertheless, the relatively new shrine of Sidi Mashhur, built in 1980, stands in the middle of the district. This shrine is visited by inhabitants of the district, especially on Fridays, when they offer votives of candles to light the shrine.

Who is Sidi Mashhur and how could his shrine be built in a time when many others were being destroyed? When the troops of the ninth Crusade entered Al-Mansura from the east in 1249 A.D. they built their camp in al-Gadila. Sidi Mashur was one of the heroes of the struggle against the Crusaders of whom many local tales are told. According to the story the people of al-Mansura bravely fought the invaders with palm tree trunks. Sidi Mashhour was a leader of the popular struggle and died as a martyr in the battle.

Many shrines are built years, even centuries after the death of the saint on the basis of dreams (see Mittermaier in this volume), and it was through such a dream vision that the mujahid Sidi Mashhur was to become a venerated saint of his district, legitimized against the Islamists by his status as a martyr. In 1980, a follower of the Ahmadiya Sufi *tariqa* built a a new shrine for Sidi Mashhour. It is said that the *wali* came to him in a dream and asked him to rebuild the shrine. He rebuilt the shrine as a part of his house. He used red bricks as construction material, a construction material of high social status in a time when most of the houses were built with mud bricks. But with the growth of the city and the labor migration of many inhabitants to the Persian Gulf countries, big economic changes took place. With influx of money from the migrants most of old houses were demolished and replaced by high buildings, and the shrine lies now between two of them. It remains the site of visits and veneration, and is lit on Friday nights in memory of the soul of the martyr *wali*.

Sidi 'Abd al-Qadir

The shrine of Sidi 'Abd al-Qadir is located in the Hasaniya neighborhood in the street carrying his name (Sidi 'Abd al-Qadir Street). Except of his Moroccan origin, little is known about Sidi 'Abd al-Qadir's life. In the past, the celebration of his *mulid* was an important event which continued for a week. The inhabitants of the neighborhood used to offer votives of food (bread, *mulukhiyah*, meat, cheese, lupine seeds, and chickpeas). At the night of the big celebration (*laylat al-mawlid*), a *dhikr* is held, poems are read, and verses of the Qur'an are recited. The *mulid* was organized mainly by inhabitants of neighborhood and adjacent neighborhoods. The procession was led by the 'Arusiya *tariqa*, followers of Sidi Abd al-Salam al-Asmar who ended their celebration with beating tambourines. With the development of the neighborhoods and the construction of new buildings and schools, the celebration became a source of disturbance for the neighboring schools in particular. Nowadays, the celebration is therefore carried out inside the shrine and only lasts one day.

At the shrine of Sidi 'Abd al-Qadir at the neighborhood carrying his name in Al-Mansura there is at the top of the shrine a hexagonal star, and in front of it there is a place for offering votives. The hexagonal star, which has a long history in Islamic ornament, has mistakenly been interpreted as a Jewish symbol by fundamentalists who have repeatedly attempted to burn the shrine.

The shrine occupies a very small place, which made impossible for the inhabitants to turn it into a mosque. Originally surrounded by a small open areal, the shrine has become surrounded by buildings over the time. And because of the high price of the land in that area, some people wanted to demolish it. It has become a very contested site, with many people opposed to its existence. Some neighbors regularly attack it by throwing garbage on it. It was repeatedly destroyed and burnt. But every time Sufi *turuq* were able to rebuild it and cover the tomb with a new green cloth (*kiswa*) carrying the names of the four Rightly-guided Caliphs (Abu Bakr, 'Umar, 'Uthman and Ali). And as the place is narrow, a structure was built outside the door of the shrine where the celebrants can put their votives.

In the recent years Islamist groups began a new attack on the shrine because there is a hexagonal star above the shrine. Gossip began to relate that star with the symbol of State of Israel, and rumours claimed the shrine belongs to a Jewish merchant. In fact hexagonal stars have a long history in Islamic architecture, and are found on many shrines and Islamic monuments. The point of interconnection between the two triangles represents justice and balance between heaven and the material world. Sultan Qalawun of the Ayubid dynasty used this star as his symbol. It also prevailed on popular products because of beliefs about the power of the hexagonal star engraved on the ring of king Solomon. In our days, however, the hexagonal star is almost exclusively associated with Judaism and Zionism, and the Islamic history of the symbol is unknown to most people.

Another reason given by opponents of the shrine for attacking it is that the square structure in front of it looks like an altar. But it is in fact the very existence of the shrine itself that incites the anger of its fundamentalist opponents. When I visited Sidi 'Abd al-Qadir Street in 2006, I asked a fundamentalist about the shrine, and he answered, "There is nothing called a shrine! It only contains a person who died a long time ago."

Despite this campaign, Sufi groups have successfully maintained the shrine. In recent years, they began to take care of a nearby shrine which was unknown because it was located inside a house. It is the shrine of Sidi Taybaq. The shrine was restored, repainted and decorated with verses from the Qur'an. New saintly legends emerged that began to connect between the history of Sidi Taybak, Sidi 'Abd al-Qadir and the Crusades. Rather than a Jewish merchant as sometimes claimed by the fundamentalist, Sidi 'Abd al-Qadir thus made an appearance as a *mujahid* defending Islam against the Crusaders—a role which gave him a new kind of legitimacy in a neighborhood dominated by an Islamist movement.

Saints of the Market: From Protectors to Providers of Services

Sheikh Hasanayn al-Shahawi

Sheikh Hasanayn (d. 1883) is an example of those shrines which were built in old market places which occupied vast areas among houses. Tales about this *wali* represent a part of the history of rich families in Al-Mansura, and how those families were related to Sufi *turuq* and believed in the *karamat* of the *awliya'*. Some members of those families built Qur'an schools which offered education for the children of poor householdsm and shrines for themselves to be buried in them after death beside those *awliya'*, thus developing the shrines into complex social sites of Divine protection of the market, identity of merchant families, and religious education.

The story of Sheikh Hasanayn is closely intertwined with the history of the merchant family of al-Qura'i Pasha. Folk tales about Sheikh Hasanayn represent a popular reading of history which depends on the name of 'Al-Qura'', a person whose head is hairless. They wove a myth related to the palace of the Pasha, King al-'Adil, and the history of mixed courts in Al-Mansura. After Sheikh Hasanayn's death, the family of al-Qura'i built his shrine with a *kuttab* (Qur'an school) beside it. Al-Qura'i Pasha himself was buried after his death beside the Sheikh, following the style of the Royal Family who built their tombs beside the shrine of Abu Shibbak (now inside al-Rifa'i mosque) in Cairo.

Sheikh Hasanayn's lineage can be traced to Musa Ibn 'Umran, the brother of Sidi Ibrahim al-Disuqi. He was a follower of the Burhamiyya-Shahawiyah *tariqa* which is stands in the spiritual lineage of Ibrahim al-Disuqi. Born in a village of Gharbiya Governorate, he was a weaver who got married and had one son called Mohammad. He traveled from village to village accompanied by two Sufi brethren called Sidi Abu Nawwar who died in Banha, and Sidi Ahmad al-Shishtawi whose famous shrine is located in al-Mahalla al-Kubra. Sheikh Hasanayn finally settled in Al-Mansura where he died in 1883.

When Sheikh Hasanayn came to the city, he built a hut in front of the house of a rich merchant Ali Pasha al-Qura'i in the place now known as Gazirat al-Ward. It is believed that it was the same place where King al-'Adil built his palace when he came to the city. Many tales exist about that palace on the banks of the Nile, on the site of which the villa of Dr. Ghayth has recently been built.

When the gardener saw Sheikh Hasanayn building the hut in front of the palace, he informed his master who, in turn, asked the gardener about the character and qualities of that man. The gardener told him that he was always glorifying God and praying. And amazingly enough he would put his praying rug on the surface of the water and pray on it—and the rug never sank. The owner of the palace sent new clothes to him, and ordered his men to take meals to him daily. He occasionally went to sit with him. On one occasion when the pasha visited the sheikh he looked upset. The sheikh asked him why. He told him that an English officer wanted to steal his palace with the pretext of it being a state property that he had stolen. At that time Egypt was under the British occupation and the foreign communities in Egypt enjoyed protection and had special tribunals known as mixed courts. The lawsuit was seen there and the judge was a Frenchman. The sheikh said to the pasha, "You will be victorious, Qura'i." Then he tapped his head delicately and compassionately. In result, all the hair from his head fell down. Since then he was called Qurai'y, as he had not been bald-headed before. The sentence was in favour of the pasha who swore to build a mosque carrying the name of the sheikh. He also built a tomb for him to be buried in after his death. He also ordered in his will to be buried beside the sheikh. When the sheikh died, he was buried in that tomb which became a shrine visited by people to get blessing.

The shrine of Sidi Hasanayn is located in the neighborhood carrying his name, in the middle of the marketplace. His *mulid* is held every year in mid-August and is attended, in addition to common people, by the Governor, notables of the city, and members of Sufi *turuq*. During the *mulid*, the sheikhs of the Sufi *turuq* gather with their banners and drums and go around the city in a big procession wearing their best clothes and reciting prayers. They are preceded by people carrying flags and followed by the *naqib al-ashraf* (the representative of the descendants of the Prophet Muhammad). The procession goes on until they reach the space beside the shrine. *Dhikr* and Qur'an recitation go on, while young men indulge in amusement, women buy things from the market and children buy sweets and play in swings.

The original shrine was a typical representative of shrines constructed in the Ottoman period, built in Mamluk style with domes and pillars. But after the decline of most rich families in the cities, there was a need to rebuild the old shrine in a way that was felt to be consistent with modern thought and the encroaching modern buildings on market places. 'Rebuilding' in Egyptian jargon of urban planning means demolition and the construction of a new building. Furthermore, with the spread of the Islamist trends and fundamentalist thought shrines standing by themselves were more vulnerable, and so the old shrine was demolished and the Mosque of Sheikh Hasanayn was built in its place. The new Sheikh Hasanayn Complex contains the shrine, a mosque, a clinic, and educational services.

Sheikh Al Bayya'

Sheikh Al Bayya' was the chief of merchants in Al-Mansura. Until early 20th century, there was a guild for each trade. No one could practice any trade without being certified by the sheikh of the guild (note that in the guild system, the term sheikh had a secular meaning of leadership which, however, could be conflated with the religious meaning of the same word in other contexts). That system of specialization led to the coherence of the members of each guild. The sheikhs of the guilds had an important role in the Egyptian towns and villages, a position which they could not reach without the acceptance of old workers of each trade. A sheikh occupied his position for life. But if the members did not accept his behavior they could ask him to step down. He was assisted by a *naqib* whose job was to implement the orders of the sheikh and to organize social events (Abu Sudayra 1990: 381).

Sons rarely practiced a trade different from that of their fathers. Craftsmen and merchants also used to marry women whose fathers practice their own trades. This must have led to a degree of social separation between different trades, and a strong social identity among the practitioners of each craft. The intervention of the state under Mohammad Ali in the first half of the 19th century led to some loosening of that structure. But the guild remained the central social and economic unit of the craftsmen until the First World War (Raymond 2005: 589).

Trades and industries never prevented those who practiced them from gaining knowledge in the field of religion, and some craftsmen were famous in the field of *fiqh* (Islamic jurisprudence), while some others practiced teaching. Craftsmen also had—and continue to have—a remarkable role in the organization of *mawalid* in the cities of Egypt. In the Middle Ages, beginning from the Ayoubid Period, and the Mamluk Period, each guild used to belong to a certain Sufi *tariqa*. The craftsmen's traditions in Al-Mansura were not different from those in Cairo. Most trades concentrated in al-Abbasi and al-Tumayhi areas, where neighborhoods were known by the trades practiced in them: *Suq al-Haddadin* (the blacksmiths' market), *Suq al-Naggarin* (Carpenters' Market), and so on (Ghunaym 1996).

Sheikh al-Bayya' was sheikh of the merchants' guild in al-Hasaniya neighborhood and a follower of the Rifa'iyya Sufi *tariqa*. After his death a shrine was built for him in the cemetery. But with the growth of the city in the 20th century, the cemetery turned into a residential area. In a way parallel to the reconstruction of the shrine of Sheikh Hasanayn, his shrine was turned into into al-Bayya' Complex. The ground floor houses the shrine and a mosque. The first and second floors house a charity association for orphans and an Azhari elementary school.

Sheikh al-'Isawi

Sheikh al-'Isawi (1904-1965) was a follower of the 'Isawiya Sufi *tariqa* which traces its spiritual lineage to the Moroccan Ibn 'Isa (Mubarak 1990: 222). Sheikh al-'Isawi was also the sheikh of blacksmiths in Suq al-Haddadin in the 'Abbasi neighborhood. His portrait still hangs in the blacksmiths' workshops. Although the guild system is now defunct, most of former guild members still practice blacksmithing. Sheikh al-'Isawi never married, and his nephews inherited his workshop.

Sheikh al-'Isawi was called 'the axis of sainthood' (*Qutb al-Wilaya*) by his followers. Many miracles (*karamat*) were attributed to him already during lifetime. When he prophesied something, it would come true. He could be present in different places at the same time. He could walk on the surface of water. His followers came from different regions to learn about religion and to memorize the Qur'an.

After his death he was buried at Sandub cemetery, and his tomb was visited by men and women who ask him to realize their hopes and offer votives on the window of his shrine. A *mulid* is held for him in March. A mosque was built next to the shrine at the entrance of the cemetery now known as al-'Isawi Cemetery. The mosque is used for the prayers for the dead before burying them. A clinic and a place for the memorization of the Qur'an are attached to the mosque. In Ramadan, a *ma'idat ar-Rahman*, (service of free food for fast-breaking), is held beside the mosque. Inside the shrine there are two big posters depicting the Ka'aba (in Mecca) and the Mosque of al-Husayn in Cairo. The tomb is decorated with green and white pieces of silk cloth on which 'Allah' is embroidered and covered with a green *kiswa* on which seven copies of the Koran are placed. There are four lanterns at the corners of the tombs. The floor is covered with green carpet.

Conclusions

The history of al-Mansura as told through the stories of *awliya'* may not stand in any direct relationship to the real events that took place in the past. They do, however, tell us very much about the group identities, the growth of the city, local values and struggles as they have been imagined and described by the people who speak of the *awliya'*: Be it with the fundamentalists depicting a Muslim saint as a Jewish merchant, Sufis turning mystics into *mujahidin*, or merchants and craftsmen uniting social with spiritual leadership—in all cases people arrange stories and meanings in a way that fits with values they hold important. The folklore they thus create—the heroes, the festivals, the popular architecture—tells us of the group identities and local histories people tell to themselves. Take, for example, the *mulid* (saints-day festival), a phenomenon rich with all the elements of popular culture. It is a means to boast of identity and coherence of a community, the bond created between its members by shared values and experiences, and its continuous existence over time and place. Each group of people adheres to some elements of the tradition that may not be shared by others. These elements become the folklore distinguishing that group. But as a street festival open to everybody, the mulid also presents a site of exchange where different groups, styles, beliefs and points of view meet. On one level creating strong local bonds, the festive culture of saints-day festivals, continuously developing as districts and their inhabitants change, also allows for a dynamic character of the folkloric imagination.

Although the tales of *Awliya'* can be considered myths or popular imagination, they still are sources of social history, especially in small towns where no one cared to record their social history in writing. More importantly, they are an important form of collective memory in a time when all old structures are demolished in order to construct new buildings, especially with the high prices of the land and the need to use those places for providing services to the inhabitants.

The struggle over the shrines between Sufi and Islamist groups is one way of contesting and telling the history of the town. In their campaign against shrines and Sufi *turuq* Islamist groups have invented new folklore, borrowed from the sands of the Arabian Peninsula and juxtaposed to the culture of the Nile valley. Holding to an ahistorical interpretation of religion that excludes notions of historical development and growth, the Islamists attempt to flatten out both the physical landscape and the historical imaginary of the city, reducing it to a simple opposition of Islam and non-Islam. The shrines, for them, are not only an improper form of religiosity, but an annoying reminder of a history much more complex than they imagine. The Sufis defending the shrines, in turn, are compelled to partially take over the Islamist imagination to legitimize the cult of saints. Turning mystics into *mujahidin* and shrines into complexes with mosques and social services, they embed the saints into the modern imagination of contemporary history as struggle, social development and public education.

This strategy has turned out largely successful. The shrines which are still attacked by Islamist groups are those which form separate buildings inside residential areas. But those shrines which are located in cemeteries are not attacked, nor are the mosques attached to shrines, be it in cemeteries or in the market. Building mosques on the sites of shrines does, however, often lead to a shift of focus. With the mosque and the social services becoming more central, people sometimes pay less attention to the shrines. In some cases people no longer celebrate the memory of the owner of a shrine, or the celebration has become a very small event.

References

Abu Sudayra, Taha al-Said (1990) *Al-Hiraf wa-l-sina'at fi Misr mundhu al-fath al-'araby hatta nihayat al-'asr al-fatimi (20-567 H./641-1171 A.D.)*, General Egyptian Book Organization.

Ben Amos, Dan (1971) "Towards a Definition of Folklore in Context". *Journal of American Folklore* 84, pp. 3-15.

Ben Amos, Dan/Goldstein, K. (1975) *Folklore: Communication and Performance*, The Hague: Mouton.

Ben-Ari, E./Billu, Y. (1987) "Saints' Sanctuaries in Israeli Development Towns: On a Mechanism of Urban Transformation". *Urban Anthropology* 16/2, pp. 243-72.

Brednich, Rolf W. (2001) *Grundriss der Volkskunde: Einführung in die Forschungsfelder der Europäischen Ethnologie* (3rd edition), Berlin.

Dundes, Alan (1980) *Interpreting Folklore*, Bloomington: Indiana University Press.

Dundes, Alan (1992) *Folklore Matters*, Knoxville: The University of Tennessee Press.

Ghunaym, Muhammad Ahmad (1996) *Al-Hiraf wa-s-sina'at al-sha'biyya*, Mansoura University, Faculty of Arts.

Hasan, Salim (2000) *Mawsu'at Misr al-Qadimah* (Vol. 4), Cairo: Egyptian General Book Organization.

Howard, Michael C. (1996), *Contemporary Cultural Anthropology* (5th edition), New York: Harper Collins.

al-Maqrizi, Abu l-'Abbas Ahmad b. Ali b. Abd al-Qadir al-Husaini Taqi al-Din (1974), *as-Suluk li-ma'rifat duwal al-muluk* (Vol. 1), Cairo: Dar al-Halabi li-n-nashr.

Mahmud, 'Abd al-Halim (1984) *Al-Madrasa al-Shadhiliya al-jadida wa-imamuha Abu al-Hasan al-Shadhili*, Cairo: Dar al-Makki.

Mubarak, 'Ali (1990) *Al Khitat Al-tawfiqiya al-Jadida*, Cairo: Egyptian General Book Organization.

Oring, Elliott (1996) "The Arts, Artifacts, and Artifices of Identity". *Journal of American Folklore* 107, pp. 424.

Raymond, André (2005) *Craftsmen and Merchants in Cairo in the Eighteenth Century*, tr. Ahmad Ibrahim and Nancy Gamal al-Din (Vol. 1 and 2), Cairo: Supreme Council for Culture.

Abstracts

Sufi Regional Cults in South Asia and Indonesia: Towards a Comparative Analysis
Pnina Werbner

This chapter examines the spread of Sufism from the Near East to South Asia. It then moves on to consider whether Sufism in Indonesia, which has been analysed using vernacular rather than analytic concepts, in fact bears significant similarities in its organizational, ritual and symbolic forms and processes to Sufi practices elsewhere. So too, the chapter argues, the legends and miracles of North African, South Asian and Indonesia holy men and Sufi saints, though set in entirely different historical and ecological contexts, contain remarkable 'deep' mythic structural similarities. In this sense, the chapter argues against Clifford Geertz's comparative analysis of the differences between local Moroccan and Indonesian Islam, that there may be underlying resemblances between the ideological underpinnings of Sufi orders and sacred centers in widely separated geographical localities, which a generate similar symbolic and organizational logics. Taking a fresh look at recent ethnographic studies of Sufi orders and cults in Indonesia, the paper compares them analytically and ethnographically with modes of Sufi thought and religious organization in South Asia, mainly India and Pakistan. In both countries the veneration of saints has come under attack from reformists, but continues to be a living, vital tradition in its reformist modes.

(Re)Imagining Space: Dreams and Saint Shrines in Egypt
Amira Mittermaier

The order of modernity in Egypt intersects with many other spaces, among them the order of the saint shrine and the order of the dream. This chapter invites to a re-imagining of space through considering interplays and tensions between these three different orders. Adopting Lefebvre's notion that neither imaginary nor material spaces can be understood in isolation, it examines how dream spaces spill over into, and are shaped by, material spaces and concrete spatial practices. While both the saint shrine and the dream seemingly subvert the order of modernity, the paper challenges materialist readings which view dreams as a form of false consciousness or which prioritize saint shrines as sites of resistance. Instead it suggests that understandings of saint shrines are incomplete unless they are conceptualized within a space which includes both the material and the imaginary. Also dream stories do not so much resist the hegemonic order of reality but rather create an alternative, but not purposively contrary, space within it.

Remixing Songs, Remaking Mulids:
The Merging Spaces of Dance Music and Saint Festivals in Egypt
Jennifer Peterson

'Mulid' dance music is a popular current that draws musically and lyrically from Sufi spiritual songs performed at Egyptian saint festivals (mulids). Amplified on large speakers at mulids as part of their carnival-like atmosphere, it is also established in other, more mundane, social realms, such as the bootleg cassette tape market, internet forums, and cell phone ring tones, as well as at ubiquitous events such as weddings, small business openings, and evening strolls along the Nile promenade.

The festive time and space of mulids is ephemeral, and they are further being gradually marginalized by various forms of Islamic and modernist discourse and policy. Yet this current of dance music has successfully drawn on them as a dynamic cultural source and, thanks to it fluid nature, enabled representative aspects of them to seep into other, seemingly disparate social realms. This music trend relocates mulids into social spaces far removed from the physical domain of the saint, extending the very idea of a mulid through time, space, and lived experience into forms and concepts arguably more permanent than those of the mulid itself. And, in the opposite direction, this music current is furthermore contributing to reshaping the features of actual mulids, offering an alternative 'modern' approach to celebrating these festive occasions and meanwhile reinforcing their social significance.

This study explores how the remixing of Sufi spiritual songs has led to a remaking of mulids, by shaping them into cultural metaphors found in a variety of social spaces as well as through contributing to an alternative 'modernization' of mulids themselves. In doing so, it follows the trajectory of this music current's developments and examines what meanings are conveyed when its social context is changed from the 'otherworldliness' of the mulid to the 'everydayness' of contemporary Egyptian life.

Notes on Locality, Connectedness, and Saintliness
Armando Salvatore

This chapter offers a few critical notes reflecting the experience of the *Yearbook of the Sociology of Islam* from a theoretical viewpoint, based on the *Yearbook*'s goal of facilitating an understanding of the ambivalent positioning of Islam in the global construction of society, and using the subject of saintliness as an entry point into the discussion.

Since its inception, the validity of a Weberian categorization of the issue of modernity with regard to Islam appeared as an inevitable starting point for the *Yearbook* project, yet also as one that needed a critical revision. This chapter departs from the issue of saintliness and discusses the interplay in it of locality and connectedness, in particular to the extent they are related to the Weberian concept of 'charisma'.

Weber's charisma as first personalized or localized and then diluted into routine practices contrasts with the knowledge we can gain from exploring Islamic traditions. The chapter mentions the example of the enigmatic character of Khidr, who plays a key role in both scholarly and popular traditions variably related to Muslim saintliness, in order to unveil Weber's notion of charisma as the outcome of a post-Protestant secularization of the chemistry of the social bond that misreads its relational nature in favor of an ongoing dialectics of inwardness (*Innerlichkeit*) and publicness (*Öffentlichkeit*). This is not a wrong genealogy or a plain anachronism, but rather a self-genealogy of hegemonic Western views. It is useful as such but can scarcely account for global modernity and the role that revitalized or reformed traditions play in it.

Saints (*awliya'*), Public Places and Modernity in Egypt
Ahmed A. Zayed

This chapter attempts to cast light on the transformations that occur in places surrounding the shrines of saints in Egypt considering them public places, and specifically to analyze the influences of modernity on them. The main questions to be addressed here are: How had the traditional mind built a sacred image for such places? How did they transform into spiritual and cultural places? How had such images structured the traditional society? What are the modes of transformation of such places and images in modern Egypt? And how do modern Egyptians reproduce local society in the festivals and rituals related to saints in different parts of Egypt. In conclusion the paper claims that the modern public sphere created at the saint's square is in many ways ever more contested and fragmented. This is due to ideological and religious struggles, urban expansion, modern economy, and the state. There are also attempts to impose fences, police surveillance, and other physical restrictions on the use of the saints' place. The chapter includes data from different places and regions in Egypt and gives specific reference to social change in the local public sphere and interweaving aspects between traditional and communal culture on the one hand and new forms of state and consumer culture on the other.

Islam on both Sides: Religion and Locality in Western Burkina Faso
Katja Werthmann

This chapter is about two sacred or saintly places in present-day Burkina Faso. It compares the sacrificial site of Dafra and the Muslim village of Darsalamy in the vicinity of Bobo-Dioulasso, Burkina Faso's second-largest city which is predominantly Muslim. These two places appear to epitomize the difference between non-Islam and Islam. Dafra is seen by many Muslims as a quintessentially pagan place where people sacrifice animals on a shrine. However, according to stories of origin Dafra was created or discovered by a Muslim saint. The village of Darsalamy was intentionally founded by Muslims from Bobo-Dioulasso in order to create a saintly place where pagan practices such as masks and dances are forbidden. The comparison of these two localities shows that they do not correspond to a neat dichotomy between Islam and paganism, but rather represent two cases of 'Islam on both sides'. For Muslims and non-Muslims alike, Islam is an important element for the constitution of collective identities or the legitimization of authority.

The Making of a 'Harari' City in Ethiopia: Constructing and Contesting Saintly Places in Harar
Patrick Desplat

The East Ethiopian town of Harar is considered the most important centre of Islam in the Horn of Africa. Its symbolic capital is reflected in its local representation as *madinat al-awliya*, the city of saints, which emphasizes the spiritual value of the hundreds of saintly places within its old walls and the many shrines in the countryside beyond them. The associated saints, their legends, and practices of veneration still play a significant role in the religious life of the town of Harar. This tradition is currently the focus of debates, in which some groups consider the local veneration of saints as an out-dated 'cultural'—and sometimes un-Islamic—practice, while others hold more ambiguous views.

Against this background, this paper concentrates on the contemporary role of locality and saintly tradition and the question as to how are they constructed and negotiated among the Muslims of Harar. The adopted approach explores changes which are expressed in phenomena of both decline and revitalization. One of the main theses of the paper is that a shift in meaning regarding the role of saints and their sites took place in context of modernity: i.e. from the more classical model of intercession between God and Muslims to the production of local and collective identity.

Merchants and *Mujahidin*:
Beliefs about Muslim Saints and the History of Towns in Egypt
Souzan El Saied Yousef Mosa

This chapter looks at the tales about a *wali* (saint) as ways of telling the history of the northern Egyptian city of al-Mansura. Different districts and social groups in the town have created different wali characters and related to them a special historical imagination. Be it with the fundamentalists depicting a Muslim saint as a Jewish merchant, Sufis turning mystics into mujahidin, or merchants and craftsmen uniting social with spiritual leadership—in all cases people arrange stories and meanings in a way that fits with values they hold important. The folklore they thus create—the heroes, the festivals, the popular architecture—tells us of the group identities and local histories people tell to themselves.

On the Authors and Editors of the Yearbook

Patrick Desplat is a researcher at the Colloborative Research Centre 295 in Mainz, with focus on the anthropological study of Islam in Africa.

Amira Mittermaier is Assistant Professor in the Departments of Religion and Near and Middle Eastern Civilizations at the University of Toronto. Her present research explores the ethical, political, and religious dimensions of Egypt's dream landscapes.

Souzan El Saied Yousef Mosa is Professor of Folklore at the Academy of Arts in Cairo, Egypt.

Jennifer Peterson holds a Bachelor of Arts degree in Anthropology and Near Eastern Languages and Cultures from Indiana University, and a Master of Science degree in Arabic Language, Literature, and Linguistics from Georgetown University. She resides in Cairo, Egypt, where she conducts independent research while working as a freelance translator and writer.

Armando Salvatore is Associate Professor of Sociology of Culture and Communication, University of Naples—L'Orientale, and Heisenberg Fellow, Dept. of Social Sciences, Humboldt University, Berlin, and Institute for Advanced Study in the Humanities, Essen. His present research explores the sociological, political and practical significance of religious traditions and secular formations in comparative perspective.

Samuli Schielke is a post-doctoral researcher at the University of Joensuu, Finland, and the International Institute for the Study of Islam in the Modern World (ISIM), Leiden, Netherlands.

Georg Stauth teaches Sociology of Islam at the University of Bielefeld and leads a research group on 'Saintly Places' in the DFG Collaborative Research Centre 295 at the University of Mainz.

Pnina Werbner is Professor of Social Anthropology at Keele. Her fieldwork has included research in Britain, Pakistan, and Botswana where she is currently studying a manual workers union, and women in the changing public sphere.

Katja Werthmann is Associate Professor at the Department of Anthropology and African Studies, Johannes Gutenberg University, Mainz and did field work in Nigeria about Hausa women and in Burkina Faso about land rights, settlement histories, interethnic relations, gold mining, and Islam.

Ahmed A. Zayed is Professor of Sociology at the Faculty of Arts, Cairo University.

Globaler lokaler Islam

Sabine Berghahn,
Petra Rostock (Hg.)
Der Stoff, aus dem Konflikte sind
Debatten um das Kopftuch in Deutschland, Österreich und der Schweiz
(unter Mitarbeit von Alexander Nöhring)
Dezember 2008, ca. 300 Seiten, kart., ca. 27,80 €,
ISBN: 978-3-89942-959-6

Georg Stauth,
Samuli Schielke (eds.)
Dimensions of Locality
Muslim Saints, their Place and Space (Yearbook of the Sociology of Islam)
Oktober 2008, 190 Seiten, kart., 29,80 €,
ISBN: 978-3-89942-968-8

Georg Stauth
Ägyptische heilige Orte II: Zwischen den Steinen des Pharao und islamischer Moderne. Konstruktionen, Inszenierungen und Landschaften der Heiligen im Nildelta: Fuwa – Sa al-Hagar (Sais)
Mit ägyptologischen Studien von Silvia Prell. Fotografische Begleitung von Axel Krause
März 2008, 246 Seiten, kart., zahlr. farb. Abb., 29,80 €,
ISBN: 978-3-89942-432-4

Abbas Poya,
Maurus Reinkowski (Hg.)
Das Unbehagen in der Islamwissenschaft
Ein klassisches Fach im Scheinwerferlicht der Politik und der Medien
März 2008, 336 Seiten, kart., 30,80 €,
ISBN: 978-3-89942-715-8

Schirin Amir-Moazami
Politisierte Religion
Der Kopftuchstreit in Deutschland und Frankreich
2007, 294 Seiten, kart., 28,80 €,
ISBN: 978-3-89942-410-2

Johann P. Arnason,
Armando Salvatore,
Georg Stauth (eds.)
Islam in Process
Historical and Civilizational Perspectives
(Yearbook of the Sociology of Islam 7)
2007, 332 Seiten, kart., 36,80 €,
ISBN: 978-3-89942-491-1

Irka-Christin Mohr
Islamischer Religionsunterricht in Europa
Lehrtexte als Instrumente muslimischer Selbstverortung im Vergleich
2006, 310 Seiten, kart., 28,80 €,
ISBN: 978-3-89942-453-9

Leseproben und weitere Informationen finden Sie unter:
www.transcript-verlag.de

Globaler lokaler Islam

Georg Stauth
Ägyptische heilige Orte I:
Konstruktionen,
Inszenierungen und
Landschaften der
Heiligen im Nildelta:
'Abdallah b. Salam
Fotografische Begleitung
von Axel Krause
2005, 166 Seiten,
kart., zahlr. Abb., 24,80 €,
ISBN: 978-3-89942-260-3

Nilüfer Göle,
Ludwig Ammann (Hg.)
Islam in Sicht
Der Auftritt von Muslimen
im öffentlichen Raum
2004, 384 Seiten,
kart., 26,80 €,
ISBN: 978-3-89942-237-5

Mechthild Rumpf, Ute Gerhard,
Mechtild M. Jansen (Hg.)
Facetten islamischer Welten
Geschlechterordnungen,
Frauen- und Menschenrechte
in der Diskussion
2003, 319 Seiten,
kart., 24,80 €,
ISBN: 978-3-89942-153-8

Heiner Bielefeldt
Muslime im säkularen Rechtsstaat
Integrationschancen
durch Religionsfreiheit
2003, 146 Seiten,
kart., 13,80 €,
ISBN: 978-3-89942-130-9

Levent Tezcan
**Religiöse Strategien der
»machbaren« Gesellschaft**
Verwaltete Religion
und islamistische Utopie
in der Türkei
2003, 232 Seiten,
kart., 26,80 €,
ISBN: 978-3-89942-106-4

Gerdien Jonker
Eine Wellenlänge zu Gott
Der »Verband der Islamischen
Kulturzentren in Europa«
2002, 282 Seiten,
kart., 25,80 €,
ISBN: 978-3-933127-99-0

Hans-Ludwig Frese
»Den Islam ausleben«
Konzepte authentischer
Lebensführung junger
türkischer Muslime
in der Diaspora
2002, 350 Seiten,
kart., 25,80 €,
ISBN: 978-3-933127-85-3

Sigrid Nökel
**Die Töchter der Gastarbeiter
und der Islam**
Zur Soziologie alltagsweltlicher
Anerkennungspolitiken.
Eine Fallstudie
2002, 340 Seiten,
kart., 26,80 €,
ISBN: 978-3-933127-44-0

Leseproben und weitere Informationen finden Sie unter:
www.transcript-verlag.de